LIFE AMONG THE MAGARS

Gary Shepherd

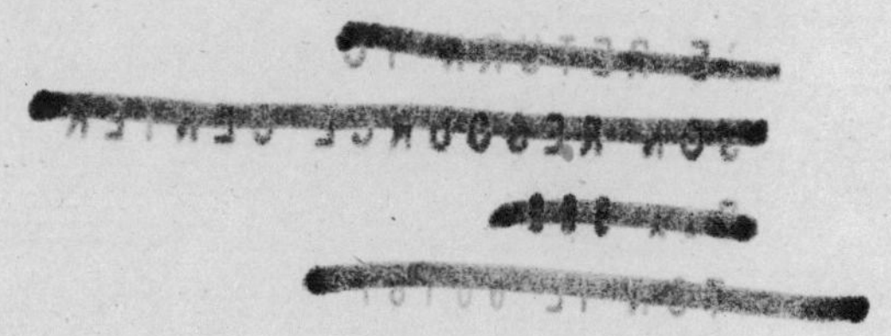

Sahayogi Press
Tripureshwar, Kathmandu.

ISBN 0-88312-921-3

First printing: 1982

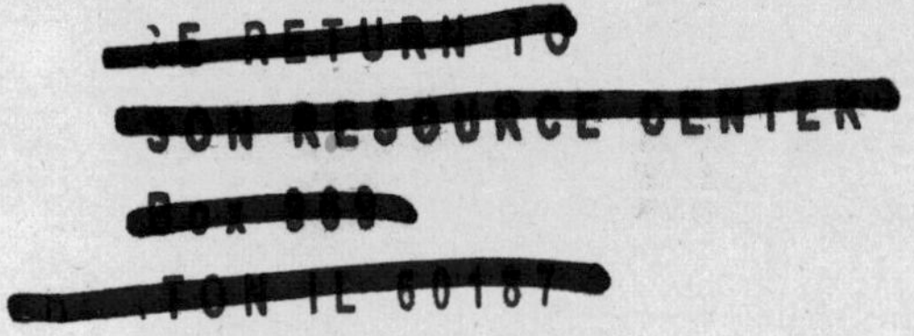

Copies available from:

International Museum of Cultures
7500 West Camp Wisdom Road
Dallas, TX 75236 USA

Sahayogi Press
Tripuwesor, Kathmandu
Nepal

Price: Rs100

Cover design by Jerry Jenkins

Cover photo: Major Nar Bahadur Thapa at a festival with Gary in 1969.

PREFACE

This book is a sharing of an experience that we as a family have had in Nepal. My wife, Barbara, and children, Adina and Michael, had an equal share in that experience. Barbara helped, encouraged and endured through the long preparation of the manuscript. She read through the chapters endless times, correcting and offering valuable suggestions. Adina and Michael, on the other hand, just lived. They thoroughly enjoyed each day they had to play with their Magar friends. If the reader comes away with a better understanding and appreciation for the people of the villages of Nepal, our purpose will have succeeded. Our family feels truly fortunate to have lived side by side with some amazing people. Though appearing to be nothing more than backward peasants from an obscure village, some of them deserve to take a stand beside the real heroes of our day.

Three men play the main roles in our book. They are: Major Nar Bahadur Thapa of Yangchok Village; from Arakhala Village, District Representative and previous Pradhan Pancha, Khadak Bahadur Lungeli (alias Daje); and his close relative of identical name, our tutor, Mr. Khadak Bahadur Lungeli (alias Pegleg), also from Arakhala village. Our sincere thanks are offered to them and the rest of our village friends for sharing their lives with us. Apologies are given where lapse of memory on our part may be responsible for any misrepresentation of fact.

Those readers who are familiar with Nepal may find the author's spelling of words of Nepali origin somewhat strange. Magar, being a Tibeto-Burman type of language, linguistically speaking has no historical relationship to Nepali, which belongs to the Indo-Aryan group of languages. Therefore, it is understandable that sometimes the Magars have significantly altered the pronunciation of the Nepali words they have adopted into their language. In not a few cases they have changed the meaning of the word considerably as well. For that reason, the author has elected to remain consistent with the Magar culture and spell the words as they are pronounced. Nasalized vowels are indicated by a tilde above the vowel, i.e., *ã*. Names and places in Nepal are generally spelled phonetically as well. For instance, *Magars* would be rendered as *Muggers* in English, and *Thapa* would be pronounced *Top-ah*.

Thanks must be given to innumerable friends and colleagues in the Summer Institute of Linguistics who taught, helped, inspired and guided us in earlier years. Fr. Lud Stiller, Fr. John Locke and Fr. Cap Miller kindly consented to read the manuscript. They steered us out of many a pitfall, both semantic and otherwise. I also wish to thank Mr. Binod Shrestha, Mr. Nanda Kumar Thapa, Mrs. Rita Anton, Dr. Harka B. Gurung and Fr. T. E. Gafney who also read the manuscript and offered valuable suggestions. Gopi Aryal is responsible for the endless hours required to type and retype the manuscript. To Fr. Jim Donnelly I am much indebted for his patient work of correcting and proofreading the manuscript. Mrs. Jerry Jenkins designed the cover and kindly assisted in the selection of photos.

Life Among the Magars is a book that at first I had no intention of ever writing. A man I have long admired for selfless dedication to the remote villagers of his nation, Professor Dor Bahadur Bista, changed that. At his insistence and with his guidance this book began. At a crucial point in the preparation of the manuscript, it was our good fortune to have the unexpected visit at our village home of Henry Materna from Austria. We are deeply indebted to him for a multitude of suggestions that have made the work more readable, as well as for many of our color pictures.

The majority of the research represented in this book was carried on under the auspices of the Tribhuvan University, Kathmandu. Thanks are due to His Majesty's Government for the opportunity given our family to have a share in the life of the Magars.

CONTENTS

Chapter 1: Angel Tracks 3
Chapter 2: Our Turn 9
Chapter 3: Major Thapa 23
Chapter 4: Retirement Years 33
Chapter 5: Arakhala 45
Chapter 6: Beginnings 63
Chapter 7: Aganda—The Life of a Shaman 79
Chapter 8: Pegleg 97
Chapter 9: Goodbye 115
Chapter 10: Home Again 135
Chapter 11: Hazards 149
Chapter 12: Deforestation 159
Chapter 13: Black Pepper and Witches 171
Chapter 14: Crow's Blood and Leopard's Milk 189
Chapter 15: The King 207
Chapter 16: "No More Sacrifice" 219
Chapter 17: Community Development Problems . . . 233

Appendix I: Hunting Deities of Arakhala 252
Appendix II: Sacrifices Performed by Hunters 255
Appendix III: Songs and Dances and their Religious Significance 258
Appendix IV: English-Nepali-Magar Word List 263
Appendix V: A Note on Onomatopoeia in Magar. . . . 267

CHAPTER 1:

ANGEL TRACKS

Out of food, and now we'd lost the trail! Before us a wall of rock sneered down through the swirling clouds. To our right we peered over the lip of a steep, narrow, snowy gorge. To the left, impassable mountains. At 15,500 feet the trail had disappeared under the hard snow. The pass was hidden up there somewhere, still another two thousand feet above. But how were we to negotiate the pathless face of a mountain?

Our Tibetan porters were on the verge of revolt. The situation looked hopeless, our plans finished. To turn back seemed the logical course. Why should we risk our lives now? We had only wanted to find the speakers of an exotic language. Since no one could tell us for sure where they lived, we had come to find out. But we hadn't found out, and to turn back now would mean a month of hardship for nothing.

This was my first experience in the wilds of Nepal. It was October 1969, Dolpo District, on the north side of the Dhaulagiri Himalayas. There were just Dave Watters, two Tibetan porters and myself. We were checking the languages spoken in the area, hoping to find where the Khams lived. We had wanted to locate a village where Dave could live to study their language and customs. I had come along because we thought there might be Magars in the same area. We were good friends and had hoped that Dave could work in one valley with the Khams and I in the next with the Magars.

Now we'd been on the trail for three weeks. We were making a circle through the Himalayas and it was still a long way back to the remote airstrip where we'd started. Twelve hours a day on the rugged trails had begun to drain the excitement out of our trip. Now we just wanted to find a suitable village for Dave and get back to Kathmandu. We would rather go over this pass as planned if it were possible. But how?

The only way was to go down into that uninviting gorge, the "gorge-of-no-return," as I termed it in my mind. Dave wandered back along the rim. Some minutes later he shouted for me to come join him. He had discovered a three-foot-high pile of rocks, a *chorten.* We knew this was what the local people built to propitiate the gods at mountain passes and other dangerous places, a place where prayer or offering was made to secure help in the dangers ahead. Dave exclaimed that the trail had to be under the snow next to this *chorten.*

Then he pointed out a single set of light footprints in the snow. They began at the rim of the gorge and meandered to the bottom. Three hundred feet below, I made out the tracks heading for the crest.

As we discussed the alternatives, our Tibetan porters began to balk. They realized too that there would be no turning back. Though we might make it safely down to the floor of the gorge, there would be no possibility of climbing back up the icy trail hidden beneath the snow.

Despite the obvious dangers, Dave and I were intrigued by the footprints. How could they possibly be there? The monsoon rains were slow to quit that year, so every afternoon the clouds had built up, bringing rain on us in the valley. That meant snow at this altitude and ruled out the possibility that the tracks were from someone who had come through the previous day.

But how could anyone have gotten ahead of us? Cramped up in a tiny, empty, herder's hut we had spent the night at twelve thousand feet. Rising before dawn, we had seen nothing but miles of empty alpine meadow above us. It was possible that someone who knew the trail had started out from his village miles below and passed us while it was still dark. But he would have had to start out in the middle of the night.

When we had offered to pay generously for someone to guide us to the top of the pass, we had been told that no one crossed the pass this late in the year. "Too much snow now," they had told us. Furthermore, villagers generally were very much afraid of ghosts and spirits. They didn't like to go out at night even in small groups, much less alone. Would such a villager hike for hours alone in the dark? It was improbable, to say the least. But what other explanation was there?

The only certain thing was that a single set of very light tracks lay in the snow before us. That was a fact we could see. If we chose to follow the tracks, either we would find the creature that had made them or they would lead us back over the Himalayas. If we chose to turn back we would obviously please our porters. I noticed that while we talked, Sheto seemed to be doing his best to change our minds; the prayer beads in the old Tibetan's hand were flying through his fingers as he awaited our decision. We'd push on!

I had a single hundred-foot-length of nylon rope with me. We tied all four of us together, and Dave, taking the lead, eased himself down over the lip of the crevasse. Quite unlike the footprints ahead of us, which were made with obvious ease, Dave had to stamp out each step deep into the snow in order to get a firm footing. Sheto, following behind me, was wearing the traditional Tibetan boots. But Angdrak, the younger porter trailing in the rear, was not so well-equipped; he had only tennis shoes. On his second or third step over the rim, his feet flew out from under him and down he came on top of us.

The older porter steadied himself for the jolt and grabbed on to Angdrak. We had survived!

What could we do to keep Angdrak on the mountain? We had no climbing gear. Dave was using his umbrella like an ice axe, stabbing it into the rocks and snow to steady himself. We had joked about this fancy piece of climbing gear, but in fact the umbrella proved quite helpful. I handed mine to Angdrak, and we continued our descent. Without the umbrella to steady myself, I slipped twice on the frozen rocks and began to slide out of control. But on both occasions Dave and Sheto were able to keep their footing when the rope snapped tight. It was a relief to reach the bottom an hour and a half later. My hands had grown numb from grasping onto the ice and rock, but soon the feeling returned as we strode rapidly up the floor of the gorge.

We knew we had a long way to go yet to reach Sisne Valley on the south side. For the next four hours we would see no trail. Where the sun had burned off the snow, we took the natural way. Where there was snow or mud, there would be the footprints to urge us on.

Dave, a severe asthmatic from birth, surged on ahead. His lung cage, enlarged from a lifetime of gasping, allowed him to inhale large amounts of the rarified air. At last breathing had become exhilarating to him. I, on the other hand, lagged far behind, lucky to climb a hundred feet at a stretch before becoming fatigued.

After two hours of climbing, we reached the crest. There we were enveloped in thick clouds. The other side of the mountain, however, seemed to be straight down. It was an eerie feeling to peer over the edge and see nothing—nothing but a cloud-filled abyss. Again the thoughts raced through my mind: "After all this, would we have to turn back? How could we?" I took out the rope again and Dave tied it around his waist. Slowly he picked his way over the edge and in a couple of steps was out of sight. When the rope became taut, he shouted back for us to come on ahead and we followed gingerly down through the loose shale. Wherever there was snow, Dave followed the tracks. Where the snow had melted, it was purely guesswork.

Slowly we made our way down the face of the mountain. The trail was treacherous. For all the times I fell on the ice and rocks I should have broken my ankle several times. But the worst I received was a badly bruised hand. In one place Dave began slipping down the side of a steep rock wall. Fortunately I was in a good spot and able to hold him. The tracks led us across rock slides and wound through a maze of cliffs, some of which plunged for a thousand feet or more. In many places we came to so-called bridges across the face of a cliff. To make the bridge, the villagers had spanned the void with two or three poles bound together with grass ropes. Although the bridges were usually not over thirty feet long, the poles were shaky and looked as if they would come apart at any moment. It was the worst part of the trip. Often we couldn't even see to the bottom of the chasm. I consoled myself with the thought that if the poles gave way, it would make little difference how many hundred feet it was to the rocks below. Our fate would be the same.

Finally, about mid-afternoon we saw our last footprint as we broke out onto a solid alpine trail. On we raced to reach Sisne Village before dark. The trail was much too narrow and precarious to sleep on; one could roll over in the night and that would be it!

Soon darkness fell and still there was no sign of the village. Cautiously we groped our way along until we came to a shallow stream bed. There it was safe to roll out our sleeping bags. But what about a fire? Every piece of wood was wet. Our porters were not dismayed, however. Out came their goatskin bellows and soon they had a cheery fire going.

Breakfast had been some small pieces of mutton, two small eggs, a little oatmeal, sugar and powdered milk. I'd mixed it all together, and we'd shared the ill-tasting porridge equally. There was nothing left for dinner now except some scraps of meat, a handful of rice and tea. But we didn't mind; we were satisfied to be safe.

At dawn the next morning we hurried on, expecting to reach Sisne at any time, but it was four hours before we arrived. We were famished and looking forward to a good meal. To our surprise, we found that the villagers were reluctant to sell us anything from their meager supply. Finally, one generous fellow agreed to let us have a small bowl of potatoes; that was all we had for the day.

Clinging to the steep mountainside, the Tibetan-style houses of Sisne crowded together in rows like a giant staircase. The thick, flat roofs of a lower row were usually the "front yards" of the houses in the row above. The trail led right across the edge of these roofs and no one could pass through unnoticed. With huge mastiffs growling from every side, it was a relief to leave the village behind.

Only then did I think to ask Dave if he had inquired about the fellow that had preceded us over the pass. He replied that he had asked, but the answer had been, "No one!" So it is that from that time onward we have referred to them as our "angel tracks."

The next three days were frustrating. The trail down the valley certainly wasn't designed for speed. But slow progress was not our biggest problem. Not only did we fail to find Khams living in Sisne Valley, but worst of all, the people would not sell us food. After three days of hiking on nearly-empty stomachs, we finally made the last turn in the loop we were making through the Himalayas.

As we headed east up the Uttar Ganga River toward our starting point, we came upon village after village of Khams. Finally we had discovered the right valley. These were the people Dave had heard about and finally found! Dave's excitement was short-lived, however. There was a more pressing problem—food! Would these people sell us food or not?

That evening we stopped at the village of Garkhani. While we were inquiring about a place to stay the night, we could hardly believe our ears when we heard a friendly voice say, "Come! You must stay at my house!"

It was a retired soldier from the British Gurkha regiments. As he hustled to sweep off the porch and lay out a mat for us, he asked, "What can I get you to eat?"

It was like a dream. Price was no concern. Cautiously we inquired, "How about eggs or a chicken?"

"Certainly!" he responded, and off he trotted. Soon he was back with two roosters and a dozen eggs. We had certainly found the right valley. In a few days everything was set up for Dave's return. We had found the Khams.

For me it was a different matter, for I had learned on this trip that the Magars I was looking for were definitely not to be found in a nearby valley. For me it meant another trip—more searching.

CHAPTER 2:

OUR TURN

Nepal, a land of mystery, full of enchantment and fascinating places. Certainly it is one of the most interesting countries that the world has to offer. Visitors flock by the thousands to Kathmandu to get a glimpse of Mt. Everest. Many others make the climb to its base in order to experience firsthand the awesomeness of this great wonder of the world.

Nepal, however, is far more than Mt. Everest. People get a glimpse of it, perhaps spend a few days on the trail with some Sherpas and then feel that they really know Nepal. But Nepal is a country of such extremes and contrasts that a lifetime is not sufficient to learn them all.

Few people realize that along its southern border there is a five-hundred-mile strip of hot jungle plains, called the Terai, which separates Nepal from India. Lying only a few hundred feet above sea level, the Terai formerly was plagued with malaria and dangerous animals, but now it is the important grain belt of modern-day Nepal. Between the great extremes in the north and south are the hills, the traditional home of the majority of the Nepalese people. These lie squeezed together like the folds of a giant accordion which have been torn and twisted every which way. Perhaps only in Nepal would such a rugged scramble of ridges and peaks be called "hills," for they rise to ten thousand feet! But if these razor-backed ripples of rock criss-crossing the midriff of Nepal were called "mountains," then what word would be left to describe the Himalayas towering two to three times their height?

The climate, the flora and fauna and the way people live vary radically in different parts of Nepal. At least eight hundred different species of birds roam within its borders. There the bird enthusiast may be able to spot such widely differing varieties as the greater flamingo and the Tibetan snow cock.

In a number of places the deep valleys cut right through the Himalayas, bringing the hot air of the Indian plains along with them. This creates some curious extremes. In the Arun River valley, for instance, live the Lhomi people. Some of their number live over the border inside Tibet. On the Nepal side, however, some of the Lhomi villages are situated just east of the Makalu Himal. Here, at fourteen thousand feet, they graze their herds of yak. But at the bottom of the slope some ten thousand feet below, their brothers are growing bananas and rice!

Some people come to Nepal to see the Himalayas, others to see the ancient city of Kathmandu. To still others, it is Nepal's position as a small, neutral, landlocked country, squeezed between the giants of India and China, that gives it special significance. What caught my interest, however, was the great variety of ethnic groups tucked away in its inaccessible valleys.

Previously, most of these groups in Nepal were not known to the outside world. In fact, only a few people in Nepal knew much about them or could tell us where they were located. The Khams, for instance, were just such a group. Though more than forty thousand people spoke the Kham language, it was next-to-impossible to find anyone in Kathmandu who had even heard of them.

Of the numerous ethnic groups in Nepal, there was one group in particular that caught my attention. These people were the Magars, a major group whose actual numbers may never be known. There were 300,000 people who spoke that language, but like the Khams and most other ethnic groups, a considerable number of Magars now spoke only the national language, Nepali. Everywhere Magars were found they had gained a reputation for honesty and hard work. The Magars were a Mongolian people who had migrated into Nepal in the predawn of history. Many of the ethnic groups had legends that told how they had come to Nepal from Tibet or some other country, but not the Magars. For them at least, history simply began and ended in Nepal.

In the sixteenth century the Magars invaded Kathmandu under the leadership of the Palpa king Mukunda Sen. In the 1750s, Prithibi Narayan Shah, the "father of modern Nepal," was consolidating the many petty kingdoms scattered across the land. For this task he counted heavily upon his Magar soldiers. The outside world, however, came to know of the Magars only after the British began recruiting soldiers in Nepal for their Gurkha regiments. The British quickly came to appreciate the Magars' qualities and they became a major part of their Nepali contingent.

But what were the Magars really like? How did they live? What were their hopes and fears? What was their society like that made them what they were? To really know them first hand meant learning their language.

On our trek through the Himalayas, Dave and I had recorded five hitherto unknown languages. The number of languages to be discovered throughout Nepal was absolutely astounding. Most people passing through the back country never gave it a thought. They generally found someone who spoke Nepali and did whatever business they had with him. What confused the language issue was how various ethnic groups would take on the same name. I was to learn that there were at least five different groups who spoke very different languages, yet each claimed they were the Magars! I presume the explanation is this: as successive waves of immigrants moved into Nepal, those who settled next to the Magars were quick to take the name of the original inhabitants, which gave them a degree of acceptance and made them insiders.

But who were the real Magars—the original ones? I found that most likely it was the Magar community which was to be found in Central Nepal in Palpa, Syangja and

Tanahu Districts. Ross Caughley from New Zealand had already begun work on the Chepang language in the mountains of nearby Makwanpur, and he agreed to accompany Dave and me on the trip to this area. Information was scarce about exactly where speakers of the language could be found, and travel was limited to the few airstrips in use at the time. I had in hand, however, a list of Magar words I had acquired in Kathmandu, from a student at Tribhuvan University.

We had come to Nepal to work under the Summer Institute of Linguistics (SIL), which was working in cooperation with Tribhuvan University. To carry on its research in the minority languages, SIL recruited volunteers from around the world to work in the twenty-five different countries where it had projects. In addition to the U.S. and Canada, volunteers for Nepal came from Japan, New Zealand, Australia, Austria, Holland, Switzerland, Germany, England, Finland and Norway.

SIL policy was to apply the expertise of its members to each country's peculiar situation, and to serve them in whatever way possible. In Nepal, the primary goals centered around linguistic research and its future application to literacy problems. However, SIL also helped with training Nepali linguists and building the University Press. In selected villages, the volunteers found many ways to assist with local health and community development. In addition, a STOL plane and expert pilots were made available to RNAC, the national airlines, at a time when a rapid increase in demand was taxing the young airline's growing facilities.

My turn to contribute to the program had come now. I was eager to go as we climbed aboard the Royal Nepal Airlines DC-3 and left Kathmandu for the Gorkha airstrip. At the mission hospital in Gorkha we were referred to a Peace Corps volunteer in Bandipur. So we headed south and crossed over into Tanahu District to see him. He, in turn, told us to see a Major Thapa, the Pradhan Pancha of nearby Ambu Panchayat.

As we walked through the forests and over the fields, I drank in all that I could. The thick forests covering the rugged mountains were interrupted by cleared areas of terraced fields. Unlike some parts of Nepal, deforestation was not yet a serious problem. Typical of Nepal's mountainous areas were the steep, narrow terraces which had been carved out of the hillsides over the centuries. From a distance, the small, closely built villages of thatch-roofed houses looked close. But reaching them by the trails, which fell into deep gorges and twisted along the uneven hillsides, took hours.

Following the unfamiliar trails was a real problem. They were constantly splitting, forcing us to guess which fork was the main trail. If there was no one to give us directions we were liable to make the wrong choice and end up stranded in the forest or standing at someone's lonely goat shed. At nearly every village there was a quaint-looking mustard oil press. Their creaking and groaning could be heard for some distance as three or four villagers pushed the heavy timber in endless circles. Carved out of the trunk of a hardwood tree, this machine of age-old design never ceased to catch my interest.

As we hiked along, I thought that this should be the area where the Magars lived. But I wondered, "Do they still speak their language?" In some places I'd heard that they had given it up in favor of Nepali, the national language. On our third day we came upon a group of people sitting on the flat stones beside the trail. The women wore blouses made of colorful maroon velvet. From their earlobes dangled flat, saucerlike golden earrings the diameter of an orange, and around their necks were draped bunches of green, blue or yellow glass bead necklaces. At first sight I knew these amiable-looking people were different. Then, as we passed the chattering group, I noticed that their speech was unintelligible. This was it! It had to be Magar; we had found the right place.

It wouldn't be easy; there wasn't a single book or course available about their language. As far as we knew, we would be the first outsiders to attempt to master their exotic tongue. That would take years, but it was the only way to learn about these smiling, friendly people. To learn their language we would have to go and live with them.

Adorned in black velvet and wearing two nose rings and two different ear rings, a village girl is ready for the dance.

When we met Major Thapa the next day, I was delighted to see a smile crease his broad, golden-brown face. His high cheekbones, bright oval eyes, barrel chest and muscular legs were all that I had imagined a Magar to be. But what about the language his village spoke? Was it the same as the list I had, or was it some other strange dialect?

He helped me check out his language. "For water, we say *di*, and for meat, *sya*. For fish, it is literally 'water-meat', *disya*," he volunteered.

As I went through a list of one hundred words, I was intent on writing them correctly in phonetic script, so that I could accurately reproduce them at a later date. When I had finished with the list, Major Thapa surprised me by asking, "Now, what is the Magar word for fish?"

I hadn't been paying attention to the meanings of so many new words and already I was being put to the test! Thankfully, somehow I was able to recall the word *disya* and repeat it to him in a satisfactory way. He seemed pleased. He offered to find us a house in which to stay and promised to help us in whatever way he could. I took him up on the offer and told him I'd be back with my wife within three weeks. As we left, I wondered, "Would he really get us a place to stay or not? This is the East, and people always want to please you and say something nice. But how should he know? I might never come back and he would go to a lot of trouble for nothing."

Back in Kathmandu we planned, shopped and prepared for the trip. Soon the time was gone and we were to leave for Yangchok the next day. How well I remember the dreadful experience. Barbara had purchased everything we would need for our two-and-a-half-month stay and had it ready for me to pack. The kerosene was in plastic containers. The flour, sugar and rice were already packed in five-gallon tins. But the rest—dried vegetables, noodles, cooking oil, our clothing, sleeping bags, books, pots, pans and a multitude of other items—was all in a mess! It had to be packed in boxes in a way that it wouldn't break, get punctured or leak on something else. Yet it had to be compact enough to fit inside SIL's little Cessna 206 aircraft.

When I finally had all the things packed up, even if they could have fitted in, we were well over the maximum load the little plane could carry. I had to disassemble it all and start again. Barbara took seriously her job of providing for the needs of the home and everything she had laid out was a "necessity." On the other hand, my job was to get everything to fit in the plane, and in the process I was ruining her future home by throwing out large amounts of "necessities." Often I would throw something out, only to find it a few minutes later slipped back under the pile to be packed! It seemed I packed and repacked innumerable times only to find that we were still overweight.

At 1:30 a.m. I quit. Two hours later I was up again, this time with more zeal for "ruining" her home. When we reached the airport that morning, Barbara was upset. Riding along in the airplane with us would be an official observer. This resulted from a new, routine government requirement for all flights with non-Nepali pilots, and meant that sixty kilos of food and "home" had to be left behind to make room for the observer. I was glad that it was the pilot this time and not me who told her to pick out the boxes she didn't want!

Weeks earlier while Dave and I had been sitting in Dhorpatan, our pilot, Wayne Aeschliman, had been sent out on a flight to pick up people in nearby Baglung. When he arrived, no one was there. He knew that just over the ridge in Dhorpatan we were anxiously waiting; with the plane empty, he badly wanted to come pick us up. It would save him a two-and-a-half-hour flight the next day, not to mention the costs involved. It would take just a twenty-minute run up the valley, and no one would know the difference in this remote area. But, no; the government required that every flight be registered in advance, and he always abided by that ruling. Likewise, Wayne made it plain that morning that he would have nothing to do with any desires we might have of flying without the observer or of overloading the plane.

As soon as Wayne landed the plane at the Gorkha airstrip, I rounded up porters for the loads and we headed for Yangchok. When we reached the Marsyandi River we found that the ferry operators of the dugout canoe had finished for the day. So we backtracked to the nearest village and spent a chilly night on a villager's veranda.

From November onwards, fog lies thick in the valleys of the inner hills, and the next morning was no exception. After crossing the river we stumbled around on one small trail after another, unable to find the right ridge. Some three hours later we finally climbed above the heavy fog. It was nice to be in the sun and soon we arrived at Major Thapa's doorstep. True to his word, he had a village house swept and cleaned, ready for our arrival. And out back, to our astonishment, he had dug an outdoor toilet.

For two years we stayed in Yangchok, living there two to four months at a time and then taking breaks back in Kathmandu. It was a rewarding time. Our "angel track" experience had been a portent of sorts for the years to come: difficulties and excitement sprinkled generously with priceless friendships.

When we moved into our house, we found that we were in a whole new world. First of all, we might as well have been people from another planet for all the interest we raised. Everyone pressed in to get a better look at the strange sight. To our relief, the crowd around us died down after a few days, but it never seemed to disappear completely. Anyone who had any visitors would be sure to bring them over for a good long look at us. Often they would stand and watch us for hours, thoroughly amused by the way we did things.

They particularly enjoyed watching Barbara cook. To their way of thinking, she was surely the world's worst cook. It never seemed to occur to them that we cooked food differently than they did; they would titter and laugh as they watched her mix things together. The best joke of all was when she made bread. No matter how many times they told her, Barbara never put enough water in. Then, instead of pouring it out like a pancake batter as they did, she made it into big lumps and cooked it! Though they thought her to be a terrible cook, it was rewarding that they always enjoyed tasting the products of her labor.

Before we had been there long, I realized that I was going to have to break my bad habit of standing up straight; either that or I would have to quit my work with the Magars. The doorways into their houses were about four feet high, and inside, the ceiling was only about five feet. (This made their houses easier to heat in the winter.) I did okay in the daylight or when I wasn't preoccupied, but the rest of the time was horrible. I'd bend my head to miss the low frame, but not enough. Sometimes the blow was such that I'd stagger back and have to sit down before I made another attempt to enter our house. And inside our smoke-blackened home it was no better. It was a rare day that I didn't stand up quickly or turn around and slam my head into the ceiling. For the first few months with the Magars, our heads never ceased to have bumps—and bumps on the bumps!

One day I got fed up with my headaches and started digging. I dug the dirt floor down until my head neatly fit under every sagging timber in the old house. As the pile of dirt in our front yard got higher each day, our landlord became concerned. He was afraid that I'd dig away the foundation of the house and it would collapse. To make him happy I refrained from digging for a couple of days, but after accumulating another big knot on my head I started back in. Eventually I finished and, to his relief, the house stood firm.

As we began learning the Magar language, we soon found that we were in for trouble. There was a sound that worked like a tone, but wasn't. It was a breathy feature that would cover a whole syllable. Discovering the breathiness was one thing, but hearing it in normal speech and reproducing it ourselves was altogether a different problem. The howls of laughter that erupted after our attempts to copy them was always a good indication that it would be a long time before we had fully grasped the secrets of their language.

There were many word pairs in the language that were distinguished only by the presence or absence of the breathiness, such as "throw away"/"buy" and "believe"/"curse." But there was another pair that amused the villagers most of all. These were the words *munga* and *mhunga*, which meant "boiled" and "tired." It didn't take long before we discovered this word pair. But even though I knew it, my tongue seemed perversely bent on spitting out the wrong word. The result was that I was forever saying such ridiculous things as "The rice is tired," or "I'm boiled!" The villagers, though, enjoyed it immensely.

In the springtime it is hot and dry in the hills. Though there is occasional rain, it is not sufficient to water a garden. This meant that the villagers had no fresh vegetables to eat for a number of months. I had grown a garden all my life, so I thought this would be a good opportunity to show the villagers how they could improve their diet. Of course, I would have to water the plants from time to time, but I thought the results would make it well worthwhile.

There was one thing, though, that I hadn't counted on, and that was the persistence of the village chickens. They were fed very skimpily and had to count on their own efforts to keep their stomachs filled. I fenced my garden as well as I could and managed to get some vegetables growing, but the larger they got, the greater the temptation became for the neighbors' chickens. Soon the largest chickens began flying over the fence and having a good meal at my expense.

I decided that in the name of progress I should take things into my own hands to discourage these intruders. I had brought a slingshot along with me, so I decided to shoot them just hard enough to teach them a lesson. The problem was that I wasn't a good shot and they always ran away before I got close enough. Then as soon as I was out of sight, they'd come right back to make a meal out of my garden.

One day I spied the biggest offender, our neighbor's prize rooster, standing right beside my garden. This time he was close enough not to miss. So, pulling back the rubber a little extra for good measure, I aimed at his wing and let loose. I watched in shock as the rooster crumpled to the ground and, with a great deal of thrashing, went tumbling down over the terraces. To my chagrin, the little boys watching me began shouting at the top of their voices, "He's killed the rooster! He's killed the rooster!"

I'd hit him in the head and killed him! Now I would have my neighbor mad at me for my foolishness. That would be just another burden for Major Thapa. When we needed water, firewood, eggs or porters, he was the one who would arrange it for us and set the price. He was the one who took so much time to help us learn the language. If there was ever a problem, he was there, ready to help. He was exactly the same age as my father and treated us as his own children. He'd spent so much effort on our behalf, but now I'd added this problem unnecessarily.

The boys raced down the hill to find the chicken, and after a few minutes brought him back. I heaved a great sigh of relief when I saw that he wasn't yet dead. After a while the rooster recovered and staggered off home, still somewhat dizzy. I had planned to teach the chicken a thing or two, but probably I was the one who learned the biggest lesson that day!

Major Thapa's house was near ours and we often went over there to see him. We were fortunate in this, because as the Pradhan Pancha of the *panchayat,* the life of the whole area revolved around him. This gave us an excellent opportunity to observe what was going on and then inquire of him about anything that puzzled us.

One of the most interesting things that happened during our time in Yangchok had to do with the Major's eldest son. Our neighbor had gone off on a four-hour hike to the village of Ambukot to arrange a marriage for his son. He and the girl's father had come to an agreement, and so they had arranged a meeting between the prospective couple at a festival held a few days later. The young people had liked each other and agreed to the marriage.

Then our neighbor went on the appointed day with a dozen or so friends and relatives to perform the engagement ceremony. But at this point, the girl's parents unexpectedly said that they wanted to wait a year or two longer before letting her marry. So our neighbor and a couple of friends sat down that evening with the girl's parents in a corner of the veranda. They had to iron out the problem. It was very embarrassing. How could they return home without completing the ceremony? Everyone would hear that they'd been put off and they'd never live it down.

Back home on leave from the army, the Major's eldest son was there that night. While the rest milled about awaiting the outcome, he nurtured his own ideas. Being a leader like his father, he decided to do something and began talking persuasively to the girl. "Don't you really like Mailha? Look at what a strong young man he is. This is your only chance! Once we have been turned down by your parents, do you think that anyone else will ever again risk being embarrassed like this? No! No one will ever dare to come again for the engagement ceremony. You will die an old maid! If you really want to marry Mailha, go inside your house with him right now!"

As soon as she had gone inside with Mailha, the Major's son grabbed the rooster they had brought along for the ceremony. Out came his sharp sickle-knife, and with a stroke he lopped the rooster's head off. Quickly he sprinkled the rooster's spurting blood over the doorposts. Then, with a thump, he threw the bird onto the yard. Hearing the dead rooster thrashing, the girl's parents looked up with astonishment from their corner of the veranda.

The party had begun. With the sacrifice given, the house god had been appeased and the engagement completed. Only a proper divorce could separate the couple now. That would have to be accompanied by a very large payment from the girl's parents. According to custom, the marriage must be completed within a few weeks. About two weeks later, I went with the men to collect the bride. The party included a big feast and an all-night celebration at the bride's house. The next day we brought her home to Yangchok, accompanied by the steady rhythm of the oboe, long trumpets, drums and cymbals.

As we stayed on in Yangchok, we began to have our doubts as to whether this was the best place to live. We had wanted to find out what the real Magars were like, but somehow we got the feeling that we were missing something. Half of the people living in Yangchok were Brahmans. They were the priestly caste in Hinduism and as such were the educated elite. When they had filtered into Nepal centuries before, they had traditionally taken the lead and dominated wherever they had settled.

Occasionally, this situation of having two different groups of people living in the same village resulted in an interesting cultural clash. One day there was a terrible wailing going on at Major Thapa's house, so I went over to see what had happened. It turned out that a little Brahman boy had come to look at the white pig we were raising. He had never seen one before and had leaned over the pen to get a closer look. The pig jumped up and "kissed" the boy on the head. The boy was distraught; the pig was an untouchable animal and now he had been defiled and lost his caste. However, Major Thapa came to his aid, sprinkled some "holy water" on him and cleansed him from the defilement. The boy regained his composure and, satisfied that all was well, trotted off home.

The Magars in Yangchok were obviously heavily influenced by the Brahman culture. Only in Yangchok had the Magars adopted the Brahman custom of abstaining from eating buffalo meat. Then there was the problem that we presented: what caste were we? Although we were educated, a privilege reserved for the high castes, yet according to their dietary laws we were the lowest, the untouchable caste. This meant that we were excluded from entering anyone's home! Major Thapa apologized for this and said, except for his mother's strong stand, he would readily invite us in. After we had been there a year and had begun to speak Magar well, she relented on this and eventually the other Magars did likewise.

That the village was heavily influenced by the Brahmans was not Major Thapa's doing; he himself held to a less severe interpretation of the Hindu religion. Major Thapa was the one we leaned upon in every difficulty. He was the one who helped and taught us so much in our first years with the Magars. As we learned more about him we found that his life read like the classical rags-to-riches story. But more than that, we found that it was the story of a great man whom success could not spoil.

CHAPTER 3:

MAJOR THAPA

Rugged Gurkha soldier, bodyguard to the Queen of England, East mingling with West. What made Major Nar Bahadur Thapa the man he had become? What were the roots which enabled him to rise to the highest military position obtainable for an uneducated Nepali tribesman?

Life was simple for the peasant lad among the remote hills of central Nepal. It meant hitching up the oxen, plowing the fields and planting the corn, millet or rice. After that, there were the fields to weed and the harvest to reap. Hard work it was, but the jovial nature of the Magar people, expressed regularly in song and dance, eased the burden. As his livestock grazed along the mountain, the Magar boy would fill the air with songs that would resound throughout the forest. After the day's work was done he would join his friends, singing and dancing for a few hours before dinner. On special days he would eat and have a short nap; then he would sing and dance with his friends till dawn the next day.

In addition to the field work, there was the daily routine of gathering wood for the fire and cutting fodder for the goats, cows and water buffaloes. As often as possible, these jobs were punctuated with regular forays along the streams for fish and crabs, and into the forest for birds and animals. Unlike their relatives higher up on the mountain,

In the nachan *dance Ludre acts the part of the King while two young men portray the queens.*

the Magars of Yangchok owned some irrigated rice fields in the valley below. These kept them extra busy, but also provided them with sufficient food in most years.

During those days under the restrictive Rana regime, it was against the law for a simple peasant of tribal blood, such as Nar, to learn to read and write. But Nar was an enterprising lad. In a nearby Brahman village lived a rich man who had hired someone to teach the Brahman children. So Nar, when he had the opportunity, would sit and look over a boy's shoulder as he recited his lessons. This was the beginning and end of his formal education. From such a start as this, who would have guessed that the barefoot lad dressed in rough homemade clothing would rise to become a friend of kings and queens, an acquaintance of ministers and ambassadors in the courts of Europe? It strikes us more like a fairy tale than the real-life story of the man who, more than any other, would become like a father to us in a strange land.

When Nar was twelve years of age, his father arranged for him to embark on an apprenticeship to a famous doctor. Based at nearby Mankauna in Gorkha District was an itinerant healer, a shaman. Nar carried the man's bag and was, in essence, his servant. As his life unfolded, it was characteristic of Nar that he always found great satisfaction in serving others, regardless of their stature and position in life.

Under the apprenticeship of the old shaman, Nar gained entry into the ancient realm of healing arts. He learned how, when and where to collect many sorts of herbal remedies. After two years, having mastered the indigenous methods of dealing with the various spirits and deities, Nar was judged by his teacher to be competent. When there were calls to go to more than one place at the same time, the shaman would send his apprentice off to one village while he himself went to another. Soon, however, an incident took place which led Nar to end his budding career as a shaman.

When a shaman is summoned to heal someone or to divine a matter, he sits down, lights some incense and appeals to the gods to come and speak through him as their mouthpiece. Soon he begins to tremble and shake uncontrollably as he goes into a trance. While in this state the god speaks out of the shaman's mouth in one or a number of different languages. Thus the divine answer is given to such questions as why one is sick, which sacrifice is necessary to bring about the healing, where to find a lost item or how to solve a pressing problem.

One day young Nar was called to go into a trance. Earnestly he began the ritual. Just as his teacher had done, Nar began to shake. He trembled and shook with all his might, but not one utterance came. Eventually he gave up in frustration and humiliation. Shamefacedly he returned to his teacher and inquired what the problem might be. The shaman replied that these things did happen, but one could save face by being very observant upon coming into a village. Then if the gods did not speak, one could say, "By such-and-such a tree is a rock with such-and-such a shape. If on that rock you will do a sacrifice, such-and-such a god will be pleased and fulfill your wishes." With a shock, the realization came over the lad that this man, who was revered by the peasants everywhere, would actually deceive them in order to protect his own reputation.

Honor, glory and personal profit aside, Nar's conscience could not condone such a practice, and after this incident his interest in the shaman business waned. He kept on, however, with the medicinal herbs and never ceased learning the usages of jungle plants from those who were proficient. I still remember the day my wife, Barbara, and I were climbing the trail up to Yangchok with him. He stopped and pointed to a plant. "See that miniature fern in the damp, shady corner beside the trail? Don't forget it! If you ever have a toothache, chew it up and place it next to the tooth and the pain will be gone in no time. It will handle the worst of toothaches!" he exclaimed.

Often I saw him with some type of root, leaf, berry or bark that he was preserving. Later he would use it to heal some ailing villager. He told me that he was familiar with a hundred or more different jungle medicines. It would be a full-time job, however, to collect and process them all. If they were not picked at just the right season they would either be too weak and useless or sometimes too strong and fatal. "The shamans," he said, "were acquainted with many of these drugs, but usually they preferred to deceive the people rather than to go to all the trouble necessary to process the drugs themselves."

Years later when he returned from the army, Nar made his own private war against the shamans, deriding them at every opportunity. When he became headman, he refused to let any of them perform in his village. In fact, he even destroyed their principal place of sacrifice. Though he was continually denouncing the shamans, one day he let slip out that there were some shamans who weren't fakes.

As a teenager, he had once been overcome by a strange sickness and was very near death. A shaman was called, and a few minutes after he had gone into his trance and called upon the gods, Nar was completely well. The real shamans had tremendous spirit power, he acknowledged. Their work was neither sleight of hand nor fake magic; their power was truly superhuman in origin.

In the old days, the big adventure of the year was the annual winter trip to the Indian border to purchase salt and other necessities. The Magars could make it through the mountains and across the plains to the border in three days of fast walking. On the return trip, however, with many men carrying over one hundred pounds of salt, it took five days. Four or five villages would band together and depart on an auspicious day. Carrying drums with them, they would sing their way across the hot, dusty miles.

The forested plains at that time were full of wild oxen, elephants, tigers and rhinos. On one occasion when Nar was along, a tiger was lurking in the nearby underbrush. Perhaps disturbed by all the noise, the tiger roared a fierce warning. The whole group pushed and shoved one another as they raced away for their lives. The tiger, however, never attacked.

On another occasion, they narrowly escaped injury when some wild elephants came during the night to drink at the water hole where they had camped. Everyone held their breath and the elephants left without incident. Danger and narrow escapes like this were a way of life to the brave Magars.

In 1929 at the age of sixteen, Nar joined the Nepali army. He was stationed in nearby Bandipur and given a salary of four rupees per month. This was the beginning of a service that would last for thirty-three years and take him throughout a large part of the world.

When he turned eighteen, he quit the Nepali army and went out to Gorakhpur in India and enlisted in the British Gurkha Forces. There he was paid sixteen rupees per month. After recruit training, he was stationed together with another man who was to play a key role in our life with the Magars. Being among the best in the regiment at singing and dancing, the two were part of a troupe which performed on special occasions. Practically every night they would get together to practice and compose new songs.

In 1935 Nar was stationed in Abbottabad, a post not far from the Afghanistan frontier. He was attached to the 2nd Battalion, 6th Gurkha Regiment. They were attempting to subdue the Pathans, who were waging a guerrilla war against their British overlords. The fighting was sporadic, but sometimes very fierce indeed. It was rough terrain, but hardship was nothing new to the rugged Gurkha soldiers. These hardy men had been used to adversity from their earliest years.

Nar's bulging calf muscles attested to his own physical strength. And no wonder; at home in the village Nar would regularly carry two hundred pounds or more of threshed rice from the valley floor fifteen hundred feet up to his ridge-top home. It was a mark of manhood and a point of competition among the men to carry such huge loads.

I once asked Nar what the heaviest load he had carried was. He told me how a Brahman priest living nearby had wanted a particular stone on which to do his daily ceremonial washings. No one could carry it, so he asked Nar. Nar put his rope around the huge, flat rock, and adjusted it on the top of his forehead. With a man on each side straining to lift the stone, Nar struggled to his feet. The two-hundred-pound loads he regularly carried felt just right and he could move at a good pace up the mountain. But this rock was different. It was so heavy that it was all he could do to move his feet. Shuffling up the trail he finally made it. For this supreme effort the priest paid him twenty-five *paisa* (two cents).

But the ability to endure hardship and the presence of sinewy rock-hard muscles were not the only reasons that the Magars were among the best soldiers of the world. Added to this was their strong sense of fate which kept them fighting against all odds. This was not to imply that they had no fear; it was just that their philosophy of life was such that they could keep that fear under control. If one was destined to die in battle, then he would die. If one was going to live, he would live. Therefore, they concluded, they would fight with all the courage and bravery they could muster. Why be a coward? That would not change one's destiny. If one was fated to die in battle, it was far better to fall with honor than as a coward.

Early in World War II, Nar was stationed in Iran and Iraq. Since the Moslems would have nothing to do with pigs, it was a great opportunity for the soldiers to put their hunting skills to the test. Nar recalls with relish the many feasts they had on the wild boars they killed along the Tigris River. In 1942 they were moved to Syria, Palestine and then on to Africa. In Africa, his unit escaped most of the fighting, but their turn was to come.

With the invasion of Italy in 1943, they were put into the worst of the battles. Nar, by then a sergeant, led his men into battle at Cassino, Gothic Line, Rimini, Montecino, Forli and Padua. The Gurkha soldiers could be depended upon like no others. Of the original twenty-five men in his platoon, hardly a one survived. He lost nine men defending the Gothic Line alone. At Rimini six died in a single day. His losses were replaced by new recruits, and they too were killed. Month after month it went on like this and so it is impossible, he said, to accurately estimate how many of his men were lost.

Often they were greatly outnumbered, but when nightfall came the tables were turned. Now circumstances were right for their specialty: hand-to-hand combat. Quiet as a cat, they would slip out of their trenches and pad off to hunt the enemy. With their *khukuri* knife they usually silenced their opponent with a stroke. Often they would return to their trenches before daybreak, having inflicted a grim toll without ever firing a shot.

In the battles, the opposing armies were sometimes faced off in trenches very close to one another. Many a time a grenade would bounce into Nar's trench. Quickly, he would heave it right back. On one occasion he was too slow and the shrapnel ripped into him, but fortunately the wounds were not serious. As soon as he was out of the hospital, he was put back on the front lines again.

The strong spirit of unity, cooperation and obedience to authority that runs throughout Magar society persisted on the battlefield as well. When the order was given by a British commander to overrun a position, the position was overrun. In some of the fierce fighting in which they were engaged, Nar's unit had been ordered to take a hill. This they did, but all of their ammunition was used up in doing so. Soon they could hear the enemy's crack troops in the trenches less than a hundred yards away, preparing for a counterattack.

Once the Gurkhas had taken the position, it was out of the question for them to retreat without orders; ammunition or not, they would not retreat. Nar ordered his men to take out their long, curved *khukuri* fighting knives. They waved them high above the trench, yelling "Gurkhali (charge)!" It worked. The enemy knew they weren't dealing with American or British troops; they would have to pay a high price to retake their position. The counterattack never came.

After the war, Nar returned home on leave for the first time in five years. Subsequently he was stationed in British India. The short time of service there must have been a perplexing time for Nar and the other Gurkha troops. In Magar society, the concept of unity is the mainspring of life. The Magars themselves, immersed in the workings of their own community as they are, might not make this abstraction so easily; but to the outside observer, it is readily apparent that what really makes their society "tick" is the emphasis on mutual cooperation.

But right next door in postwar British India it was quite different. India was getting its independence and the communal riots between Moslems and Hindus had begun. Nar had just been through the Second Great War, and somehow it was not too difficult to understand how nations could war against nations. But this was neighbor against neighbor. People who had occupied the same land and the same villages together for centuries; people who spoke the same mother tongue.

Nar, who had fought in some of the bitterest battles that war can offer, said that he was aghast at what he saw in India; the killing in the worst battles in Italy seemed like child's play. One day he was ordered to conduct a trainload of grain to a certain Indian city. He and his men sat with their machine guns on top of the train. As the train meandered its way across the country, no one bothered to attack them. The people seemed interested only in killing one another, all in the name of religion! On entering a city, it was not unusual to find the place absolutely deserted except for the thousands of unburied corpses lying about the streets.

After India's independence in 1947, The Nepalese soldiers were split between India and Britain. Nar continued with the British and was sent off to fight the guerrillas in Malaya. Because of the swamp and jungle terrain they were obliged to fight in, those were the worst of all his fighting days. He enjoyed, however, the times off to hunt and fish in the jungle. One day he hid beside a game trail and waited expectantly for a deer to come along. But suddenly, instead of a deer, a tiger appeared. Being an expert marksman, he killed it with one shot. The trophy was not to be his, however; from headquarters came an order to turn in the skin. Who knows where the trophy ended up? I can only imagine that it is gracing some officer's den somewhere, but I don't know. Nar doesn't know either, but if he did, he is the sort of man who wouldn't complain anyway.

Of all his army experiences, the year 1957 was one never to be forgotten. As he stood there among the distinguished men of the British Empire the contrast was remarkable: they—tall, slender, pale-faced with long protruding noses; he—short, stocky, solid as a tank, his brown face graced with a short pug nose. They—graduates of Oxford, Cambridge, and Sandhurst, many tracing their aristocratic blood back for centuries; he—not a day of regular schooling to his credit, a simple peasant's son of the remote sub-Himalayas.

What was he doing there? Was he out of place? No; he wasn't a peasant lad now; he was Captain Thapa, Queen Elizabeth's personal bodyguard! It was the greatest honor offered any Gurkha soldier. For two years, as the Queen's Orderly Officer, Nar went wherever the Queen did. Ambassadors, ministers, the royalty and society of Europe all were known by him. This European high society lifestyle was as far removed from his simple village as it could possibly be. Beyond his wildest boyhood dreams, Nar had made it.

After completing his service with the Queen, Nar was promoted to the rank of Major. This was as high as he could go; no Gurkha soldier was allowed to go any higher. His last assignment was at the Transit Camp in Calcutta where he stayed until his retirement in 1963.

Leaving the army must have felt strange after thirty-one years in the British Forces. His total adult life had been spent in the army, and he had reached the top. Now, he could settle wherever he liked. He could get a plush job and have a life of ease and pleasure. He deserved it. If anyone had earned it, he had.

But no; though he'd been to the top, he'd not forgotten his origin. He'd not forgotten his people and their problems. Retire he would, but he had work to do. He would return to his remote little village.

In England Capt. Thapa attends the wedding of the son of Wall Saheb, his pre-WWII commander.

CHAPTER 4:

RETIREMENT YEARS

While he trekked day after day across the hot dusty trails, what thoughts occupied Major Thapa's mind? Civilization, as the modern world knew it, was left behind. Ahead was his village and his people, living not much differently than their ancestors centuries before. Never mind, changes were coming. His life had been one of service in unquestioned obedience to the British officers and the will of a foreign country. Now he would choose to devote the remaining days of his life to serve HIS people, HIS nation.

In the years that Major Thapa had been in the army, one enormous change had taken place in Nepal. The country had virtually stagnated under a hundred years of Rana rule. But in 1950, with the help of the Indian government, King Tribhuvan escaped from the capital, and in February 1951 he returned to take over the reins of the government. King Tribhuvan's aim was to establish a parliamentary democracy. Perhaps no one ventured to doubt that democracy would soon perform miracles for Nepal. As the years wore on, however, this common hope was rudely shaken.

Political parties, free to operate for the first time, shifted their efforts into high gear to secure power for themselves. Near-chaos resulted. Cooperation was as hard to find among the politicians in those days as the proverbial needle in a haystack. Progress for the nation at large was minimal; political intrigue and self-seeking politicians ensured that.

Sick of it all, King Mahendra, who had succeeded his father, ordered the parties disbanded in 1960. His hope was to replace politics with performance.

The King then instituted a partyless government called the *panchayat* system. It aimed at shifting power away from political party leaders and back to the people. Each small village was to elect a single representative, the man they found best among themselves. He was not to be elected upon the merits or power of a political party but upon his own personal ability. This system was well-suited to the cooperative spirit of the Nepali people. The representatives of nine villages elected from among themselves their Pradhan Pancha (chief) of the *panchayat* council. The Pradhan Panchas of each area then elected a representative to the district *panchayat,* and the district representatives, in turn, elected one of their own men as representative to the national *panchayat,* their parliament. Thus, in order to reach the top, a man had to secure support from his peers all along the way.

When he first arrived home, Major Thapa settled in the nearby town of Bandipur so that he could study this new system. In 1966 he was elected as the Pradhan Pancha of his local *panchayat.* When we arrived in 1969, he was hard at work doing his best to implement improvements for his people. Twice while home on leave from the Army, he had built and started a school with his own money. Twice it was disbanded soon after he left.

Now once again he had a school built, which under the new government was open to all castes and levels of society. The school wasn't necessary for his own children; his daughter and four sons had been educated in Malaya and India. It was his villagers he was concerned about. Now their children would have opportunity for schooling right in Yangchok. Major Thapa was such a dynamic leader that soon his counterparts in the other *panchayats* wanted to elect him as the Chairman of their District. He declined, however, saying that he must first build up his own village area before he could accept greater responsibility.

Soon after we arrived in Yangchok, Major Thapa began thinking about what could be done to reduce the long walk for us from the Gorkha airstrip. Often we had to stay overnight on the trail and he didn't like that. Having had field engineering training in the army, he had ideas. In the spring of 1970, he reported that he'd found the place.

Down beside the Marsyandi River lay a small flood plain, about a hundred feet above the river level. It had been farmed at one time, but was now abandoned and overgrown with briars and trees. He told me, "It will cost you about two thousand rupees to clear this land and to smooth it off so the plane can land." So we went to work.

In the beginning, I didn't keep an exact account of the wages paid, but figuring it up later, I discovered that my costs to build the thousand-foot airstrip came to within a rupee or two of the two thousand rupees he had estimated. In honor of the reigning Queen, the Major named the place Ratna Chowk.

Major Thapa and his wife care for Tara while we await the arrival of the small plane.

From behind the Annapurna Range of Himalayas comes a swift-flowing river named the Marsyandi, which forms the border between Gorkha and Tanahu Districts. The only way to get across it used to be in one of the dugout log canoes that served as a ferry. For the villagers of Yangchok, this meant a detour of many miles upstream. Since they had many relatives across the river further downstream, it meant a considerable amount of extra effort for them to visit back and forth. When Major Thapa returned to Yangchok, he combined his leadership ability and engineering skills to build a log bridge to span about sixty feet of rushing river. The first year we were there, I heard the announcement for everyone to come help build the bridge, so I went with the men to drag the long logs down to the river. When we got the logs to the river's edge, I looked across with great skepticism. I couldn't possibly imagine building a bridge under such crude conditions.

However, in carefully selecting his site, the Major had found a narrow spot where there were some huge boulders standing slightly out into the river. Upon these boulders he made the bulwarks for his bridge. To build up the bulwarks, he first constructed a huge basket like container out of long, heavy stakes and wove them together with vines and limber branches. He then filled this "basket" with large stones to make the bulwarks for his bridge.

Then, from the top of the rock-filled baskets, the men slowly pushed out four logs, two from each side, until they overlapped in the center of the river. These logs formed a cradle to support the heavier spanning logs which were pushed out next. When all the logs were in place, they were bound together with vines. Finally, a firm walkway and railing were constructed on the span to complete the job. Within two to three days the whole bridge was built, and all without a single nail or piece of steel. I was amazed.

Unfortunately, the first heavy rain of the monsoon always washed the bridge away, so that each year the villagers had to build a new one. But being closer to their families and relatives for six months made it worth the effort. Their troubles, however, came to an end in 1974, when they were able to have a permanent two-hundred-foot-long steel-wire suspension bridge built, culminating many years of effort to this end by Major Thapa.

Another life-long desire of the Major's had been fulfilled back in 1971. Ever since he had joined the army, he had vowed to himself that when he returned, if he did nothing else, he would at least do something about the difficult water situation in Yangchok. He told me it often happened to a Yangchok lad that the girl he loved would sadly say, "I would marry you and come live in your house, but I just can't face the thought of hauling water up your steep mountain every day for the rest of my life."

Carrying water is the women's responsibility and a six-hundred-foot climb up from the spring to the village takes no small amount of effort. A small family might get by with using only two sixty-five pound jugs of water each day. Otherwise three, four or more would be needed.

Major Thapa knew of a cold, clear stream which trickled out of a limestone cave in the cleft of the mountain behind Yangchok. With 6,600 feet of one-inch galvanized pipe, the water could be brought to the lower section of the village. So the Major started his campaign. First he raised twelve thousand rupees from among the villagers themselves. Then another eighteen thousand rupees was granted from the district fund. In order to make the money stretch, he himself went to Calcutta and purchased the pipe. He accompanied the pipe up to the Nepal border and on to Narayan Ghat. From there, the villagers ferried the pipe over the mountains to Yangchok. The money, however, had been insufficient. Before the job was finished, Major Thapa had expended more than ten thousand rupees from his own pocket for transportation and personal expenses.

In those days, it was quite a job to buy pipe and get it trucked all the way up to Narayan Ghat, so it took him nearly three months to get the pipe up from Calcutta. During his absence, those who were envious of his position took advantage of the chance to spread the rumor that he had absconded with the funds! Because he had introduced many changes into the village society, the Major naturally became a target of those who wanted to keep the status quo.

There were many ways for him to get back at his enemies when he returned, but I never knew of him to retaliate against them. In fact, I don't think he even thought of them as his enemies. He simply commented, "They are like children; they are ignorant," and left it at that; he refused to allow his mind and his relationships to be sidetracked by other people's pettiness.

Digging the trench through the rocks and laying the water pipe turned out to be quite a job. We were in Yangchok during part of this time and often I went with them to help. After many weeks of hard work the pipe was finally in. It was a happy day indeed for Major Thapa when the clear, cool water began flowing just a few hundred feet down the trail from his house. The girls would no longer use water-hauling as a reason for not marrying the boys in Yangchok.

No one can have good health without a pure water supply. Major Thapa had provided this for his village. To cure the villagers' diseases, he had learned to use a multitude of medicinal herbs. This initial knowledge he continued to build upon as he had opportunity. While in the army he learned as much English as possible and read all the medical books and manuals he could get his hands on. Thus, as best he could, he brought together the West's science of medicine and the East's understanding of the Ayurveda (an ancient Sanskrit treatise on herbology and careful diet balance).

Often he would give me a large shopping list of medicine to bring from Kathmandu. The people from two days' walk away would come to him in preference to hospitals closer by. He understood them and had compassion, being a villager at heart himself. He understood the terms they used and could reinterpret what they said into medical facts and treat them accordingly. He turned no one away. If they ran short of food, he gave them his own. If they paid him back, fine; if not, that was okay as well. But no one was turned away for lack of food or money.

In 1965 an epidemic of cholera swept through Nepal. It had reached a village called Baghe, some four hours' walk away. Major Thapa sent their Parliament member into Kathmandu to arrange for vaccine and stationed a local *panchayat* man at the Gorkha airstrip to await its arrival. When it came, the Major rode his horse straight to Baghe Village. There he found that the people from the surrounding villages had attempted to contain the plague by barricading the trails going to Baghe. When he broke through the barrier, the villagers all warned him to come back, but he paid no attention.

When he arrived, the dead and dying were lying everywhere. People had fled to the forest and caves, abandoning livestock and relatives to their fate. The Major shouted out for everyone to return to their homes and when they did, he gave them the vaccine. Then they began burying the dead. Twenty-two had already died, but the rest he was able to save.

When he was telling me of this tragedy I asked him, "What did you do to keep from getting the dreaded disease yourself?"

He declared, "I took along garlic and kept a clove of it in my mouth at all times. Garlic fumes are able to kill cholera before they get into you," he replied solemnly.

I smiled to myself in disbelief when he gave me that explanation. I never dreamed that I would be the one searching for the garlic years later.

Along the valleys of Nepal, rice is cultivated wherever water can be brought by canal to the fields. In the hills and mountains of central Nepal the amount of high-producing irrigated land is severely limited. Thus the grain production of the hills is insufficient to sustain the growing population. To help meet this need, wheat was being introduced as a winter crop in Gandaki Zone. It was to be grown as a second crop on these irrigated fields. The rice fields, however, which were the villagers' customary winter grazing land, were almost impossible to properly fence. So those enterprising farmers who began to plant wheat often found their fields devoured by the neighbors' cows and goats.

To counter this serious problem, Major Thapa had a law passed in his *panchayat.* It stated that whoever found another's animal eating his wheat should take that animal home. The animal would then be held until the owner paid for the damages. Such a law was easy to pass but very difficult to enforce under the prevailing social conditions. Major Thapa, however, was determined to effect the necessary changes in his *panchayat.*

One day I was sitting with him on the little platform that overlooked his flower garden asking him questions about his language. Since his house was the focal point of the village and the panchayat, often I got in on what was happening. On this day the runner had come with a message from some hours away, concerning two very rich men living near Ambu, one a Brahman and one a Chhetri, the two higher castes in the Hindu system. The Major, being of a tribal caste, was a long step below both of them. One of the men had planted a field in wheat and the other had a large herd of valuable goats. The goats had been caught feeding on the wheat and were brought to the wheat-grower's house. The wealthy owner of the goats was indignant about the matter. He told the other fellow to keep the goats because he would never humble himself to pay the fine for the wheat they had destroyed.

When the Major received this message, he wrote with characteristic decision that the fine WOULD be paid. He would not allow the goats to be kept in place of the fine. Furthermore, if it weren't paid within two days, the Major would be there with the police and take the offender off to the district jail. The fine was paid. The next year, as a result of the enforcement of that law, the Major's *panchayat* received first prize as the leader in wheat production among the forty-three other *panchayats* in Tanahu District.

We hadn't been in Yangchok long before we came to realize that Major Thapa was one who would not draw back from hard decisions. It was what was right that counted, and if bringing about justice meant personal loss to him, so be it. Many were the stories I heard of how he had come to the aid of the poor and defenseless. Though some of those of higher caste often ridiculed and poked fun at him behind his back, he did not allow their derision to make him one-sided with his justice. If one of low caste came for help, he gave it; if one of high caste came, he gave it equally.

I well remember the short, stout, grey-haired Brahman widow who used to drop in to visit with us from time to time. She has since died, but I still recall her little thatched house and vegetable garden with dill growing beside the trail. Her sons, daughters, husband and relatives had all died one by one, leaving her the lone survivor. The old widow, however, had been left with a nice piece of rice land. This was rented out, and her share of the crop was sufficient to meet all her needs. As a result, she quietly passed her days tending her small herd of cows.

One day she got the idea to sell her land and live off the proceeds. This was a foolish thing to do, and the Major instructed her not to sell it. But she kept insisting that he purchase it. It was choice land and a great opportunity, but still the Major refused to buy. The other villagers in the surrounding area followed his lead, and refused to purchase it. This, everyone presumed, was the end of the matter.

But during harvest time some months later, she came to the Major. "So-and-so has come to take my rice!" she moaned, "I'm going to starve to death!"

Ignoring the Major's advice, the old lady had gone across the river to a rich man in Gorkha District and had offered him her land. He agreed to buy it and accompanied her to the land office where she signed away the deed to him. Though he was the wealthiest man in the whole area, he had convinced her that he was short of cash. She would have to wait until after the harvest before he could pay her. But now, with the deed in hand, he had come to collect the owner's portion of the rice, claiming that he had already paid for the land. This, in fact, was so stated on the deed. Nevertheless, everyone knew it was a lie and that he hadn't paid for the land. Otherwise, the old lady would have been spending some of the money she had supposedly received.

Major Thapa sent someone to bring a policeman and went down to the threshing floor with the widow to handle the problem. Though the rich man was adamant that the land was rightfully his, the Major won, at least partially. He told the swindler that the old lady would collect her portion of rice this year and the next and the next, up to the day she died! And, until that time, if he ever came to take away the rice again, the Major would solve the problem with his gun. As far as he was concerned, the land remained hers for as long as she needed it, deeds and technicalities aside.

I learned that the usual Magar way of doing things is not at all with threats, which are given only in extreme circumstances and are meant to be carried out. Major Thapa was no different; his threat was not an idle one. Probably everyone realized that except myself. The following day I asked him what he would do if the rich man came back next year. Without hesitation he answered, "I'll shoot him, and that will solve the problem!"

I replied, "But what will happen to you then?" He knew he would go to jail for murder, but figured that he would probably be set free after about two years because of the extenuating circumstances.

The rich man had done everything right by law and was willing to leave the old lady to her fate. Presumably, she would have starved to death within a couple of months. The Major, on the other hand, was willing to accept the ignominy of a trial and two years in prison to see that she didn't. She was already over seventy years old and in fact only lived for another four years or so. The Major, though, was the sort of man who was willing to trade two years of the prime of his life in order to redeem the widow's last four!

There is another incident in Major Thapa's life that shows, as well as any, the greatness of the man. He himself would not place much significance in it, but it reveals clearly his inner thoughts and where he places his values. Before retirement, his father died and he came home on leave to take care of household business. His father had been one of the more wealthy Magars in the area, and over the years he had saved a little cash which he had loaned out.

Behind Yangchok, on the south side of Chimkesori Peak, lived a number of people who called themselves

Ghartis. They were not the Gharti who had been slaves, but a separate ethnic group, eking out a living on the mountain's high, rocky slopes. The language they spoke was called Bujhel. When my colleague Ross Caughley compared it to the Eastern Chepang he was studying, he was able to determine that it was a dialect of the Western Chepang language.

Through the years, the Major's father had loaned a considerable amount of money to these people. So when he returned home, the Major climbed up the ridge to make the yearly collection. Like the Chepangs, they were extremely shy and the poorest of the poor. They had borrowed the money in the first place because they had had no food to eat. While going from village to village to collect the money he found that they had nothing to give back. The only recourse was to take their only goat or laying hen in payment for the interest that had accrued. This he refused to do, and after a couple of days he turned back for home.

When he reached the top of the ridge that separated "Bujhel" country from his village, he stopped. There and then, he determined that no one from his family would ever again exact any greater burden upon the Ghartis' poverty. They owed him more than two thousand rupees. But lighting a match to the loan papers he was carrying, he ended their indebtedness. At that time the rate for a day's labor was only one rupee. In any society two thousand days' worth of wages is no small amount!

Over the years, the Major's crowning achievement probably was in his efforts with the local school. He had already established a primary school in his village, but after the fifth grade, the children had no choice but to go off to Bandipur. Very few of the villagers could afford to pay the room and board for a child. The Major's dream was to provide local schooling through high school.

When we left Yangchok in 1972, our little airstrip on the bank of the Marsyandi River was abandoned. So he talked to the owners of the Ratna Chowk area and they agreed to sign over their land for the benefit of a school. This land was then given over to interested villagers who farmed it on a fifty-fifty basis. They cleared the land and planted corn. In the fall they planted oilseed. One-half of the crop went to support the school, one-half the villagers retained.

At just this time, the education system in Nepal was being reorganized. Because of lack of funds, only a certain number of schools were being allowed in each area. There was already a high school a few hours' walk away in Bandipur. Since there was a relatively small population in the Yangchok area, the government would not support another middle or high school there as well. What should he do?

In order to get permission for his school, the Major agreed to operate it without any financial aid from the government. However, as the number of students grew, the corn and oilseed profits were not enough to pay for all of the teachers' salaries. So in 1976, the Major organized the villagers and they dug a long irrigation canal around to Ratna Chowk. The next year they repaired the worst parts with forty bags of cement to insure that there would be plenty of water for the whole area. The result was that some three hundred *muri* (about nine acres) of rice was reaped the following year from those fields. This was sufficient to support the school.

When we went out to Pokhara in October 1978, we were able to drive right to the school grounds, which overlooked Ratna Chowk. It was satisfying to look down on the fields, lush with ripening rice. The hundred-foot embankment, which ran from the school down to the paddy fields below, was completely covered with banana trees, the proceeds of which also went to the school. The slate-roofed, nicely-designed school and wide play area were all constructed in typical professional fashion.

The Major's dream is now fulfilled. The 275 students at Friendship School pay the same nominal fees that children in other schools do. Other than this, the school is entirely operated and the nine teachers all paid from the profit made on a piece of previously abandoned land. This stands as a testimony to the imagination, foresight, drive and dedication to his nation of a man who has few equals.

CHAPTER 5:

ARAKHALA

Soon after we had begun our work in Yangchok, we realized that it was not an ideal place to learn the Magar language and customs. About twenty years previously, a nearby Brahman village was twice razed to the ground by fire. After the second occurrence, the Brahmans asked permission of the Magars to settle alongside them in Yangchok. This they were granted, so long as they agreed to allow the Magars to keep their pigs, the untouchable animal for Brahmans.

So it happened that in Yangchok half of the villagers were Magars and half were Brahman. The Brahmans had Nepali as their mother tongue and a high form of Hinduism for their religious practice. The result was that the Magars' own Tibeto-Burman language, animistic religion and social customs were rapidly being overlaid, replaced or disguised by those of the Brahmans. Some ancient Magar practices had already been dropped, while others had been mixed with the Brahman practices. Thus, it was difficult for us to decipher the underlying system that was governing the Magars' lives.

It was in their language that the changes were most easily identified. Many of the verb stems and adjectives they used, such as "big," "small," "long" and "short," were all Nepali words. The breathiness feature in their words, a sound that was not found in Nepali, was being either dropped or else shifted into an aspirated form, such as was commonly used in Nepali.

The areas where they did differ in religious and social practice were much harder to determine. They, like the Brahmans, had decided not to eat buffalo meat because it was too much like the sacred cow. Also, they were cremating instead of burying their dead. Many had also taken up the habit of putting on a huge feast and procession at their marriages. Their rules of marriage, however, they had refused to alter. The Brahman custom which allowed brothers and sisters of one family to intermarry with brothers and sisters of another family was greatly offensive to them. But basically these were surface ceremonies, practices and changes which could be readily recognized.

What about their thought patterns and value systems? Ceremonies were one thing, but if I were to understand the Magars, I had to understand the Magar mind. One occurrence in the village had given me some clues. Major Thapa had called a meeting to discuss village business. They had sat up half the night without coming to a conclusion; the representatives of two houses had not shown up for the meeting. "How could they possibly have reached a decision?" I overheard the Major exclaim in exasperation.

He disciplined the two men involved by ordering them to cut down the nettles growing beside the main trail. The next night everyone showed up and the business was finished. From this experience I realized the value the Magars put on community spirit and consensus of opinion. But I had been lucky. If those two men had shown up for the meeting, I might have gone on for years without fully understanding this. On the other hand, one could say that the old language forms and social practices were still there in Yangchok to some degree. That was correct, but it was exasperating to try to distinguish them from the Nepali language and the Hindu practices with which they had become so intertwined.

True, the children were still learning Magar as the language of the home—that was clear when they went to school. They were dumbfounded hearing the Nepali language spoken by the teachers. If there happened to be a Magar teacher, he would try to bridge the gap by first explaining things to the Magar children in their own language. But despite that help, most of them sat for three or four years before they passed first grade, and then the majority of them quit without becoming literate. Later on, when these children became older and mixed with Nepali speakers, they would learn Nepali quite well. But that would be too late, for by then their opportunity for schooling would already have slipped by.

But just because they were continuing to speak Magar did not solve all our problems. Yangchok was also atypical in that they had a goodly number of rice fields in the valley. This meant that they were forever busy with their work in the corn fields on the mountain or the rice fields below. They had very little free time and this caused our biggest problem: we couldn't find anyone to hire regularly to teach us the language. The only exception was when we took someone into Kathmandu to stay with us for the monsoon.

The Major, of course, helped when he could, but he too was busy most of the time. So we were forced to follow the people to the fields or forest to ask whatever questions we might. This was good for learning their way of life and getting some types of information, but for linguistic analysis it was difficult and frustrating. I was glad for the opportunity to be out with the villagers. They taught me all about plowing, planting, cutting wood and the like. But I found that while the headband was squashing my skull from carrying a heavy load on my back, such times were just not conducive to deciphering the meaning of some complex verbal particle!

One day we met Gwen Coventry, an Australian nurse attached to the mission hospital in Tansen. She had been travelling throughout the mountains of Palpa District on a project to eradicate tuberculosis. In the course of doing this, she had established a small station at Bojha in East Palpa to facilitate the work. She kept telling us that this was a center of the Magar population and that it was an ideal place for us to work. I was anxious to see the area but by then our first child, Adina, had been born. "It would be a three-day trek for us from the nearest airstrip to reach that area," I thought. "That would be difficult with a small baby."

Some time later we met Gwen again. She had found a place to build a small airstrip and she urged us to come out and look it over. At the same time, the person in whose house we were staying in Yangchok decided he wanted it back. We would have to give it up. Since there were no other empty houses in the village, that meant we would have to build a new one. Obviously, now was the time to move if we were going to do so.

Taking along a Canadian colleague, we set off with two porters to find Gwen's station. We didn't know the trail and in the end we spent many more days walking than necessary. From Yangchok we toiled over the rocky, steep trails for three days, finally arriving at Narayan Ghat in the Terai. Someone along the way had given us directions to reach Bojha from there, so the next day we marched westward across the flat hot plains until our feet were numb from walking.

The next morning we were feeling good; Bojha should be just over the range of mountains north of us. After a couple of hours we came to Kirtipur, a small Magar village couched in a small bowl at the foot of an impossible-looking mountain. When we inquired, we were happy to learn that we were indeed on the right trail to Bojha. Then the man asked, "By the way, which Bojha do you want to go to? The trail to the left goes to Chuli Bojha, the trail to the right goes to Tedhe Bojha!"

I had no idea which one Gwen was living in, so we opted for the closest one and started up the steep grade. Even in February it was sweltering on the southern side of the mountain. We were thankful for the shelter we had from our umbrellas as we struggled up over endless stretches of loose rocks on that steep trail.

From the pass, which formed the backbone of the Mahabharat Range, we had a breathtaking view. To the south the flat land stretched out to the horizon. Somewhere among the jumble of forests, patches of rice fields and the wide meandering Narayani River, lay the border of India. North, stretched from horizon to horizon, lay the magnificent Himalayas. Closer by, perched like an eagle's nest on a promontory of a nearby ridge, was the village of Arakhala. It looked as if we could reach there in an hour's easy walking, but distances are deceptive in the mountains of Nepal; Arakhala was three long hours away yet. Just over the pass the trail wound down to Bojha—Chuli Bojha. Of course it was the wrong one and it was another day before we reached Gwen's place.

Arakhala, which we had seen from the crest, was among the villages she recommended for us to live in. It had almost a hundred houses, nearly double the size of most other large Magar villages.

Along the Kali Gandaki River, we saw a place for an airstrip and met Damodar Birtakoti, the owner of the land, who was a Brahman and the Pradhan Pancha of Buling *panchayat*. He told us we were welcome to use the fallow land for an airstrip. My companion and I picked up the few

Chule Bohja village: forty miles away stand the majestic peaks of Manaslu, 26,658 ft.; P 29, 25,705 ft.; and Himalchuli, 25,895 ft.

rocks that were lying on top of the grassy plain, and the airstrip was built! No doubt it was the quickest and cheapest airstrip ever made in Nepal. From Buling, I knew my wife Barbara could make the three-thousand-foot climb up to Arakhala in three or four hours. The leaders of the village invited us to live there and it seemed like an ideal situation to me, but would Barbara approve?

A month later I returned with Barbara and our little daughter for a look at the village. To my relief, Barbara agreed that we should move to Arakhala. Our daughter had been given the village name Tara, meaning "star." The people loved that. Tara, a chubby, blue-eyed, seven-month-old baby with a fuzz of golden hair, was certainly the star attraction. We had a swinglike affair called a "Jolly Jumper" which had a long rubber spring and could be attached to the rafters in the ceiling. Tara was quite proficient by then and could leap nearly a foot into the air with this bouncer. As the villagers crowded around to watch, they laughed as she jumped. Tara, in turn, would laugh back and leap all the higher.

Barbara and Adina on the trail to Arakhala, followed by our village "grandfather."

As the sea of people crowding around us increased, their sing-song, animated speech was like music to our ears. Never did we hear them conversing in Nepali, and their intonation was so different from that of the Magars in Yangchok. The slow rollicking way they spoke made it hard for us to understand at first; it reminded us of the southern drawl of English spoken in the southern United States.

As for customs, one thing was certain—there had been a minimum of influence here from Brahmans and others. I noticed that many of the women still braided their hair beginning at the crown rather than at the back of their heads, something I'd seen nowhere else. Apparently, even Nepali styles were slow in reaching this isolated area.

Furthermore, there were other advantages in living here. As we walked around the village, we found that every house had its own hand loom. Here they still spun and wove cotton for their own clothes; in Yangchok that was a lost art. Also, with so many people to talk with, it was an ideal situation for learning their language. This was the heart of Magar land; this is what we'd been searching for. When the people readily invited us into their humble dwellings, I felt sure that this was the place for us. The villagers urged us to live with them and promised that if we did they would lend us a piece of land to build a house on.

In September 1972 I returned to Arakhala with a Finnish colleague to begin work on our house. The day before we arrived, a family left the village and moved to land that they had purchased in the Terai. Thus we had their empty house to stay in while we built our own.

Gopal, the secretary of the *panchayat,* continually helped and made all the arrangements for us. The custom was to hire builders at a daily wage and feed them three times a day. This was impossible for us to do, so I suggested that we would give them a lump sum payment to build the house, but that they should feed themselves. To work on a contract arrangement like this was new to them, but in the end they agreed to it. I told them that this way, if they worked quickly, they could make a good profit. On the other hand, they could also stop for a few days to attend to any of their own work at home that might come up. Now, some years later, it is their preferred way of working.

We had our house made just like the village ones, with the walls constructed of mud and rock. It was different, however, in that we had brought from Kathmandu the frames for full-sized doors and plenty of windows. I had had my fill of banging my head on the low door frames every day. And instead of a mud floor, we laid down cement. It also had the addition of an inside toilet and a cast-iron, wood-burning stove.

Since we had decided that the downstairs would be open to the public, the room was usually crowded with people. They came to gaze and wonder at the bright kerosene lamps or other gadgets we had. Just as in Yangchok, I often overheard someone volunteer that Barbara was cooking something the wrong way—too much flour in the bread, etc.

Twelve men carry a timber brought from the forest many miles away.

Daily, the villagers, who had suffered so long from some of the simplest ailments, came to us for first aid. In anticipation of this we had taken some basic medical training and had brought along common medicines for them, particularly for worms, goiter, diarrhea and sores.

In early January I decided to go down to the airstrip at Buling to meet the plane which was bringing us mail and food. At the same time, I figured it would be a good chance to go across the river into Tanahu District for a short visit to see my friend and his wife, who had started work in the Darai language. The Darai were a small ethnic group that totaled only a few thousand. Their language was peculiar in that it had some very complex items which my friend found to be similar to Persian.

I went down to the Buling airstrip and waited for some time. When the plane didn't arrive I hurried down the trail and across the river to see my friend. By the time I returned to Buling in the late afternoon, the plane had come and gone. At the airstrip I found Damodar, the Buling Pradhan Pancha, along with our Arakhala Pradhan Pancha sitting there with sad faces. It turned out that the Buling High School was ready to begin a new term, but their copy of the test results for the previous term had never arrived in the mail. No one knew who had passed to the next grade and who hadn't. Only that morning they had received a letter in the mail saying that the copy of the test results had been sent from Tansen via Pokhara to Kathmandu.

Hearing that the plane was to come, Damodar rushed down to the airstrip, arriving just after I had left. I had told the Buling leaders that any time they had business in Kathmandu, they were welcome to ride in on the plane for free. Unfortunately, that day a new pilot brought the plane in. When Damodar, the Buling Pradhan Pancha and owner of the airstrip land, asked to be taken to Kathmandu to get the test results, he was refused. And this was the very day that it was urgent for him to get in to Kathmandu.

The problem was that Damodar generally dressed in simple peasant clothing. He just didn't look like an important man. Day after day, wherever the pilots flew they were regularly asked for free rides into Kathmandu. This they couldn't do. So the new pilot, not understanding the situation, had refused Damodar. I was very upset over the incident. We had missed our opportunity to repay our friend for the kindness he had shown, but it was one of those things that couldn't be helped. Damodar realized that if he had been able to inform me ahead of time, I would have gotten him on the plane, so he chalked it up to bad luck. We found out later that some others were not as magnanimous as he was.

I left Buling in the late afternoon. By trotting on the flat stretches, I climbed to Arakhala in an hour and twenty minutes. I had never been in such good physical condition in all my life. It was exhilarating to walk into our house not feeling the least bit tired. Little did I suspect that it would be three years before I would be capable of doing that again. A few weeks later we returned to Kathmandu. There Barbara and I both came down with infectious hepatitis. It took two and a half months for me to recover sufficiently to return to Arakhala.

Normally, before the plane came in I would go to the airstrip ahead of time to clear off the sticks and stones that had accumulated and to chase away the grazing cattle. This time, though, I was coming in the plane. We were loaded up with our food, kerosene for lights and some building materials. The pilot took a swing over the airstrip to see if all was clear. Everything looked fine, so on the next circle around he set the little Cessna down. Barbara got out with Tara, while I helped unload the cargo. The pilot then went to check out the airstrip before takeoff. When I saw him puzzling over the place where the plane had touched down, I went to see what was wrong.

As I came close, my heart leaped. There was a hole right in the middle of the airstrip. Less than a foot past the center of the hole were the marks where the left wheel had hit the ground! In my mind I could see the plane cartwheeling down the airstrip, ablaze with gas and kerosene. "Were the angels back with us again today?" I wondered.

At first, I thought the hole was just an ant hill that had collapsed in the recent spring rains. But after a second glance, it was apparent that someone had dug the hole in the airstrip. Lying half-hidden in the grass was a long pole that had been placed upright beside the hole.

Later on, I learned who was responsible for digging the hole, but I also knew that they did not realize what the consequences could have been. Apparently the idea of erecting the pole was to point out the hole they had dug and to force us to land from the other end of the airstrip. It was their way to express their displeasure and relieve their frustration over not having taken Damodar to Kathmandu in the plane. However, because of our delay in returning, the spring storms had blown the pole down and new grass had grown up through the dirt that had been dug from the hole. That was why we had seen nothing unusual from the air. We never made the incident public, but from then on we were much more cautious.

By now, our second child was on the way. Up in Arakhala, I spent much of each day fixing the yard to be a safe, clean place to play for Tara and a hoped-for brother. I never considered the blazing heat nor the fact that my liver still had a way to go to recover from the hepatitis. Early one Sunday morning, I was awakened in the dark by the strangest feeling in my lower back. In a few minutes, it had turned into an excruciating pain that I knew must be a kidney stone attack, the natural result of a weak liver and of working in the hot sun without drinking enough water. We had some codeine and aspirin pills, of which I took a double dose, but it didn't help at all.

In childbirth, the pains come and go, giving the mother a period of rest. But with a kidney stone, there is no such period of relief. As soon as it was light, I stumbled down to the Pradhan's house and asked him to get me a man to go to the outstation at Tedhe Bojha for medicine. He said he would, and I made my way back home, stopping only to vomit on the trail from the overwhelming pain. The man came for instructions at 6 a.m. He had two mountain ridges to go down and two to climb. I knew that if he didn't miss the small trail on the second ridge, he might be back after seven hours. But while I was racked with pain, every moment seemed to last for an eternity.

Finally the runner left for the medicine, leaving me to my thoughts while the crushing pain brought forth the sweat in torrents. Kidney stones usually take a few days or as long as weeks to pass through to the bladder. Sometimes they hang up along the way so that only surgery can remove them. In my condition it was impossible to walk. I could arrange to get carried down to the airstrip all right—that is, if Gwen had a drug strong enough to stupefy me for the trip. Should I send for the plane or not? Sending a man out to Narayan Ghat to the telegraph office would make it possible, if all went well, to get picked up in three days.

I kept looking at my watch. Where would the runner be now? Would he lose time on the unfamiliar trails over by Tedhe Bojha? Would he pick the right one? Three days to wait after sending a man off. It didn't seem that I could endure three minutes more! "Pray that God will heal me," I groaned to Barbara. She put her hand on my back and prayed something. Twenty minutes later, I lost consciousness.

An hour and a half later, I awoke as though out of a bad dream. The stone had obviously passed into my bladder. As the pain had begun to tail off, apparently I had fallen asleep from exhaustion. Two hours later when I returned from the bathroom, I had a trophy to show my wife. It was a spiney, black, football-shaped kidney stone! "If there are no more stones hiding in my kidney, my troubles are over," I thought. But I was wrong; they had just begun.

Meanwhile, the villagers all recognized the source of my kidney stone. *Char kacha*, they all said. "The witch has put her curse on you!"

They had ways to deal with a witch. First of all, they would offer sacrifices to one of their favorite gods or ancestor spirits. The arrangement they had when making sacrifices was that they would feed the deity the blood, which was the life, while they themselves would eat the flesh. If the first deity they fed neglected to return their favor and failed to destroy the witch's spell, then they would try giving a sacrifice to another god. If that god couldn't or wouldn't do it either, then they would try others.

Before long it could get quite expensive. A large rooster could easily be worth a man's whole week of labor. As a last chance, they would offer a sacrifice to the witch herself. They could never hope to satiate her appetite for blood, so they only used it to trap her. While her spirit was busily lapping up the blood, they would put a magical curse on her, thus forcing her to leave them alone. If that didn't work they had no other recourse. Most of the time it was only at this point that they would consider trying modern medicines, if they were available.

In Western countries the reference to witches has been largely relegated to fairy tales and Halloween. But with the Magars, we found that there was probably no single thing they were more concerned about. In the village society, witches were still very much alive and well. At first it was extremely difficult to get much information about witches. When someone would dare to tell us something, it was with guarded speech and in soft whispers. We hadn't been in Arakhala long though before we had another conflict with a witch. It was a nerve-racking experience for Barbara.

When we came out to the village, we brought our flour, sugar and rice packed in five-gallon tins. These were highly prized by the villagers for storing their grain. When it came time to return to Kathmandu, we always sold them for a small price to the villagers. Because there was such a demand for them, Barbara would make a list of those who asked and give them out in turn, according to who had asked first.

One night when I dragged in exhausted from a hunt, I found Barbara in a quandary. "What have I done wrong? Something terrible has happened today," she said anxiously.

Sailha's mother had come in about noontime and asked for one of the five-gallon tins. In those days we did not know that Sailha's mother was considered to be the strongest and most fearsome witch in the area. Her name, however, was not on the long list of those to receive a tin. Nevertheless, she insisted that she be given one immediately.

Even if Barbara had decided to give her one, she couldn't have, since all of the tins were still partially full of supplies. When Barbara refused and wanted to wait to consult with me, the witch insisted all the more. When this didn't work, she began to point out other things in our house that she would take instead of a large tin. "Then give me this! Give me this! Give me that!" she barked.

When Barbara found that the witch wouldn't take "No" for an answer, her patience came to an end. Tara had been crying and wanted to be nursed to sleep. So using a tactic that is common in Nepal, she just ignored the woman and went upstairs to put Tara to sleep.

Not long afterwards, Barbara heard some wild screams coming from the empty schoolyard a few hundred yards away. Looking out the window, she realized that the noise was coming from Sailha's mother. Amidst the undecipherable curses and pitched screams, Barbara recognized the word *goroni* (white woman) being repeated again and again.

Barbara felt bad. We had come to be friends with the villagers and now she had made a terrible enemy. When I heard the story, I suspected that the villagers had tabbed the woman as a witch, so I wasn't overly concerned. The next morning I went to see the Pradhan Pancha and asked him for advice. "How will Sailha's mother react the next time we meet her?" I inquired.

To my surprise, he told me that she would smile and laugh as if nothing at all had happened. Later on in the day she came by. Just as the Pradhan Pancha had said, she was as sweet and nice as ever!

For some time I wondered why the witch had gone off to the empty schoolyard to vent her anger. Eventually I learned that with the Magars, only the children become angry in front of others. One is allowed to argue or show displeasure in their society, but never anger. To show anger would be to lose respect and standing in the community. It would be a sin and disgrace that could never be lived down. That is why the witch had gone off in semiprivate to do her screeching. Nevertheless it was interesting to note that she made sure to remain within earshot of our house; this ensured that her displeasure was duly registered.

By the end of June it was almost time to return to Kathmandu, but I still had not found a language assistant. I was getting worried. Whom could I get from Arakhala to be my teacher during the monsoon?

Gopal, the *panchayat* secretary, agreed to take care of it for me. A few days later he announced that his older brother would be the man to go in with us. He was a sixty-year-old man who had lost his left leg. Because he stayed up on Deo Chuli Mountain herding his cows and goats, I had only met him twice before. It seemed to me that surely there must be someone younger and better able to teach me. But I had given Gopal the job of finding me a man and now I abided by his decision. Later on, I often thought how fortunate I was not to have interfered. This man, Khadak Bahadur Lungeli, turned out to be a living storehouse of information.

On the 5th of July, 1973, I began work with my new language assistant. A few days after I began studying with him, I noticed that my liver was swollen and tender once again. At the hospital, the doctor discovered that it wasn't a relapse of the infectious hepatitis. Instead, it was amoebic hepatitis. In the village I had been too slow in taking the dysentery medicine, and so some of the amoebas had migrated to my liver for a change of diet. A course of medicine took care of them, and in a few days I was back again studying with Khadak.

I was looking forward to a fruitful summer of working out some confusing parts of the Magar verb system. In Arakhala, Tara had begun to speak Magar as her first language. I was astounded one day when she toddled in the front door and poured out a sentence to a little friend. Only after years of struggle was I able to discover the meaning of the very particle she had spoken with so little effort!

After a few weeks of work, I came down sick again. This time the weeks crawled by and I had to go to the hospital to stay. The days blurred together into one long nightmare of mononucleosis and measles with daily shots of morphine and pills swallowed by the handful. We would have to go home just when things were finally beginning to look good. Back in Arakhala I knew what they'd all be saying: "It's the witch. She's put a curse on you!"

Those last few days in Nepal we stayed with a friend out at Kirtipur on the Tribhuvan University campus. Barbara and our friends had packed everything and moved us out of our flat in town. Someone tipped me off that when our SIL Director came to see me, he was going to ask me to return to Nepal after six months. He couldn't know how deeply the hurts of the last few months had cut. Furthermore, there had been the constant frustration of having no language helpers in Yangchok. I hadn't progressed nearly as far in the work as I had planned. The next day when the Director came, I had my answer ready. With a weak voice but strong resolve, I murmured, "I'm not coming back!"

After all, I was a volunteer. I could do what I thought best. This wasn't the armed services where you had to do everything that you were told. Following college, as a junior officer in the Navy, that was the way it had been. I gave orders and I followed orders. The immediate obedience to them could mean life or death for one's self and all the others on the ship as well. Now it was different. I wasn't under that sort of orders, and I could quit if I liked. Nevertheless, I had learned there was value in discipline and obedience, so I modified my first statement. I told him that I MIGHT return if the situation changed for me, but under no circumstances would I come back in six months.

With that in mind, we left for home. I had no desire to think of the future. All I wanted to do was sleep—fourteen hours a day! As the plane lifted off for Bangkok, I felt nothing. After four-and-a-half years—nothing. I only wanted to recover, to forget the miseries of Nepal and get safely home.

My parents were there waiting for us when we arrived at the little local airport. Just a day or two before, they had received the news that we were coming immediately.

My home of Oak Harbor in Washington State was nestled in the upper end of a large island in Puget Sound, near the Canadian border. From my youngest days, my father had taken me with him into the forests and out on the water for hunting or fishing. As I grew up, all my spare time had been spent traversing the mountains and valleys. Now I was dumbfounded as we flew north from Seattle in the small plane. The towering Olympic Mountains on our left and the Cascade Range on our right appeared to be but ripples. Sitting behind the pilot, I could see that we had climbed out to only a thousand feet. From that altitude the state looked through my eyes like one flat plain!

What had happened in my absence? Then I remembered. In Nepal, Arakhala was in the lower hills. It was on the first hill up from the plains, yet on the thirty-five-minute flight we were required to climb to at least seven thousand feet. If there was any wind or clouds, we often went up to nine or ten thousand feet just to reach a valley in the lower hills! This was higher than most of the peaks in either the Olympic or Cascade ranges. The contrast was remarkable indeed.

We stayed home for a year. I had kept kidding Barbara that I had already endured all the pains of childbirth for her when I had given birth to the kidney stone. "Child number two will be a cinch for you," I predicted. Just like I had said, I had hardly gotten all the papers filled out at the hospital that morning before the doctor came by to tell me that we had a son. His name at home was Michael. But for Nepal, we named him "Hukum Singh" in honor of one of the Major's sons and after a policeman friend from a village near Arakhala.

After six months I had recovered sufficiently to ponder the future. Friends had continued to encourage us. The charm and uniqueness that belong to Nepal began tugging at us to return. Yes, we would go back again. There were things we could do, numerous ways that we could be of help to our friends in Arakhala.

CHAPTER 6:

BEGINNINGS

When we returned to Nepal in August 1975, it was in many ways a new beginning for us. We found a nice little house to rent in Kalimati, a suburb of Kathmandu, and were ready to make a fresh start. My Canadian friend accompanied me again to Arakhala to bring old one-legged Khadak back to Kathmandu. Khadak was full of information and eager to help me in my study. One of the many things that I learned from him was the origin of Arakhala.

In the Magar language *arakhala* is the name for one of the three types of oaks found in their mountains. The village was located where there had previously been a large stand of *arakhala* oaks clustered around a clear-running spring. That seemed like an amazing similarity to me. My home town of Oak Harbor on the other side of the world was named for the huge oaks surrounding the harbor. And here, I had unknowingly built my house in a village named for the oaks surrounding a spring.

About 1850, the area around my home town of Oak Harbor was being settled by men looking for free land. Some fifty years previous to that, the men in Nepal too were searching for new land and a new beginning. They had climbed a mountain, found a suitable site and began cutting down the grove of *arakhala* oaks. Khadak was able to tell me better than anyone else; his great-great-great-grandfather was among those original settlers.

But to start back at the beginning, before men even came to Arakhala: "Long, long ago," so the old men say, "there were seven sister goddesses. They lived on that highest, snowy peak north of Arakhala, called by them *Him Chuli,* meaning "Himalaya" or "Snow Peak". The goddesses were called *mayu*, all virgin girls, the most powerful gods of the land. One day these goddesses decided that they should send one sister off to live on *Deo Chuli,* which translated means "Peak of the Gods." That steep jagged peak rose high above all others in the range. It overlooked much of the Terai plains, and from there the goddess could

Peak of the Gods rises through the morning mist over the Terai plains.

rule all the land under her gaze. However, when she arrived at Peak of the Gods, she found a *daintya,* a monster demon, living there. The demon was ravaging the villages in the surrounding mountains, catching and devouring much of the population. He was so terrible that it was reputed he would regularly eat three bushels of ground iron at a meal.

"The *mayu* goddess attacked the demon, but fight as she might, she could not overpower him. One day on a nearby ridge she spotted two fine virgin Magar girls dancing the *ghãtu* initiation dance. She swooped down in a whirlwind and carried them away to Peak of the Gods. There she transformed the girls into *mayu* goddesses like herself. Together the three goddesses then attacked the demon and successfully drove him away."

Ever since then they have been referred to collectively as the *Tin Kannya Mayu* (the Three Virgin Goddesses). They have been the strongest of all deities, the rulers and protectors of the land. Even the Tharu people, the original inhabitants of the malarial jungle to the south, agreed on this. To this day, the Tharus continue to come yearly from far and wide to climb to a cave near its 6,300-foot peak. There they offer sacrifices to these most powerful of all gods.

The queenly girls with popcorn crowns keep their eyes shut while dancing the ghãtu.

Onto this scene, perhaps around the year 1750, the settlers came. It was new land, the lure that through the centuries drew men from everywhere. The Magars who settled there were men with subtribe names of Ale, Pulami, Gora Saru, Gharti and the like. When they found a place that suited them, they set about felling the ancient trees. Lacking any other peculiarity about the area, they simply named this village *Ban-Kata,* meaning "cut-down-forest." After burning them up as best they could, they planted their crops of millet, corn, buckwheat, highland rice and various types of lentils and beans. As the years went by, they gradually erected more substantial houses to replace the temporary shelters they had built at first. Using the plentiful rock cemented together with mud, they would erect an oval-shaped house with a sixteen-inch-thick wall. A five-foot-high ceiling covering the single room helped keep the warmth in during the winter. On top of this, the steeply sloping roof was covered with thatch.

The fine grains were put in large, round, woven bamboo containers and stored on the attic-like upstairs floor. The ears of corn were generally hung from the rafters or simply stacked up along the wall. The whole extended family ate, slept and lived in the downstairs room. Sometimes, however, a son with a new bride would sleep outside on an enclosed part of the veranda or else upstairs. Their few utensils for eating and their tools of iron—sickle-knives, short-handled hoes and an axe—were set on a board shelf, hung up on pegs in the wall or just slipped between the wooden rafters in the ceiling.

About this time in the village of Bhartipur on the opposite ridge lived another Magar named Kirtiya Rana. He was a short, stocky man and exceptionally brave. He joined the Nepalese Army, and in the fighting one day he found himself standing alone before a house full of enemy soldiers. He challenged them to come out and fight. As they came out the narrow doorway he slew every one of them with his sword. For this feat of bravery the King awarded the short little soldier some land around his village. As a result, Kirtiya Rana became very powerful and came to own the choicest rice fields along Phulmadi Stream.

Some years later disaster struck: exceptionally heavy monsoon rains fell that summer. On the bare mountainsides around Ban-Kata, the running water cut deep into the shallow topsoil. Before long, the water was carrying tons of mud and rocks to the fast-moving Phulmadi Stream a thousand feet below. The rampaging mass of rocks, mud and water tumbled down the stream bed and washed up over the fields owned by Kirtiya Rana. The damage to his rice fields was so great that he ordered the settlers to abandon Ban-Kata immediately.

Magar villages are often built along the crest of a ridge or else at the top of a steep outcropping. Some say that this is because the gods will not bless a person who has fields higher than his village. Thus the village was generally built on a high spot above the land that its people cultivated. In addition, another practical and important reason in those days was that a village thus situated was easier to defend in time of war.

A mile and a half away from Ban-Kata stood a grove of *arakhala* oaks covering a promontory above a very steep section of the ridge. It would make a good site for a village. On the west and south sides for five hundred feet or more the ridge fell away so abruptly that one could scale it only by holding on to the brush—not a good situation for an attacking force. The knoll itself was flat for this country, providing suitable farm land. On the east for some six hundred yards the land sloped off gently before giving way to another steep drop-off. Yes, a village built here could easily be defended against a superior force. To make it all the more inviting, a spring of cool pure water gushed out of the ground in the middle of the grove. As an extra blessing there was the refreshing breeze that continually blew across the ridge during the hot spring months.

On the opposite side of the world, freedom and new land had called settlers to America, where the Revolutionary War was raging about this time. Here too, in Nepal, there was a war of a different sort in progress. The villager usually didn't see it as a war, but nevertheless the results of the conflict were just as surely life or death.

A few miles to the north, across the Kali Gandaki River, was the village of Bhũwarkot. There lived a man of the Rana line of Magars. He, like the rest of the villagers, was engaged in a lifelong war. His, however, was not a battle of flesh against flesh; that would have been easy. His struggle was with the multitude of witches, ghosts, demons and forest elves. It was the lot of every villager. These evil forces were constantly after his livestock, his crops, his family, his health and life itself. The powerful *mayu* goddesses, the ancestor spirits and the other gods and goddesses of their pantheon would help him in this battle. That is, they were supposed to. But first he must be successful in fulfilling their numerous and sometimes capricious desires for blood sacrifices. Otherwise they too would turn on him with even more drastic results.

Most likely, this man had been doing rather poorly or he wouldn't have been wanting to move. Manipulating the good deities so that they would bless and protect one from the evil deities was a tricky business. A grudging ancestor spirit could demand virtually all of one's chickens, pigeons, goats and pigs for sacrifice. After that, one would have nothing left with which to please the rest of the spirits. Thus he would incur their displeasure as well. It was an endless circle from which one could seldom find escape.

New land would do much to solve that problem. The witches would stay in their village, while the local deities, ghosts and powerful ancestor spirits would remain on their portion of land. If he moved, any grudges or ill feelings they might have towards him would have little or no effect. New, uninhabited land would be virtually free of ghosts and ancestor spirits, at least for a generation or two. New land would give him freedom from this oppression. It would be a new beginning, where he could cherish bright hopes for a future free of disease, free of crop failure and free of fear.

We know nothing whatsoever of this man's wife, but since the men usually married in their teenage years we can presume that he had one. It would not have been unusual, however, if that wife had died in childbirth or from some sickness. In that case he would be expecting to find another one from the Ban-Kata people or from some village nearby. Whatever the case, hearing that the people of Ban-Kata were to clear land among the *arakhala* oaks, he decided to throw in his lot with them.

Down at the river nowadays there are long, dugout canoes in which one crosses the two hundred yards of swiftly moving water, but in those days there were none. So, going down to the bank of the mighty Kali Gandaki, the man from Bhũwarkot cut some trees into lengths with his heavy, all-purpose sickle-knife. With vines that he found nearby, he lashed the poles together to form a crude raft. Then he fashioned a paddle and cut a long pole for pushing through the shallows.

Now he was ready. Poling easily to the end of the back eddy, he pushed off strongly into the swift water. Like his own ancestors, this river had its beginning on the Tibetan side of the great Himalayan Range. Facing south, his back was to those great white peaks as he paddled furiously for the far shore. His life was in the hands of the gods now; doubtless he was repeating their names as fast as he could recall them. He would reach the southern shore with their blessing or be swept to a watery death in the rapids below. Later on his son would meet that latter end on a flimsy raft like his own.

Safely across, he wrapped the rope of his headband around his cone-shaped bamboo basket. Heavy with his supply of food and life's possessions, he let out a grunt as he rose to his feet under the load. Perched on top was his woven straw sleeping-mat and his *li,* a strong bamboo hunting bow. His knife-like sickle hung in a wooden carrier riding on his hip. And like the odd person one might still meet on the trail today, in his hand he likely carried his *khurli*.

The *khurli* was a unique little three-foot-long pellet bow used for shooting birds. Its projectile was a round, sun-baked clay ball the size of a marble. The bowstring was a single piece of slender bamboo attached at each end of the bow with a short string. This flat bamboo bowstring was made with a pocket-like affair in the middle. From the midway point the bamboo was split two or three inches in each direction. The split was then forced apart and four crosspieces were woven in to make a little pocket for the clay ball to rest in. In effect, it was a high-powered slingshot. With it the men and boys were regularly able to add birds of all sizes to the family pot.

In this deep valley only nine hundred feet or so above sea level, lurked the dreaded malaria. During the winter, though, as now, there was nothing to fear because there were no mosquitoes. Up out of the river gorge he climbed and moving across the few hundred yards of flat land he soon reached the foot of the mountain. It felt good to be climbing; it was natural. Flat land was not his home. He didn't even notice the sweat running profusely off his brow as he climbed the steeply winding trail. Carrying heavy loads on the mountain trails had always been a part of his life; unless he was sick he took little notice of the exertion. As all the herder boys do when they are out alone, more than likely he sang to the forest with a resounding voice, which would prevent the chance meeting of a bear, leopard or tiger. He was a man of the wilds and although his mind no doubt was dreaming of the new opportunities before him, his unconscious mind was ever alert to the jungle signs and sounds.

When he arrived at the grove of *arakhala* oaks he had a beautiful view of the wide, blue Kali Gandaki River to the north some 2,700 feet below. It was running due east here and in another fifteen miles it would join the Trisuli River. The Trisuli itself had just previously conjoined with the Marsyandi, a few miles east of Yangchok. As one large river, now called the Narayani, it swept past the last section of the Mahabharat Range and surged on into the Terai. From there it wound lazily into India. After joining the mighty Ganges downstream, it finally reached the Indian Ocean, some four hundred miles away at Calcutta.

Looking across the river, the newcomer could see another series of ridges four to six thousand feet high. They were similar to the Mahabharat Range upon which he stood, but for the most part not so steep. Farther north were the higher ridges, rising suddenly to collide with a wall of rock, ice and snow. This was the Himalayan Range, stretched out as far as the eye could see in an unbelievable panorama, visible for two hundred and fifty miles to the west and another hundred and fifty miles or so to the east. North of them lay Tibet, the land of mystery, magical medicines and in those days, land of that precious commodity, salt.

Arakhala was good to the man from Bhũwarkot. He was able to raise two sons to adulthood and probably a daughter or two as well. The youngest son had a speech impediment, but this was not unusual. A relatively large number of people were mentally retarded or handicapped with various degrees of deafness, dumbness or both. These conditions could often be attributed to a period of severe sickness, often during pregnancy. It was aggravated, however, by the fact that handicapped persons were married to others with similar handicaps. Their offspring usually were normal, but very often the deafness and dumbness cropped up again in following generations.

History does not record such at this time, but according to the old men, news came of an invasion from Tibet. Our oral history might be referring here to the war with Tibet in 1856. In that case, the dates in this section should be advanced by about twenty years. Young men joined the Nepali forces to repel the enemy. Among those who volunteered was the eldest son of the settler among the *arakhala* oaks. Besides his parents, he left behind a young wife and Jokhya, his infant son. His chief weapons of war were his bow and arrows and a sling that could throw large stones with a deadly force. If there were enough to go around, he might also have been issued a sword. However, he never returned. He survived the war only to perish on the return trip home. As he attempted to cross the Kali Gandaki River, his clumsy craft was swept into the rapids. Word came back that only a few miles from home, he drowned when his raft broke up beneath him.

After this, his wife returned to Rising to live with her parents. They tried to persuade her to stay near them and remarry someone close by. Custom, however, required her to give up her son for the father- and mother-in-law to raise. Baby Jokhya was the rightful heir to his father's land and even if a new husband were to agree to it, the grandparents would never allow their grandson to be raised in another's house. More important, he was the grandparents' "Social Security," the one they would count on to take care of them in their old age. The young widow, though, could not bear the thought of giving up her only child, so sadly she returned with little Jokhya to her deceased husband's home.

Magar custom provides for just such a situation, and she, no doubt, knew what the solution would be. Her husband's younger brother was not yet married. Furthermore, his speech impediment made it more difficult for him to get a good bride. It was the obvious solution: marry the widow to her husband's younger brother.

A widow, particularly a young one, would be constantly torn between her desire for a husband and her love for her children. But how could she abandon her children in favor of another husband? However, if she remarried within the family, this would solve the problem and keep the extended family intact. Even if the younger brother already had a wife, he could (and often would) be politely forced to marry his elder brother's wife. Just such a situation was to occur at least twice more in Jokhya's line.

From this marriage with his uncle, Jokhya's mother raised three additional brothers to adulthood. Those three were to be much more prolific than the offspring that came from Jokhya's own line. However, though fewer in number, it was Jokhya's side of the family which was destined to exert the most powerful role in the future of the area.

Little Jokhya was born in 1829 or thereabouts. He grew up, married and like the rest of the villagers, continued to clear the forest for more fields. The less steep portions of the mountains were terraced and made into permanent fields to plant corn, millet, buckwheat and highland rice. On the steepest places, people would simply cut the forest down and burn it up. The resulting ash provided the fertilizer for their crop.

While almost any crop might have been planted on these slash-and-burn fields, this is where they traditionally planted their cotton and their *bhotiya* corn. The *bhotiya* corn was a slow-growing variety, taking five to eight months to mature. It was particularly well-adapted to producing in the ash and thin soil of the steep mountainsides.

One day something strange happened that brought about a drastic change in Jokhya's simple life. Without warning his body began to shake uncontrollably. "A god," they said, "was riding on his head." Jokhya had been selected by a god as his personal intermediary. As such, Jokhya would be the mouthpiece for this god and the rest of the supernatural realm. For this privilege, Jokhya was required to give up certain things in order to keep himself holy and useable by the gods. In return, they would bless him if he was obedient: he would have supernatural power to use as he liked. This would bring to him a position of respect, authority and awe among the villagers.

So Jokhya became a shaman, the intermediary for Bishnu Bhaguwan, as the god called himself. To keep himself holy, the god ordered Jokhya to make periodic fasts of three, five or seven days in length. In addition, he was never to drink liquor or eat pork. He could eat rice or grain only if cooked by himself, and that but once a day. Eating any sort of grain product the rest of the day was forbidden—only fruit, yams or milk products were to be his fare.

However, Jokhya went a step further up the ladder of holiness. He refused to kill anything, not even the lice or fleas that crawled through his uncut hair; to do so would be a sin. The one exception was fish. "Fish pollute the stream water we drink," he said. "That causes us to become unclean in the sight of the gods. Fish are born and die in the water. They eat, excrete and urinate all in the same water. In doing so, they pollute the water we drink. It is no sin at all to kill them," he declared. So, day after day, Jokhya could be found down at a stream catching the fish and freshwater crabs, which he would eat with his single meal of grain. Other meat he was prepared to eat, but only if someone else had cooked it for him.

Because of this higher degree of holiness, he was called a *tapasi*, an ascetic, and the gods consequently gave him special power. If anyone lost anything or if one of their animals had run off, they would come to the shaman, "Jokhya Lama," as he was called. Using the thumb of the same hand to point with, he would count his knuckles over and over again. Occasionally he would interrupt the counting and glance up at the sky. Finally he would say something like, "Well, your goat is dead, but you will find it near the *mhorjyak* tree on Dabar Streamlet." He was always right when it came to divining whether a lost animal was dead or alive, or where a lost thing could be found.

One day Jokhya was sitting on the mud veranda of his home puffing on his huge bamboo *huka* pipe. As he was sitting there, a *jogi*, a Hindu ascetic who lived on the bank of the Kali Gandaki, happened to be passing through the village. No one knows the particulars, but the *jogi* said something to Jokhya that threw him into a rage. Suddenly Jokhya leapt up and began beating the *jogi* with his pipe. The *jogi* fled, but later he gathered his friends together and complained to the government overseer, the *jimmal* in nearby Singchang Village.

When Jokhya heard of this, he became frightened and hid away in the forest. It was two days before his half-brothers finally found him. They reassured him that all would be well and brought him back to tell his side of the story. During the interrogation at the *jimmal*'s house, Jokhya was able to answer the questions in such a way that the *jimmal* laid all the blame on the *jogi*.

As the shamed *jogi*s went back down the mountain to their riverside abode, they began to fight and quarrel among themselves. By the time they reached the river they were violently sick with severe vomiting and diarrhea. Before long most of them were dead. What black magic Jokhya had performed no one knows, but that was the fate of those who had chosen to attack him.

There was another thing, however, that really set Jokhya apart from other shamans in the area. This was his power to prophesy the future. "What does this mean, boys?" he used to say. "The gods are telling me that there will come a day when men will actually set fire to a wick they have placed in their own mouths!" Perplexed himself, he often asked the villagers if they could figure it out, but they couldn't. This was some years before the advent of cigarettes in Nepal.

Another time he prophesied, "One day you might have to work standing on the point of a sword and walk on the edge of a knife." The meaning of this was clear to everyone: some day their job may be such that a single slip could mean instant death. Only later, when the British began recruiting the village men as soldiers and they went off to war, did it actually come to pass.

Some things that he predicted, he never lived to see fulfilled. Under the Hindu system, one of the unthinkable things to do was to intermarry with someone of a different caste. Jokhya, however, prophesied, "One day there will be no distinction made between the castes. There will only be one caste." Now, by law this is true, and in practice, intermarriage among the castes, which used to be rare, is not such an unheard-of thing now.

Another prediction concerned money. Years ago, most trade was done by barter and very little money was minted. In those days, things were very cheap and even when they used money, not much was required. Yet Jokhya had said, "Some day, money will become cheap! Nevertheless," he warned, "though money will come easy, it will go the same way. You will not be able to keep hold of it for long." Nowadays, as he said, people are walking around with hundreds of rupees in their hands, but as soon as they buy something, it is all gone.

Concerning the end of the age, Jokhya prophesied two things that his people should know. First of all, "In the end time, even those of the same family will fight with one another and kill each other." To a people who are highly family oriented and cooperatively biased, this must have sounded particularly unreal. The other thing was, "At that time when everyone is killed, everyone will be together in the same place." These prophecies, among other things, are what is remembered today about Jokhya. The villagers' judgement of Jokhya is that he was a good shaman and a holy man.

During Jokhya's time, more people were moving into the area and clearing away the forest for villages and farms. To the east across Desot Stream, on the very shoulder of Peak of the Gods, two brothers of the Gurung tribe settled. They were the very first to clear land and build a house over there. One day Jabar Singh, the eldest, was sitting on the veranda at the stone handmill, grinding grain in the predawn darkness. Suddenly a tiger leaped out of the dark and plucked him off the veranda. It carried him straight to the nearby forest and devoured him.

Since that time, no one has ever again been so presumptuous as to build a house on the Peak of the Gods. It was quite obvious to all that the *mayu* goddesses were offended by the house that had been built on their mountain and had sent the tiger in reprisal. Looking over there now, one might think that there are many houses built on that steep ridge. But no one ever calls them houses. They are "herders' sheds," they say. Except for the fact that there are no wooden doors placed in the doorway, some of those sheds could not be distinguished from the smaller houses found in Arakhala. Nevertheless they are called sheds. To call them houses would be to risk the danger of angering the *mayu* goddesses.

Sometime after Jabar Singh was killed, a shaman in a trance reported that Jabar's spirit was in need of sacrifices. He had become more than just a *bayu* ancestor spirit in the other world. He was now Jabar Bhũyar, a god of power to be reckoned with. Through the decades, from time to time Jabar Bhũyar would manifest himself in the mouth of a shaman. He would report things to individuals present at the seancelike meeting which only they and the Jabar Singh of real life had done. The tone of the voice and mannerisms of the shaman as he spoke were Jabar Singh's. His close friends and relatives were unable to distinguish any difference between the god Jabar Bhũyar and the man Jabar Singh that they had known so well. Thus, the veracity of the spirit speaking was proved beyond a doubt. No one would dare to refuse the sacrifices that he demanded. The fear of his power over them has continued through the decades to this day.

No one is really sure just how many children old Jokhya had. It is remembered that his first wife was of the Kanhu clan. The children she bore who survived were a boy named Aganda and a girl, Dama. When the first wife died, Jokhya took a wife from the Bereta clan in Tedhe Bojha. (This was the same village where, a hundred years later, Gwen set up her outstation health clinic.) The second wife was referred to as Tungkuni Budiya, meaning the "short, stout old lady." Her ancestors had given up their previous clan name and had taken the name Bereta. This happened when someone had performed a valuable service for the King and had been given the *birta* land grant as a reward. Their name Bereta came from the corrupted form of *birta*. This wife bore Jokhya a son, Bir Bahadur, and two daughters, Ramita and Deoma.

Of all of Jokhya's descendants throughout the generations, none had an impact on the history of Arakhala like that of his first son Aganda. Like his father, Aganda was destined by the gods to become a shaman. As such, he would have the support and power of the gods with which he would be able to confound and overcome the forces of evil. These opponents of mankind appeared primarily as the jungles elves, the ghosts, demons and their human ally, the witch. The impact that Aganda has had on Arakhala up to the present day cannot be fully assessed by an outsider like myself, but it is clear that among all of Arakhala's ancestors, no one can compare to Aganda.

CHAPTER 7:

AGANDA--THE LIFE OF A SHAMAN

Born in 1849, Aganda's early years were no different from those of the other Magar boys his own age. He learned the ways of the forest and, like most of his friends, became an avid hunter of the small barking deer and goral mountain goat. If they were lucky on the hunt, they might kill a wild pig, or serow, a large type of mountain goat. And from time to time the unexpected would happen: they might even kill a small sloth bear, a Himalayan black bear, a leopard or a tiger. In those days their primary weapon, of course, was the bow and arrow.

More so than today, sheer physical might was of utmost importance. Aganda's bow, made of the *li* bamboo, was very powerful. His grandson Khadak told me that when he joined the army at the age of sixteen and a half, he was still not strong enough to draw Aganda's bow. The bowstring, called *lipya*, made from the inner bark of a tall slender bush of the same name, was extremely strong and durable. On his left forearm Aganda wore the *bhalthok*, a wooden armguard to keep the bowstring from stripping the skin off his arm when he shot.

The arrows were made either of a length of the slender *ninggala* bamboo or else of a split piece of the larger bamboo. Onto the arrow, called a *meyasar*, was attached either the *meyã* or *thingkya* arrowhead. The *thingkya* was simply a straight, slender rod of iron, and arrows with this type of point were used for target practice. The *meyã* arrowhead was used on big game. It was a three-inch rod of iron with a long V-point tip. The iron was heated and pressed into the bamboo shaft. When it was securely seated, the bamboo shaft behind the iron point was wrapped tightly with a strong string and covered with the gluelike sap from a tree. Properly done, the arrowhead would never separate from the shaft.

Next the iron arrowhead was sharpened and washed with poison. No one can remember how they made the poison, but they do know that there were three types. Each was called by its name, "one-step," "two-step" or "three-step" poison. The name of the poison indicated how far an animal was expected to go before it died. When the poison had been applied to the arrowhead, the men would blow a secret spell over it that made it certain to kill instantly. When an animal had been killed, they would blow another spell on the carcass, in order to nullify the effect of the poison so that they would not also die when they ate the meat. The arrows were carefully kept in a hollow section of bamboo called a *thokoro*. When hunting, they strapped the arrow-filled *thokoro* to their back.

During his lifetime Aganda married three times. His first wife, Sanapurna, of the Aslami clan, bore him eight children which survived. The first two were girls named Padu and Narmati. Sometime after Narmati was born, Aganda lost control of himself; they say he went crazy. He was just sitting there around the fire one day when suddenly he began to tremble and shake; a god was putting him into a trancelike state. Jokhya was there and grabbed him by the feet and asked, "Are you all right, son?" But immediately Jokhya too began trembling while his own teacher-spirit, as it is referred to, began to take control of the father.

Whether it took place on that same day or a little later is not known. Anyway, the two gods did not get along, for the father and son began to fight while under the control of their respective teacher-spirits. Jokhya was determined to show the superiority of his god, so one day he pounded a stake firmly into the ground. Then jumping onto it, he began leaping and twirling as he danced on its top.

It would take much practice for one to learn to balance himself like that on one foot, much less dance on it. So, when Jokhya had finished his performance he said to his son, "Okay, now you do it!" But Aganda, shaking and staggering as he was in the trance, could not stay on the stake. This conclusively proved to everyone the superiority of Jokhya's god.

Because the gods did not get along, Aganda was not able to live with his father any longer. In his madness he rejected his rightful portion of the family land and gave up his inheritance to his younger brother, Bir Bahadur. On the southern edge of the village lived a family of the Gora-Saru clan into which Aganda's half uncle's sister had married. He went to them and obtained permission to build a house for himself on their land next to the spring, in the shade of the *bar* and *pipal* trees around which a resting place had been built. On the west side of the house where the small stream ran, he constructed a rock-wall fence.

About a hundred years later Aganda's grandchildren once again asked permission to build a house. This time it

An empty basket sits on the veranda of an oval-style Magar house.

was mine. As the foundation was being dug, the workmen pointed out the remaining stones of a house that had long since been torn down. It was only after five years had passed that I learned that it had been Aganda's house. The remains of the rock wall that fenced my garden had been built by him as well.

Aganda didn't stay in this small house for long. Financially, things were going well for him and in a few years he had the means with which to buy two pieces of land and a large house on the western edge of the village. After he left his father's house, Aganda was periodically driven into the forest by *Saiyambu*, his teacher-spirit, and by the other gods that used to ride on him. Compassionately, Jokhya would go out and search for his son and lead him back home, but before long he would go mad once again. One day the gods finally drove him into the forest for good. Unbeknown to him his wife was then pregnant with Parthama, their third daughter. That proved to be a cause for trouble later on.

Aganda was gone for twelve full years. He spent most of this time in the deep forest up around Peak of the Gods. Occasionally someone would see him, stark naked, wandering through the forest, his long, tangled hair trailing down to his hips. At other times someone would come across the spot where he had made his bed in the thick grass. He was as elusive as a wild animal and twice as frightening. Only after Aganda returned to the village did they find out what had happened.

Later he told how the gods attended to him and fed him fruit, milk and whatever he desired. Though there are only a few places on that steep mountain where water can be found, he said that wherever he went the gods would provide water for him to drink. Sometimes the gods would show him a small hole in the earth and tell him to enter it. He had protested the first time, saying that it was impossible. But when he had tried to do so he suddenly found himself popping through the entrance. Once inside the earth he would wander through a labyrinth of caves. In this way he had been able to travel to the home of the *mayu* goddesses inside Peak of the Gods.

During the years on the mountain, the gods taught him many supernatural secrets. Though it appears that Aganda had no real choice in the matter, the fact that he was living the life of an ascetic obviously pleased the gods. In return they looked after him and taught him their secrets. Apparently, on occasion Aganda would leave his mountain retreat to visit the gods in other areas. Toward the end of his twelve years of solitude he borrowed a torn fish net which he wrapped around his waist like a skirt and left for Kathmandu.

In Kathmandu, Aganda visited all the temples, including Swayambhu, the home of his teacher-spirit. Then he travelled on east of Kathmandu for three months, visiting Tatopani, Chisopani, Jaliwa and Maliwa—places unknown to the villagers of Arakhala. When he returned to Kathmandu after six months' absence, some of the people there recognized Aganda as a true ascetic—a man truly pleasing to the gods. These people bought him a shirt, pants and blanket, and combed his matted hair for him.

The gods had told Aganda that he must endure twelve years of penance. This period was nearing completion, so he returned to his relatives' village of Tedhe Bojha. There he asked for a large spool of thread from every household and went up to the nearby peak of Badai Chuli. His reason for doing it has since been forgotten, but Aganda tied a thread to a stone on Badai Chuli. Then, unraveling the thread as he went along, he walked down to the Kali Gandaki River many miles away. There he tied the string onto a rock and put it in the water, making a single thread of string connecting Badai Chuli with the Kali Gandaki River.

After this, Aganda walked a day and a half west of Arakhala to the Magar village of Biyaghan. There he told the villagers that he was going to celebrate in their village the completion of twelve years of penance. They in turn would have the honor of feeding him his first rice meal since he had begun his period of asceticism. So on the appointed day, each of the sixty houses prepared for him a meal of rice, chicken, curds and one banana. Aganda began in the morning and went from house to house. Before the day was over he had eaten a meal at everyone's house.

After returning from Biyaghan, Aganda first went to the smaller village of Lower Arakhala. There he ate a meal of one *muri* (about 320 cups) of red chili peppers. Finding that he was burning up from the chilis, Aganda walked back down to the Kali Gandaki River and lay immersed for seven days and nights in the cold water. It was at this time that Kalabir Masan, the king of the demons who lives in that river, taught him all about black magic.

From the river Aganda returned to his home for the first time in more than twelve years. When he saw eleven-year-old Parthama, he asked his wife, "Who is this?" She answered that it was his youngest daughter. Try as she might, she couldn't persuade Aganda; he was convinced that someone else had fathered the child. So back to the river he went, his wife in tow. Holding her by the hair, he immersed her three times in the river. Taking her home, he dug a deep hole and made her stand in it while he filled the dirt back in and compacted it around her legs. Then he left her to stand there, buried half to her hips in the hole. When he felt that she was sufficiently purified by this penance, he finally took her out of the hole.

Once again Aganda joined the mainstream of life in Arakhala. However, he was no longer just another villager. No one in the whole area had known of someone who had done twelve years of penance for the gods. Some shamans might do two or three weeks of fasting before completing their training; others were known to have done various types of penance for a few years. But as to severity and length, Aganda was beyond compare. As a result, he was considered to have far more spiritual power than anyone else. He was often called to faraway villages to perform a divination or healing and his fame spread far and wide.

Among the Magars there is another religious officiant in addition to the shaman, called the *muthyar,* meaning "blower." He is a healer who divines things by means of magic and signs. The healing he does is effected by blowing spells upon the patient and by giving him medicinal herbs.

One day Aganda was at Chharchharya, a village just below the Mahabharat Range's crest, two valleys to the east. In Chharchharya at that time there was a healer called Tokolok Gurung. He challenged Aganda to a contest, saying that he could eat more at a sitting than Aganda could.

Aganda responded to the challenge. For the contest they each agreed to take a goat yielding about twenty-five pounds of meat to the upcoming sacrifice at Dargaon, a day's walk west of Arakhala. On the appropriate day after the sacrifices were over, each man chopped the carcass of his goat into small pieces. Then he cooked it and sat down to eat. Tokolok Gurung consumed every bit of his goat and won. Aganda lost because there was one bone in his goat that he was unable to chew up and swallow. Returning to Chharchharya, Aganda stayed with a man of the Phal clan. Burning with chagrin at losing the contest, he asked them to grind up eight pounds of a black bean and make a single piece of fried bread. When they had it cooked, Aganda ate the whole thing and went home.

Many are the stories of men of old who could consume huge quantities of food. This ability is always attributed by the villagers to the power of a demon residing in that person. Such a man would have the ability to do the things that the gods themselves could not or would not do. That gods would operate out of the same men that demons do, such as in Aganda's case, does not seem to cause any conflict in the villagers' minds. It is just an idea that they accept.

When Aganda's ancestor first hewed down the old oaks and built his home in Arakhala, life with the supernatural was not burdensome. There were the yearly sacrifices to be made to the *jhãkari,* the jungle elves who owned and ruled over the forest which the villagers hunted in. There were the few sacrifices to the spirits of the ancestors—those which had not been able to reach their eternal rest in *boikunthaũ,* the "place-of-our-fathers." And there was the occasional sacrifice required by a god, goddess, demon or ghost to satisfy their hunger. That was about it; that much they could handle. But before Aganda had left the scene, he had them deeply "buried in debt," as his grandsons later termed it.

Surely no one thought of it that way. The gods ordered it and the people responded. Most often the command came while Aganda was in a trance. When shamans went into a trance, usually they were unable to remember what had taken place. So, the first thing they did on regaining their senses was to ask the spectators what had happened. Homan, my neighbor who owns the land our house is on, told me that he did not lose his senses when he was in a trance. On the contrary, it was by listening intently to the god speaking through his mouth that he learned what was expected of him. While the god was speaking some unknown language, there was nothing to listen for, but when he began speaking in Magar, his mind would be alert while his mouth talked on. In fact, he had to be alert; he could never know when the god might order him to fast or to perform some other act of penance.

It is not certain what Aganda's experience was; perhaps sometimes he lost his senses, while at other times he didn't. Anyway, as the gods spoke through his mouth, the orders to the villagers would come. At other times Aganda himself simply reported that the gods had privately told him something the villagers must do. Certainly it was most common for the gods to speak for themselves. On the other hand, Aganda was in contact with them constantly, so the villagers didn't consider it out of place for him to simply pass on what they had told him.

At this point the chronological order is lost from focus, but that makes little difference in terms of the total effect on the future generations. One day (they think it was while Aganda was in a trance) he said, "In order that all will prosper and be well in Arakhala after I'm gone, you must honor Kala Bhairum, the god who resides in my head."

There are two main entrances in and out of Arakhala. One entrance is on the north side where the trail comes up the ridge from the river and the other is on the south side where the same trail continues on up the mountain to the pass to the Terai. Near the north entrance Aganda built an altar to Kala Bhairum by putting a squared post in the ground. In the top of the post he stuck an iron trident similar to the one he had carried during his twelve years of penance. At the base of the post he laid a flat rock that served as the god's plate from which the deity could eat the blood. Aganda ordered that each year a male pig be sacrificed at the post. At the same time a rooster must also be sacrificed, but its blood was to be sprinkled crosswise on the nearby trail. Then Kala Bhairum would stand in that spot. Like the blood of the rooster, which symbolized an obstruction of the trail, the god would stand as a barrier to stop all the evil forces which would enter the village by way of this trail.

On another occasion, Aganda ordered that the goddess who resided in his chest, Chhattisa Debi, must be honored on the upper trail. There he built a similar altar and ordered that a female goat and two hens be sacrificed yearly to guard the upper trail. In this case the extra chicken was required for Boksiman Budiya, the spirit of an old witch. The name, being nonspecific, was probably given in the hope that all of the dead witches would be satisfied by this sacrifice. To distinguish this sacrifice for the benefit of the recipients involved, the hen for the witches was sacrificed at a post off to one side of the main altar.

Up at the spring, which flowed clear and cold, a tragedy occurred one day. There was plenty of water from this source for all the villagers' needs and more besides. Aganda and the other men sometimes swam in the small pool which was formed by the free-flowing spring. But a foolish tailor woman washed her dirty skirt right there in the pool, which displeased the gods so much that they caused the spring to dry up. Instead, the spring began to flow out of the ground in an inaccessible spot some four hundred yards down the steep slope below Aganda's house. To reverse this stroke of bad luck, Aganda ordered the villagers to carry up some clean sand from the river. In order to cleanse the area, he took a bottle of *gawõt* (cow urine blessed by a Brahman) and sprinkled its contents, along with the sand, around the dry spring.

For the altar, he set up a square post with two entwined snakes carved on it. An iron trident was stuck in its top and around this centerpost were set four other posts forming a square. "This is the altar for Seti Nag, the Great White Serpent. He requires of us a male sheep, a white chicken and a pigeon, white if possible," Aganda announced. Then he prophesied, "Seven days after the sacrifice the water will return again." But he was wrong. Though the villagers have faithfully continued to make the sacrifices every year, the water has yet to begin to flow as Aganda promised. In fact, since then, getting sufficient water has been a very difficult problem for the villagers.

For their crops too, water is of perpetual concern for the people of Arakhala. Only a very small portion of their fields are situated where irrigation water can reach them. The rest are all found on the steep mountainsides far above any running water. If rain doesn't come at the right times or in the right amounts, their crops might be reduced to one half or one third of what they would otherwise be. When the spring rains are sparse and late, their major crop, the corn of their terraced fields, does poorly. One helpful thing about their agricultural cycle is that they also plant the *bhotiya* corn on their burned-over mountains. This corn usually produces well when the weather cycle is such that the corn on their terraced fields yields poorly.

One year when their recently sprouted corn was being burned up by the hot spring sun, Aganda announced that the gods had given him the remedy. Obviously the gods were displeased about something; that was clear to all. Otherwise they would have brought the needed rain for their corn. First of all, on the very edge of the ridge coming down from Peak of the Gods right above his own herding shed, Aganda built an altar of three stones. The stones were very heavy and each had some resemblance to a head and neck of an animal. Then with the big drums booming and the cymbals and long-arching trumpet-horns playing, the men left the village and made the fifteen-hundred-foot descent to Desot Stream. Some of the men stayed at the stream and prepared the altar there while the rest made the 3500-foot climb to the new altar on the ridge top above.

At the stone altar they sacrificed a pair of pigeons and a female goat to the three *mayu* goddesses. To Indra Debi they sacrificed a rooster. At the time the goat's head was severed they gave a signal to their friends at the stream. Nowadays they signal by shooting a gun, but then they presumably did it with the drums. Immediately, down in the stream bed their friends sacrificed a male pig at the *pipal* tree to Jala Bhũyar, the god of water.

The *mayu* goddesses were a holy type of deity, so they were offended by pigs and beer or liquor. For a midday meal, beer mash of fermented corn and millet is the villagers' most convenient and common food. But Aganda forbade anyone to take their beer mash or liquor onto the holy mountain or to allow pigs to be kept on that side of the stream. That would court disaster, as was amply shown by the case of Jabar Singh and the tiger.

This day, however, was the exception. While the goddesses were gathered round the three stones lapping up the blood sacrificed to them, Aganda had a cup of beer sprinkled about the altar. Presumably the goddesses were so intent on drinking the blood that they never saw the beer. When the droplets of beer suddenly landed on them they became defiled. This was supposed to make the *mayu*s furious. In revenge, the goddesses would send a heavy rain storm to drench the offending villagers before they could return to the village.

Nowadays when they go to do these sacrifices, many of the men take an umbrella along. If it has not yet rained by the time they reach the village the girls take jugs of water and stand above the trail to splash the men as they return. Perhaps this is to remind the *mayu* goddesses of what is expected of them.

Sometime after his return to village life Aganda became concerned about his continued failure. He'd been married many years yet he had fathered no sons. One day the gods offered him a solution to this problem. He went to the men in the village of Lower Arakhala and told them, "If you give me seven of your unmarried daughters to sleep with, the gods have promised me that my wife will finally bear a son." The men agreed to his request and on the appointed night he took all seven of the girls down to the water hole below their village.

It wasn't supposed to happen that way, but it was one of the seven girls, a girl of the Garangja clan, who became pregnant. When this became known, she was married to Aganda. True to the god's word, the child she bore was a son. The boy was named Bhuwan Singh, but the girl's father had demanded of Aganda the token bride price of one *mana* (two cups) of rice, so the villagers called him "Mani" instead. This second wife, however, never bore another child, for soon after she contracted tuberculosis.

Before long, the poor girl was debilitated to the point that all she did was lay on her back and gaze at the ceiling. They knew that if she died in the house looking at the ceiling like that, her spirit would rise to that spot on the ceiling and remain there to plague the rest of the family with tuberculosis. So when it became apparent that she was going to die soon, the family took her down to Phulmadi Stream and built a shelter there for her to sleep under. Daily, someone from the family made the long trip to the stream to give her food and drink.

The problem was, she didn't die as soon as they had expected. After six or eight weeks of feeding her like this, someone came one day with the food to find nothing but a headless corpse. No one could guess who had cut her head off. Aganda himself was not accused of the crime, and it was presumed to have been the evil work of a *laguwa*. The *laguwa* were shamans who had the ability to turn themselves into tigers whenever they liked. The shamans of the Tharu tribe, living in the plains to the south, were particularly noted for this ability. To back up this conclusion, it was noted that female tigers always ate a person from the feet up, whereas male tigers always started with the head. "And see! It was the head that was taken. Surely it was one of those Tharu shamans," they concluded.

Sometime later Aganda became dissatisfied with his first wife, Sanapurna. So, one day he told her, "Either make a friend for me out of a stone or else let me bring home another wife."

Not being able to do the first, Sanapurna thought, "Well, at least a second wife will give me some relief from the household work," and she gave her consent. So Aganda went to his mother-in-law's family in Tedhe Bojha and brought home from the Bereta clan a girl named Khagi. Khagi, however, never produced a single child—a cause for deep humiliation in this part of the world.

About two hundred yards down the hill from the dried-up spring stands a huge old *simbal* tree. It towers far above the small grove of trees of various varieties which cluster around its base. It was near these trees that the outflow of the spring used to run. Here Aganda built another altar. He marked out a square with four posts and placed the fifth at the center. "Here," he said, "we must do the *pancha bali* Five-Blood sacrifice. Twice a year we must give it, then the *mayu*s will finally be pleased. Then they will bring us rain and good crops, as well as keep us from plague and sickness."

With booming drums, long trumpet-horns and clanging cymbals they came, leading the major sacrifice, a male buffalo to be offered to Bishnu Bhaguwan. A rooster also was given to him. In addition, a female goat and pair of pigeons was offered to the *mayu*s and a bottle of liquor and a duck to Aghori Deota, the death-god. In the Magar language, however, they called him *Jyamarat,* meaning "night-eater."

This was the minimum sacrifice. It was given, like the others that Aganda instituted, as a cooperative effort of the whole village. The meat of these sacrifices was divided up and a portion given to each household. Individual offerings for personal needs and desires were made in addition to these and the meat belonged to that person. For the cooperative sacrifices each house took turns providing an animal or fowl. If they had none to spare, they were to give money to purchase one from a neighbor. At one of the recent *pancha bali* sacrifices I witnessed, in addition to the cooperative offerings, there were an additional thirteen goats and numerous chickens sacrificed by the individual villagers.

One day Aganda left for Chharchharya with some drummers. He was going to get another god, this time for himself. From Chharchharya they climbed up the sheer mountain trail to the peak of Badai Chuli, where he picked up a heavy rock of sparkling iron ore. With drums pounding, they escorted the new god back home. In his back yard he built a small house and altar around the rock, which he called the abode of Madusara Deota. It was for his own family's benefit alone. From that time onwards they were ordered to offer it a male goat at the spring *Dasain* festival and a rooster at the fall *Dasain* festival.

To further honor and placate the various deities of the area, Aganda called for regular holidays to be observed. This meant that there must be abstinence from the regular work schedule. Every Monday was a holiday, as were the first Saturday, second Sunday, third Wednesday and fourth Tuesday of every month. The full-moon day was to be observed as well. These are the days observed by the people of Arakhala; other villages have their own days to observe, depending upon how their particular deities have instructed them.

Aganda's neglected god-house for Madusara Deota.

For Arakhala, Monday was to honor the *mayu*s so that they would keep the villagers free of sickness. Tuesday was for Manggala Debi so that she would thwart the evil eye of the witches. Wednesday was to please Budhabariya Deota and thus keep plagues out of the village. Also included in that day was Churamani Barajyu, a notorious family of witches, to keep them from sending leopards to kill the village livestock. Saturday was kept for the benefit of Sansari Debi so that the villagers would get protection from illness. Sunday was kept for the sake of the *tin khukhuriya sayari mantar*, so that others' evil spells would be repelled from the village. The full-moon day was kept to honor the moon god.

In addition to these regular holidays, there are numerous festival days, death ceremonies, marriage ceremonies and other holidays which are celebrated as well. Thus, there is a minimum of nine to ten holidays per month and usually quite a few more. On these days the priest, an unmarried Magar boy, goes and prepares an altar for the sacrifice. If there is no blood sacrifice to be given on that day, he will give *dhar* on one of the many altars.

The particulars vary, but basically *dhar* amounts to placing a flattened ball of cow dung on the altar. Two depressions are then made in it with the fingers. The one on the left side is filled with water, the right side one with rice and milk. Between the two a string is laid. On the right side of the cow dung, a leaf cup is placed. In it an oil-soaked string is lit. Then in front of the dung a live coal is placed and incense is sprinkled on top. As the smoke comes up the priest is to pray, "Lord, we've given you this today. Now we won't work in order to honor you. Don't let sickness come on us, and bless our crops and livestock."

About sunrise or a little later, the boy finishes and returns to the village. In those days the town crier went immediately throughout the village proclaiming, "It's a holiday! Cease from all work!" From that time onwards, the only work allowed was to cut grass and feed the livestock. A sentry was set at the resting places at both ends of the village. He would ensure that no one entered the village carrying a load and thus defile the holy day.

Although field work of any type was strictly forbidden, there was a loophole by which some would do certain types of work. What these people did was to eat early and leave the village before the crier had ordered the ceasing of all work. Then, since they had not heard this order to cease work, they had an excuse. When they returned to the village carrying a load, they would be told by the sentry to leave it at the resting place. The villagers would leave the load and go to their house to eat. In the late afternoon the crier would call out the news, "The holiday is finished!" Only then were they allowed to retrieve their loads from the resting place.

Aganda must have gained a great deal of power and authority in his long life in Arakhala. No doubt this was a point of burning resentment in the heart of the headman who was supposed to be the village leader. One day the headman was sitting under the trees at the upper resting place drinking beer with his friends. When Aganda came along they got into an argument. The headman leaped up and began to fight with the aging shaman. During the fight he managed to pull out a little of Aganda's long uncut hair. Aganda, realizing that his head had been defiled by the loss of the hair, went home in disgrace and had his head shaved. From that day onwards he never again wore long hair like the other shamans. Though he remained strong and robust until he died, that incident was something of a premonition of the end for Aganda.

One of the most terrifying things the shamans can do is to shoot their *ban*. Basically this means to put a powerful curse on someone or something. The villagers understand it to mean to send off a familiar spirit to kill the object cursed. The *ban* itself was a special marble-sized rock. A shaman could acquire it only when its hiding place in the forest was pointed out to him by one of the gods. Once a shaman had found a *ban* it became his and he would take it home with him. When he wanted to activate it he needed only to intone the magic spell. Then the stone would begin hopping up and down and with a loud humming noise shoot off to its mark, often miles away. With this powerful magic the shamans would often fight one another. Like the god of

Jokhya and the god of Aganda, who couldn't get along in the same house, the gods of the other shamans often urged them to fight with one another to see who was the most powerful. Whether Aganda had a *ban* or not we don't know. It seems very unlikely that Aganda did not have this ability, but today we have no remembrances of him using his *ban* in a fight.

The thing we do know is that one day Aganda went to a sacrifice of the Five Bloods up the ridge at Chuli Bojha, the village of the retired Inspector General of Police, K.J.S. Baral. There Aganda got into an argument with the local shaman who said it was not proper to offer a bottle of alcohol to Jyamarat, the death-god. The argument got so heated that eventually the local shaman stormed back to his house in a rage. He took out his special stone and mumbling the secret spell, made his shot.

Then and there Aganda fell ill with a high fever and became so weak he had to be carried home. The curse was so powerful that until he died seven days later, Aganda was unable to eat a thing. Before he died, though, he prophesied, "The gods had allotted me only six more months to live, so though I'm dying prematurely I don't have much to lose. He (the other shaman), though, had yet another seven years left, but he will die long before his time." Though mortally wounded himself, Aganda had been able to turn the *ban* back onto its owner. As he predicted, within three months the other shaman also was dead.

In the history of Arakhala, many more shamans were yet to make their mark in the years to come, but none would compare with Aganda. New generations were coming, and new things which Aganda had never dreamed of would become common experience for his grandson. That grandson to whom he taught so much would ride in cars and on planes, and he too would become a man of influence upon the generations to follow.

CHAPTER 8:

PEGLEG

Aganda's third and last son, named Antabir, was born in 1890. Twenty years later, in November 1910, Antabir's wife bore their first child, a son named Ratna. Old Jokhya, who at 81 was still strong in body, saw that great-grandson. But before the month was gone, Jokhya had passed away. Three years later, which was the common time span between bearing children for these mountain village women, a second son, named Khadak, was born. He is the one who many years later would become my tutor, advisor and friend. Khadak was an invaluable source of information on the Magars, ranging from history to witchcraft.

Before Khadak reached the age of five, he, his older brother Ratna and a cousin were all sent up to the herding shed to assist Grandfather Aganda. So, for the last ten years of his life, grandfather and his three grandsons were together day and night. Grandfather, the forty-five cows they herded, the forest and the Peak of the Gods were their life. The village and its life were two-and-a-half hour's walk away. They went there only occasionally, usually on the big sacrifice days. So it was natural that as they sat around the glowing fire at night, Aganda should pass on his life story and knowledge to his grandsons.

It was most often at night that the spirit would catch Aganda away into a trance. The boys just watched and listened. They didn't understand much, however, because the gods and spirits would usually speak in Kham, Tibetan, Gurung, Nepali or some other language that they didn't understand. If Grandfather had a reason to call the deities, he would first put on his *ludreche* necklace of nut-like balls. Then after lighting some incense, he would place a metal plate on his head and begin beating it with a stick. In other areas of Nepal the shamans usually had a special drum, but here, more often than not, they didn't. In place of the drum Grandfather beat the plate, and how it ever stayed on his head while he shook and leaped about was always a wonder to the boys.

There are a few things that stand out in Khadak's mind about those early years. In those days, the majority of their corn crop came from the slash-and-burn agriculture which they practiced on the steep mountainsides. Thus, cutting and clearing the forest year after year was one of their big jobs. One day when their mother and father had come up to relieve Grandfather for a few days, Khadak and his brother were left on their own at the herder's shed. Being energetic little boys, they decided that they ought to get to work. The closest thing at hand was their neighbor's corn field, in which the ears were just beginning to form.

The boys started at one end of the field, Ratna cutting and Khadak methodically piling up the corn stalks as if they were brush for burning. Only when the field was completely cleared did the eager boys quit work for the day. The neighbor came back that night to the shock of his life. Khadak, hiding his head in his mother's skirt, vividly remembers the neighbor sobbing to his father, "What will I eat this year?" Father told him to count the corn stalks and when their own corn was ripe, he would pay him back accordingly.

In Arakhala, springtime is a time of thunder and hailstorms. The hot winds blow across the scorching plains of India, and a few miles short of the impassable Himalayas this hot air is halted abruptly by the steep Mahabharat Range. The quick change in altitude and temperature creates massive, rapidly moving black thunderclouds. It is from these thunderstorms that the Magars get spring rains for their corn. Some years, however, the hail from these small cyclonelike storms can be very fierce, leveling the corn to the ground and even killing the livestock. Typically the day will begin calm and sunny, but in the afternoon one will hear the faint thundering in the west of a far-off storm racing down the ranges. I have heard them come, the thunder and lightning repeating so rapidly that it makes me think of a stampeding herd of celestial horses charging across the mountains.

One year Grandfather prophesied to his neighbor, Old Man Sorti, "Today the gods say there will be a furious storm. Don't take your cows out too far from home," he warned, but Old Sorti didn't pay any attention to him.

Grandfather was especially alert that day, but while in search of pasture for his animals, he strayed too far from the herding shed. It was about 3 p.m. when Grandfather's old ears finally picked up the fierce rumbling of the storm racing down upon them. Khadak still remembers Grandfather's strong fingers wrapped around his little arm. Leaving their cattle to fend for themselves, they fled for their lives. The wind tore at them wildly as Grandfather towed Khadak and his brother down the narrow, winding trail. The lightning flashed everywhere. The ground trembled under the awful roar of the thunder. Down, down, down they went, as fast as their bare little feet could take them. No sooner had they entered their shed than the huge hailstones began pounding down upon the thick thatch roof.

As is typical with these storms, in less than an hour it was all past and the sun was once again glaring brightly down. This time, though, the world was brilliant-white with hail. Grandfather left the boys in the shed, and he himself went back up the mountain to retrieve their cattle. He was lucky; at dusk he returned with the herd intact. Other herders were not so fortunate. Some of their young calves and old or weak cattle had succumbed to the pounding of the enormous hailstones.

Later that evening, word got out that Old Sorti and his grandson had not returned home. Early the next morning everyone was out searching and had soon located the cattle. Shortly thereafter, the little grandson answered their calls from under a huge tree where he had taken shelter from the driving hail. He pointed out the way he had last seen Old Sorti going. Many of the places on these ridges are so steep that if a cow loses its footing, it is likely to tumble down the mountain to its death. At the bottom of such a steep place they came across Sorti's corpse. Presumably the hail had struck him down, and the fall had finished him off.

To perform the last rites, the men put an oiled wick into his mouth and lit it. Then they put out the light by striking it with the leafy branch of the *rhum* tree. Laying the branch then on his mouth, they poured in water to satisfy his spirit. If this last ritual were not performed, the spirit would not qualify to go to heaven. Instead, it would be destined to roam about as a ghost. After this ritual was completed, the men carried the body down to the stream bed and buried it in the sand.

No one was surprised sometime later when a healer announced to his client, "Your aches and pains are similar to the ones Sorti had when he died in the hailstorm. Old Man Sorti has returned!" So a chicken was sacrificed and a piece of bread was offered to his hungry ghost. The villagers all said, "After all, he died a tragic death. Not only that, but during the night before the wick was put in his mouth, his corpse surely was touched by an insect or a snake or something else that has disqualified him from going to heaven. That's why his ghost returns now to trouble us."

At the base of an oak tree in the forest, one man who was particularly afraid of Sorti's ghost built an altar. After making a platform from a small heap of dirt, he fenced the mound with stones and placed a long flat rock on top on which to present the sacrifices.

Others would not be bothered to go clear over on the mountain to this altar. Instead, they would take a large stone and set it at the edge of one of their terraced fields and sacrifice a young rooster there for Sorti. If an animal or one of the family was sick during the year and Sorti was discerned as the cause, they would sacrifice another rooster. After the sacrifice, they would throw the stone away so that their field wouldn't be encumbered by it. The next year they would simply pick up a new stone on which to sacrifice for Old Sorti. That was sufficient.

Khadak recalls how terrified he was at five years of age on the day they were to perform his hair-cutting ceremony. A relative from his mother's side of the family had made a brand-new rope of the type used for tying up the cows. They had tied it around his neck and had made him hold a leaf of the *bar* and *pipal* tree along with a piece of *dubi* grass between his teeth. Little Khadak was certain that they were preparing to sacrifice him to some deity! Only with great difficulty was his father able to convince him that they were only going to cut his hair and not his neck as well. After promising him lots of the tasty fried bread they had made for the occasion, his father was finally able to stop Khadak's loud wailing.

As Khadak remembers it, it was in 1921 that the big locust plague came. The locusts came out of the west with an eerie humming sound in clouds so thick that they blacked out the sun. Landing on the trees for the night, they would pile up so heavy that occasionally a large limb could be heard breaking and falling with a thud to the ground. When a villager walked near such places, the defecation of the locusts was so constant that it sounded like rain falling.

It was practically useless to try to drive them from their fields. The locusts would only fly a short way and land in another part of the same field. As a cloud of them flew past, Khadak and Ratna killed some by waving a long stick in the air. These they roasted and ate. "Very tasty!" he proclaimed.

The hordes came and went for three days, leaving the land devoid of green vegetation. The millet and other crops were completely devoured. Only the mature field corn which had already begun to dry escaped. The people survived the famine that year by digging and eating the *lakuwa,* a round hairy root that must be boiled in ashes to take the worst of the bitterness out of it. About 1925 another plague of locusts came, but it wasn't nearly as severe as the previous one.

After Grandfather died in 1927, fourteen-year-old Khadak and his older brother looked after their cows alone. Their only other job was to cultivate the few mountain fields which they had claimed from the forest.

In the mountains of Arakhala, all of the surrounding forest area has been divided up among the respective villages. Thus the people from one village cannot cut wood or graze their animals on land belonging to a neighboring village unless special arrangements have previously been made. Of this forest land, most of the original trees have been chopped down to make their temporary slash-and-burn fields. Even the steepest of the mountainsides have been cut for these *khoriya* fields. The tradition has been that whoever clears the forest for the first time becomes the owner of that land, that is, as far as planting crops is concerned. But the grazing rights and use of the forest products belong to everyone in that village.

In 1930, Khadak's father arranged with a man in the village of Lower Arakhala to rent his forest field for a small sum. Then Khadak's family, which included five brothers, slashed down the forest growth. After it had dried for a while they set it ablaze. Then on the ash-strewn slope they planted their *bhotiya* corn. The next thing to do was to build a *thara,* a lookout from which someone could continually guard the field against monkeys, bears, wild pigs and other predators. Thinking that no one would mind, Khadak and his father cut twelve slender poles for their lookout from the adjacent forest. That forest, however, belonged to the other village.

A man from Lower Arakhala, one who was noted for bringing legal suits against others, found out and brought the case to the headman. Khadak and his father were called up to trial. With heads hung in humiliation, they sat in the center of a circle as the important men of both villages discussed their case. They were fined thirteen silver Indian rupees and a clay jug of beer.

It was a severe fine, considering the value of the poles and the pettiness of the offense. But far worse than the fine was the great shame they felt at being brought to trial before their neighbors. In fact, it was so great that Khadak could think of nothing except getting away. Two months later the chance came. He left with some others for Gorakhpur to enlist in the British Indian Army. He told me that the recruiters didn't believe him when he said his age was eighteen. But when he passed the physical requirements with flying colors, they enlisted him nevertheless.

Khadak was recruit number 5339 assigned to the 2nd battalion, 6th Gurkha regiment. He enlisted under the name of Khadak Bahadur Thapa, but in fact his last name was not Thapa at all. Khadak was of the Rana clan of Magars, belonging to the Lunggeli subclan and the Sunggarpak sub-subclan. But none of these clan or subclan names were readily recognizable as Magar ones. So all of the men enlisting from his village had started the habit of enlisting under the name of Thapa. The Magars were highly valued as good soldiers, so the villagers had instructed everyone to say their name was Thapa. This was the name recognized as Magar and it ensured that they would be recruited.

A year later young Nar Bahadur from Yangchok was enlisted. He was recruit number 5469 and was assigned to the same unit as Khadak. Both Khadak and Nar were well known in their respective villages for their singing and dancing abilities. In the army they became fast friends and with other young men of like ability, formed a dancing troupe. Every spare minute they would spend in practicing and composing new songs and dances. On weekends and

Gurkha dancers in 1932. Nar, dressed as a queen, on left end behind drummers; Khadak, same row, eighth from left.

holidays they would perform before the various brigades, which would give them a donation. They saved this money towards a big party which they threw each year.

In 1935 their unit was moved up to the Afganistan-Pakistan frontier town of Abbottabad. There Nar was assigned to a different unit while Khadak became a signalman. His duties as a signalman put him up with the front-line soldiers much of the time. One day he was standing at the top of a ridge waving his flags to those in the rear, reporting that all was well. Suddenly the boulder behind him was showered with a hail of Pathan bullets. He dived for cover, rolled up his flags and escaped by wading down a stream. He recalls now with astonishment that at the time he thought, "I could have gotten a bullet in the head! I'd be much better off if I could just get wounded in the leg or arm."

Two days later that unspoken wish was fulfilled. Khadak was leading his unit down a dry streambed when danger struck. They ran into a mine field hidden under the dry sand. Khadak stepped on the first mine and he was thrown into the air. The explosion sheared off his left foot and shattered his left arm. Back at the field hospital, his highly regarded officer, Captain Wall, pleaded with the surgeon not to amputate Khadak's arm. The doctor heeded his request and as a result they did indeed save it. His leg, however, was a different matter. In the hot weather, gangrene set in and so a second operation was necessary. But a piece of shrapnel had run the length of his leg and the gangrene continued to spread. On the third operation, the surgeon amputated his leg just below the hip joint; only then did he succeed in stopping the gangrene.

One of the reasons Magars are good soldiers is that they know how to be good followers. In their close kinship relationships they put a high value on obedience to the family leader, obedience to the village decisions and obedience to their gods. In the village, their difficult living conditions require that they work together with mutual regard for the goal chosen by their leader. In their close society, Magars learn to bear with the quirks, habits and faults of others.

Captain Wall had a good relationship with his men and that probably saved Khadak's life. For Khadak, the shock and pain of losing his leg was so great that for three months he refused to eat a thing—he simply wanted to die. He would have died except for the intravenous feedings he was given. One day "Wall Sahib," as he was called, came to the hospital to visit Khadak. "Here are five rupees. Buy yourself some rum and have a party before you die!" he told him. Just as Captain Wall had no doubt hoped, Khadak was so taken by the generous gift from his beloved officer that he quit wanting to die!

After recovery and rehabilitation training, Khadak was retired in 1939 with nine years of service to his credit. However, Khadak was very disheartened when it came time to return home. Just a few months before, Captain Wall had been transferred back to Europe, and Khadak was sure that had the Captain been there at the time, the amount of his pension would have been increased. His pension amounted to twenty-one Indian rupees per month. However, eight rupees were deducted: first, to fix an artificial leg for him whenever he might need a new one; and secondly, to pay for his transportation to and maintenance at the hospital whenever necessary. The result was that his pension was no greater than a soldier who retired without a disability.

Khadak's reduced pension gave him the right to stay at the Poona Rehabilitation Center for as long as he wished. There he would receive first-class food and treatment and have a life of ease. Many of those who were completely disabled did stay on. But that was no life for a restless young man of twenty-six, so he left Poona and went back to Arakhala with his thirteen rupees a month. There the pension was enough to buy the corn to feed himself and his wife; that was all. For clothing, salt, oil, meat, lentils, beans or anything else they might want, they would have to find the means themselves. In the end, he discarded his artificial leg because he found it too heavy a load for climbing the steep trails. The crutches he had were much more useful; with them he could still easily carry a thirty-pound load up the mountains. His remaining leg was powerful enough to get him wherever he wanted to go. Fifteen or twenty miles across the mountains wasn't too long a trip for him in the winter, but during the warmer months he was limited; the perspiration caused his crutches to rub his armpits raw on longer journeys.

Back in Arakhala, he became known as *dūdiya*, meaning "Pegleg." Khadak told me that they never use that name in his presence; that would be less than kind. But when he is not around this is the name that others sometimes use.

When he returned to Arakhala, Pegleg moved back into the herding shed that his grandfather Aganda had built. He plowed his own fields up on the mountain, slowly hopping along on one leg. As he followed behind the oxen he held a stick in one hand and the plow handle in the other. He and his wife looked after the fields they had up there and took care of the cows and goats. His older brother and family stayed at the house in Arakhala with Mother, Father and Aganda's third wife, Khagi. Pegleg's third, fourth and fifth brothers all joined the British forces and went off to war. His third brother was among the nine men from Arakhala *panchayat* who were killed in heavy fighting along the Irrawaddy River.

When news came that his brother had been killed by an artillery shell in the bitter fighting in Burma, Pegleg was shocked and filled with grief. A Brahman priest in a nearby *panchayat* reminded Pegleg that whatever gift he gave to him as one of the priestly caste would be sent on to his brother in the afterlife. Accordingly, Pegleg gave the Brahman some clothing, a pair of shoes, an umbrella and many other generous gifts for the benefit of his beloved brother.

One day there was a serious illness in the family. Pegleg called for some shamans to come to his house and inquire of the gods as to the cause. The chief shaman was a man from Raikot, a village on the ridge to the west side of Phulmadi Stream. The incense was lit, and soon all the shamans began trembling as they fell into a trance. The *mayu* goddesses came, spoke their piece and went. Other gods and goddesses appeared and left. The villagers were crowded into Pegleg's house, expectantly waiting and watching to see what would happen.

All at once the head shaman began shaking more fiercely. Crying out suddenly, he said, "I am Aganda! And YOU are my grandson! You haven't been praying to me. You haven't asked me to protect you. You've given me neither incense nor sacrifices. I am going to destroy you!"

Pegleg was stunned. There was no mistaking the voice. The tone and manner were exactly as Grandfather had spoken. Furthermore, it was out of the question for that shaman, who lived so far away, to have known the name of the man who had died some fifteen years previously. Even those in the village had known him only as Bõlha Budha, the Mad Old Man.

Someone pleaded, "Now tell us please, give us wisdom and understanding and tell us what we must do." Aganda was the one who had caused the illness and he answered, "I will not accept a chicken. Give me a male goat sacrifice and then I'll leave you alone." From that time onwards, Pegleg was sure to see that the Mad Old Man got the blood of a male goat to drink at least once a year.

In 1941, smallpox struck Pegleg's house in the village. His older brother's wife and all six children died. The villagers fenced off their house, which was on the edge of the village, thus containing the plague. For three months the only way they could get to their house was by climbing up over the steep terraces. They were instructed to draw water only from the lower water hole; the rest of the village dipped their water from the higher seepages.

The men of friends and relatives usually volunteer as pallbearers to carry the body off for burial. However, in this case no one volunteered. Since Pegleg himself was unable, only his older brother and father were left to attend to the sad task of burying the seven bodies. One of the advantages of a kinship-oriented close society like this is that people are seldom lonely—at least not like people in an industrialized society often are. The psychological impact of being fenced off from the rest of one's friends and relatives in such a time as this must have been great indeed.

As was the custom, they ate no meat or food with salt in it for the thirteen days of mourning for the wife; this assists the departed in reaching heaven more quickly. For the eldest son, however, the mourning period was five days, and for the other children only three.

At the end of the mourning period, a death feast is required. The family is obliged to butcher a pig and feed the pallbearers and all the clan relatives who have abstained from salt and meat. This is an expensive affair for a family. When Aganda died, sixty men volunteered as pallbearers. As a result, they had to prepare a large buffalo in addition to the pig. If the family is able, they also invite a large number of friends and nonclan relatives to the feast. One gets the feeling that the larger the feast, the more pleased the departed one's spirit. This has a practical side, for if the deceased is happy, his spirit is not so likely to cause sickness to his family at a later date. In this case with Pegleg, a pig was killed for his brother's wife, and a baby pig for the eldest child. For the remaining five children, they killed only a chicken for the death feast.

When I inquired as to the cause of the tragedy, Pegleg said that it was not attributed to the spirit of Aganda. This sort of thing is supposed to be the work of a demon or of the spirit of a person who has died a tragic death. On the other hand, it is the job of the ancestor spirits and various deities to turn back such evils, but they hadn't done so.

He didn't say it, but I imagine that this experience had a lot to do with Pegleg becoming the most religious person in Arakhala. Not only did he do far more sacrifices than anyone else, but he also learned to become a proficient healer and astrologer.

Many a time Pegleg paid the whole amount to buy the sacrifices and pay for the musicians required for the Five-Blood sacrifice, in order to impress the gods with his devotion and to merit favor for his benefit. The meat he divided among all the villagers, though he could have kept it for himself.

Among the various deities, after the *mayu,* the *bayu* or ancestor spirits are considered to be the ones most important to appease. So Pegleg was careful to keep each of them satisfied with an annual sacrifice of one chicken. Those who died while young seemed to go right on to heaven, but the older the ancestor was at death (particularly if he were a shaman, healer, astrologer or witch), the longer that ancestor spirit seemed to stay around. If the person had died a violent or tragic death, soldiers excluded, he never made it to heaven at all. Instead, that person would become a *mari,* the worst type of ghost.

The result was that every time someone got sick, there was always at least one sacrifice to give to some deity or other. Though Pegleg was forced on occasion to borrow from the rich to perform all the sacrifices he made, he was always able to repay the principal eventually. His yearly army pension was of great help in this. Of course, the main reason the villagers made so many sacrifices to the deities was to enlist their assistance and not be forced into debt. The facts, however, seem to indicate that this custom was actually counterproductive.

How many sacrifices Pegleg made in a year is hard to guess. To give some idea, though, I remember a friend over in Yangchok telling me that his family alone had to make twenty-three ancestor sacrifices a year. That excluded any eventuality of sickness in the family, which would of course require additional sacrifices.

For Pegleg, to perform so many sacrifices wasn't quite so difficult. Grandfather Aganda in his madness had given up all his rights to old Jokhya's land and belongings. Nevertheless, as a shaman he had become quite well off and had left many cattle and sufficient land for his sons. But others who didn't have so much could expend nearly all of their livestock in making sacrifices. I have often seen villagers offering a chicken so small that it was yet to get all of its feathers. This is okay, they say, because the deity is only really interested in getting a taste of blood. Even the small amount of blood from a chick may be sufficient to satisfy its hunger, they reckon.

As a shaman, Aganda had known the art of black magic and used it. Pegleg himself actually saw him doing it only once, and then he didn't immediately recognize it as such. Aganda's eldest son's wife had died, so the son went off to

Nuwakot. There he found a woman who was unhappy with her husband. By charm and flattery he persuaded her to coming home with him as his wife. Sometime later, the woman's ex-husband came to Arakhala to collect the payment due him for his wife. Aganda didn't want to pay for his son's new bride, so he went inside his private room which was attached to the side of the family house. A little later, young Khadak wandered in to find Grandfather bending over a rag ball. Muttering an evil spell, Aganda stabbed fiercely at the ball with his long knife. When he was finished he burned the rag to ashes.

Immediately something came over the ex-husband. He began to get dizzy. Soon he decided to head for home, but he was only partially successful. Staggering and stumbling down the trail as if he were dead drunk, he stopped occasionally to tear at the ground like a wild animal. In telling me about it, Pegleg thought that the man had died soon after reaching Nuwakot. But as he was questioned later on, Pegleg wasn't really sure whether the man had died or not. Anyway, the man never came back again to collect payment for the wife that had been stolen from him.

The *muthyar,* or healer, is also able to perform feats of magic, black or white. If he knows the proper spells, he can cause health or sickness and make others love or hate one another at will. Pegleg had not been called by the gods to become a shaman like his grandfather, Aganda. But to become a healer did not require a call from the gods, so he set himself to learning some of this magic, and became proficient at it over the years. He was so good that sometimes the villagers would carry their sick and dying over to him on the mountain to receive help.

Pegleg is the sort of person who, when he sets his mind to doing something, puts his whole heart into it. Hunting was the major sport and favorite pastime of the men in the village. When Pegleg returned from the army, he never thought of participating with the rest of the men. His artificial leg was too heavy; he was a cripple!

Then came the day that he swallowed his pride. He was a cripple, and he would give up all pretense of trying to look like everyone else. Packing his wooden leg away, he strapped his gun to his back, picked up his crutches and joined the men on the hunt. That must have been a day that gave new meaning to his life, for from then on, whenever the men went off to hunt, Pegleg was with them. In fact, he was such a skillful hunter that he became the leader of the hunters. As such, he was the one who made the decisions on where and how they should make the drives up the mountain.

Before continuing with Pegleg's exploits, it would be good to understand the sort of weapons the villagers hunt with. When the muzzle-loading guns first became available in the 1920s, they were relatively cheap as well as accurate and powerful. Except for a few die-hards, the guns soon replaced their bows and arrows. Bali Bhadra Ale, the headman's uncle, was the last of those who refused to lay down his bow. Although the others were using guns, he preferred the ways of his ancestors. When he died in 1942, the art of bow hunting died with him. From then onwards it was guns only; an era had come to an end.

But in 1947 there came another drastic change. With India's independence came the end to the availability of accurate and powerful muzzle-loaders. In addition, the villagers were no longer allowed to purchase the good powder and caps that they had bought in India. In its place they began to manufacture their own powder from charcoal, saltpeter and sulfur. It burned slowly and irregularly, but it shot. However, if it got damp, which was often the case, it wouldn't ignite at all.

I had many opportunities to observe the performance of their decrepit old guns. When I first came to Arakhala, the men kept asking me to go hunting with them. They loved to hunt and fish, so sometimes I agreed to go up on Peak of the Gods with them. We chased the small barking deer and goral mountain goats up and down the mountain all day long. On occasion they would shoot at the animals as they passed by. Sometimes they fired nine or ten shots, yet never hit a thing. Sometimes the cap would not fire; sometimes the charge wouldn't go off. If both did, the irregularly-shaped rocks they used for bullets went any direction except straight. I often thought that they would be far better off with their grandfathers' bows and arrows, but no one knows that art any longer.

Because of the poor quality of weapons, when the hunters meet a dangerous animal such as a tiger, leopard or bear, they may be afraid to shoot. If they do decide to fire, they wait until the animal has come to within ten yards or less before they dare to shoot. At a longer range their guns do not have the shock power to kill a large animal quickly. Pegleg was well aware of that fact when his chance came.

One day Pegleg was stationed at the Lower Pass, waiting in ambush as the drivers came beating the brush from below. Suddenly his sharp eyes spotted a movement. It was a tiger, moving stealthily up the mountain. He watched it move toward his friend, who was hidden in the boulders above him. His friend, though, was looking another way and failed to spot the tiger silently drawing near. Just before it reached the boulders, the man went into a coughing spasm. The startled tiger whirled around and came for the Lower Pass. Seeing it turn his way, Pegleg recalled, "All my hair stood up straight on end and the goose bumps sprouted up all over me."

Pegleg had doubts about his gun. What if he failed to kill it on the spot? He knew first-hand that a tiger could take down a large bull with ease. He would be nothing before it. Once it was on him, its powerful jaws would crush his neck in a flash. Even if he had had two legs to stand on, there would be no chance! Nothing could compare with the vengeful fierceness of a wounded tiger. "Nope, I won't chance it," Pegleg thought. "I'll just let him pass me by." Then a few seconds later, a flood of courage surged through him. Perhaps remembering how the leopards and tigers devastated their livestock, he determined, "One of us is going to die today. It's either you or me!" Steeling his mind to that decision, he slipped back the hammer of his old gun and pressed his body even tighter against the tree trunk behind which he was crouching.

The tiger was moving quickly, his head constantly turning as his eyes pierced the forest for any hint of danger. With pounding heart Pegleg lay frozen against the tree. The tiger was coming straight toward him. He could see every hair on its body now as it glided silently along. The closer the better, Pegleg thought.

The tiger—just a few yards away; Pegleg—gun steady, his eye on the target. Deliberately, the veteran soldier increased the pressure on the trigger. Now! The cap went off. The charge fired. Two bullets catapulted down the barrel, followed by a rag and a cloud of smoke. The shot echoed out across the deep gorges and valleys. The acrid smell of burned gunpowder pervaded the air. What had happened? He couldn't see a thing! Where was the tiger?

When the smoke had wafted away, Pegleg raised up slowly on his crutches for a look. Forty feet below, the tiger lay dead, sprawled across the trunk of the tree that had stopped its downhill roll. One bullet had broken the tiger's right shoulder, the other had gone right between its eyes. The animal was nine feet, eleven inches long, and so heavy that it took eight men to carry it down the mountain. Later, someone purchased the tiger skin from him for the grand sum of two rupees (twenty cents).

Pegleg had one other lucky day at the Lower Pass. This time it was with wild boar, another animal which is extremely dangerous when wounded. When wild pigs are running, they make a curious sight. The largest takes the lead with the second largest next and so on down to the smallest, which brings up the rear. Each pig runs nose-to-tail with the preceeding one so that at a distance it reminds one of a giant snake winding through the forest. It was a thrill of a lifetime to see the herd of pigs coming towards his ambush. Nine of them were winding their way up the mountainside.

Silently he waited, and soon the lead boar reached the pass abreast of him. Steadying the old blunderbuss, he took aim. As the gun fired, the boar squealed loudly, and leaping high into the air, charged straight ahead. Pandemonium broke loose as the eight other pigs scrambled every which way. When everything quieted down, Pegleg wondered where his pig had gone. Was it wounded or not? A little while later, some three hundred yards down the other side of the mountain, Pegleg's friends found the pig. It was stone dead—shot through the heart!

CHAPTER 9:

GOODBYE

This, then, was the man from whom we were to learn so much in our life with the Magars. Veteran soldier, reknowned dancer, proficient in magic and healing, repository of village history, expert hunter, simple herdsman and cripple; all of these he was and more. Gregarious, loyal Pegleg. We couldn't have found any better help. A "pegleg" he was, but in our family he was affectionately called *Bajyu,* meaning "Grandfather."

Starting work afresh after our return from the United States, we thought of all the progress we could make—all that we could accomplish in the following four years. We didn't know how soon that dream would be shattered. Before half that time was up, an abrupt end would come to those expectations.

This time when we planned our future, we were more realistic. In the first four-and-a-half years, we had taken a single twelve-day vacation down in India. Although we had taken other times of official vacation, these always seemed to turn into times of catching up on correspondence and other work that we had been putting off. This certainly contributed much to the serious deterioration of health I had experienced. Now we were realizing that the best use of our time required that we take a good break once a year. Furthermore, at last we admitted to ourselves that it was going to take more time than we liked to get a trial literacy program laid out. Nevertheless we were encouraged.

Pegleg would work with us whenever we asked him. That was real progress. He was eager and mentally astute. Soon we were getting many of the complexities in the grammar figured out.

One of the misconceptions that people commonly have is that the language of an underdeveloped agricultural group such as the Magars would be very simple indeed. Nothing could be farther from the truth. It's true that they do not have terms for things of science, mathematics and other areas outside their culture, but when it comes to grammar and verb systems, they can be extremely complex. In the area of expressing speakers' attitudes, compound actions and exact modes of movement, I find English to be a third-class language when compared to Magar. Their language can be so precise that one could take pages in English to explain the use of a single particle and even then not do it justice.

Just to ask a proper question wasn't easy. Often when I had asked what I thought was a straightforward question, I would either get a puzzled look or some unanticipated answer. I knew that I didn't have a complete grasp of the difficult interrogative system. How could we help them with literacy or in any other way unless we had most of these problems solved?

In the Magar language there is much variation in pronunciation from village to village and person to person. I learned that a word could still have the same meaning although pronounced somewhat differently. So when I found that there was a question word *kudhangcha* and one *kudhingcha,* I wondered if there was really any difference at all. The villagers couldn't tell me any difference, so I was confused. When I asked a simple question, it seemed like they'd tell me everything except what I wanted to know!

One day, one of the Magar school teachers was at our house when I was mulling this problem over in my mind. Hardly expecting a productive answer, I asked him, "Is there any difference between *kudhingcha* and *kudhangcha?*" I expected him to say, as everyone else had,

"Nope, they are both the same." But to my surprise he replied, "Sure, they're a little different, but I can't tell you how."

That was all I needed. With that clue, I kept at it until I had the answer. I found that the question using *kudhingcha* inquired into the attribute or quality of the **subject**; i.e., "What sort of person is he?" The word *kudhangcha,* however, questioned the quality of the **verb**.

If the verb was a transitive type, the question was about the manner of the action; i.e., " **How** did he throw the ball?" On the other hand, if the verb was from a large class of verbs in Magar (which are not even verbs in English) such as "good," "bad," "cold," "hot," "light," "dark" and colors, etc., the question asked for a description; i.e., "How dark was it?" or "What sort of red was it?"

Living in Arakhala, we became involved in village life again. Whenever there was a holiday, the men were always eager to go hunting. One day I agreed to go with them. Eleven of us set out from the village that morning. We made the long descent to the stream and climbed the three thousand feet up to Pegleg's little shack. From there we climbed at least another thousand feet up the mountain, following the narrow trail until Arakhala looked like only a speck below.

When we got to a heavily forested area we all sat down on the rocks to lay out plans for the hunt. Pegleg wasn't along that day and another man was the leader. He ordered each gunner to his stand, describing to him in detail from which direction he could expect the game to come. Then, ignorant of the history behind it, I was assigned to Pegleg's lucky spot: the stand at Lower Pass. The shooters then left for their places up and down the ridge and the beaters disappeared into the dark forest, leaving me alone on the mountain.

As I took stock of my situation, I became less and less happy about it. The forest was so thick and the pass so narrow that I couldn't see more than a few feet in front of me. Any animal emerging from the forest would be right on top of me. A deer or wild goat would be okay, but what if it was a dangerous animal? I backed down over the side of the pass and dug my feet into the ground so I wouldn't slip. Now my head was just level with the ground at the pass. This would give me a split-second more to shoot before an animal landed in my lap. I thought to myself that if the beaters were to jump a bear today, I would be much happier if he came by someone else's stand!

Patiently, I waited while the shouts of the beaters drifted in and out of the steep ravines below. A shot high on the mountain above me broke the suspense. Then all was quiet. I couldn't even hear the beaters any more. Quietly I sat there, straining my ears to catch any sound of approaching game.

Then I heard it. A rustling in the leaves...but how could that be? The noise had come from behind me, but the game was supposed to come from the direction of the beaters. All was silent again as I wondered what it could be. My eyes pried between the leaves to see something, but nothing was there. Perhaps it was only a squirrel or lizard. As I sat there the leaves rustled again. Then I saw him! A barking deer was standing well-camouflaged in a bamboo thicket some forty yards below me. I took aim and fired. The little .22 rifle cracked and the deer made a bound and was out of sight.

I heard the deer crashing through the brush below me for a moment and then all was quiet. Had I hit him? Was he dead or not? From the way he had leaped I felt sure that he was mortally wounded. I was anxious to go find him, but what if he wasn't dead? Perhaps he'd run away and we'd lose him altogether. I decided to stay where I was. Besides, another animal might happen along my way.

A half-hour later, everyone showed up and asked the usual questions. When I told them that I'd killed a barking deer, they wanted to know where he was. I pointed out the bamboo thicket where the deer had been standing and they scoffed increduously. They were hunting the east side of the ridge. What was a deer doing coming up the west side? It would have been going the wrong way. Maybe I just imagined something was a deer. Besides, the distance at which I'd fired was too far, particularly for my tiny gun.

The Pradhan Pancha, the leader of the *panchayat,* was along that day. We had become fast friends and it had been at his urging that I'd come hunting with them. His name, Khadak Bahadur Lungeli, was identical to Pegleg's, and in fact, they were close relatives. I had first addressed him as "Pradhan," but he refused that honor. He was but two years older than myself and he insisted that I call him "Daje," meaning "older brother."

Daje was an eager hunter, but since he had been elected as the Pradhan Pancha he hadn't gotten to hunt much. I was glad that he was there that day; no one else believed me. While everyone sat down for a rest, he and a companion picked their way over to the bamboo thicket. Immediately they found the deer tracks in the dry, rocky soil and carefully followed them down the mountain. They had only gone a few yards before they called out excitedly, "There are blood spots here!"

I was relieved. At least I'd been exonerated; I wasn't just telling tall tales. A few minutes later they found the deer and in great excitement carried it up to the trail. At home in my country, we were always excited when we had a successful hunt, but the reaction of the hunters that day took me by surprise. They were far more elated than I would ever have expected. It was several days before I pieced it all together.

There was plenty of game up on Peak of the Gods and despite their next-to-useless guns, I had presumed that they occasionally killed something, but that was not the case at all. It had been eleven years since they had shot anything, and Daje himself had been the one who had shot that one. Since that time, they said that they had been under a very strong curse from a witch. Despite all the sacrifices they had done, they still had not been able to break that curse. But what they had failed in, I had accomplished: I had killed a deer and broken the witch's curse! This had been their cause for rejoicing.

When an animal was shot, an elaborate ceremony had always been performed, which called for offering various portions of the meat to different gods, including the jungle elves who were the "owners" of the wild game. I knew nothing of this at that time. I had only heard that the one who shot the animal received the two hind legs. The rest was to be divided up evenly among the other hunters.

My friends that day were in something of a quandary over what should be done. They asked me if it was necessary to perform the ceremony to honor the gods. They were using words and terms that I'd never heard before and so I didn't understand their question very well. I answered that when I had shot deer before, I had just dressed them out and taken them home. They would never do such a thing, but since it was my deer, that was fine with them; that was far easier. Anyway, I would be the one who would have to face any wrath of the gods or jungle elves.

Having decided to drop one ancient custom, they saw this as an opportunity to eliminate another. Huddling together, they discussed how to do it. I should get only one hind leg, they announced. In place of the other leg, they would give me a portion equal with the other hunters. I was hurt by this decision, but tried not to show it. I thought they were just taking advantage of me. Later, I realized that it was simply their big opportunity to change an old tradition. It was just that I was the first shooter they had found who would agree to break with the traditional division of meat and relinquish half of his due portion.

Later on, I delved into the various sacrifices and gods related to hunting. In doing this I came to realize how important a place hunting held in their society. There were yearly sacrifices over the guns, a special sacrifice and ritual for removing the curse of the witch from their guns, a yearly sacrifice to be made at the stream and another to be made on the mountain. And for every eleven animals shot, another big sacrifice was performed. To make certain they wouldn't forget anyone, they had a written list of fifty-eight different gods to be honored in one way or another so that they would have a successful hunt. These rituals and sacrifices were so involved that it would take chapters to properly describe them. It was no wonder that they were happy to abandon them, as long as any possible curse for doing so should fall on me and not them!

Among the villagers, instead of "Hello" or "Good morning," a common greeting was, "Have you eaten today?" It indicated in some way that people didn't always get to eat. The question also seemed to show the deep-down social responsibility that the villagers felt toward one another. They would generally feed someone who hadn't eaten.

In their agricultural economy, it was natural that they were very concerned about how their crops were doing. Like them, we also learned to anticipate what the outcome of the next harvest might be. Good crops would mean that they were short of food for only two or three months of the year; a poor yield would mean food shortage for several months. Food, clothing and health were their concerns, and so in a real way they became our concerns too.

When their local remedies and solutions failed, they would come to us for medicine. We encouraged them to go to the clinic in Tedhe Bojha and later to the new government health station in Buling. They could make it to either one and back the same day, but more than likely they didn't or wouldn't go for medicine. Barbara did most of the health work while I concentrated on other jobs. Unfortunately, the villagers had a very poor hygienic situation. For lack of sufficient water with which to wash, small cuts and sores often festered for months on end.

Roundworms were a real problem for many. The villagers claimed that worms came from eating sweet things. But just how the sugar was supposed to turn into worms, we never discovered. Because of that belief, the mothers were very reluctant to feed their children the piperazine worm medicine, figuring the sweet syrup would just cause more worms. Then someone got the idea, "No, don't you see how tricky these white people are? They have mixed the poison with the sweet stuff. When it goes into the stomach, all the worms come running to eat the sugar and they swallow the poison as well!"

The medicine worked wonders on worms, so eventually there became a heavy demand for it. Nevertheless, we still had a problem when we gave a proper dosage to the older children. The mothers were very anxious. "That much!" they'd exclaim. "You're sure it's not too much?" Some mothers would refuse to allow us to give the full dosage to their children. It took us a while to learn what the real problem was.

According to Magar legend, within everyone's stomach there lives a "great worm" which aids in digestion. If the "great worm" dies one can no longer digest his food and he will die in just a few days. It turned out that the villagers were afraid that our medicine would be so powerful that it would kill their child's "Great Worm" and he would die. Apparently, on more than one occasion their children had succumbed when they had been given the local herbal concoctions for worms, so it was natural that they presumed this could happen with our medicines as well.

We discovered that the villagers were all too well acquainted with overdoses. When we first arrived in Arakhala, the fat, happy baby next door was our daughter Tara's playmate. Through the years, this neighbor's children had all died except one ten-year-old boy and this new baby girl. One day I noticed that the baby had a cold. This was common in the village, so I thought nothing of it. But the next morning when I saw the mother, her baby was gasping for air. My friend Daje was there and I asked him what was wrong. He replied that she had taken the baby to a healer that morning, and evidently the herbal medicine he had given was too strong.

That evening Barbara came back from next door and asked me quickly to take a look at the baby. She couldn't feel any pulse. When I arrived, the family was sitting very quietly around the fire. My flashlight picked up the glazed eyes of the child and I knew what the family already did: another baby was lost! Unfortunately, that was by no means the last time we saw a neighbor's baby die.

The worst tragedy we personally encountered in this regard involved Pegleg's family. His youngest brother, Gopal, the *panchayat* secretary who helped us so much in getting the house built, had a little girl whose name sounded like "Pretty." She was the same age as our Tara. Gopal loved carrying Tara and Pretty about the village, one on each hip while they giggled and cooed.

While in Kathmandu during the monsoon we received a letter one day from Gopal. The letter started out with the usual: "Greetings to you from us. We are all fine and in good health here. We hope and pray that you are too." Then in the middle of the letter he broke the news, "Pretty and the other two babies in our house are dead!" A cold virus which was followed by pneumonia had swept through the village, leaving thirteen children dead, all of them within Tara's peer group. Included was the third and last surviving son of a hunting friend whose wife was now too old to bear any more children.

It was no wonder that most of the villagers had little use for "family planning." They thought it was wonderful that we could be married all those years and have only one girl and one boy just when we wanted to, but they were realistic enough to know that they could lose most or all of their children in a bad season.

In a society where the family is the "Old-Age Pension Plan," it is absolutely necessary that they have at least one surviving son. Their daughters would all go to live in their husbands' families' homes, but the sons remained at home with the parents. Usually the elderly folk would work productively up to the time of their death. But if and when they became too old to look after themselves, their sons and grandchildren would take care of them. The man whose third and last son had died in the epidemic that took Pretty was a living reminder to the villagers that three sons is not always enough.

It appeared that on the average, not many more than half the children survived, and often less. The worst case we heard of was with Pegleg's second wife. His first wife had only one child, a son. After she died, he took another wife who was estranged from her husband. She had given birth to eight children, each of whom had died as a youngster!

When she came to Pegleg's house, perhaps they both had secret hopes that there might still be a chance for one more child, but that never happpened; she remains childless to this day. Fortunately for the family, Pegleg's only son survived, grew up and joined the army. Now there is even a grandson to give security to their future.

Perhaps one might think that it was just as well for many of the children to die off, for wasn't that the only thing that helped hold down the population explosion? Unquestionably, under the present circumstances, if there was any place where the land could not support the increased population pressure, it was Arakhala. But there was another factor: many of those children weren't just statistics; they were real people whom we had grown to know and love. Some had been Tara's playmates and Hukum's buddies. They were our friends' children. Who can count the sorrow of losing the last son or of seeing eight children die, one after another?

Over in the health outpost at Tedhe Bojha, Gwen apparently felt concerned about this problem. In a village like Tedhe Bojha, which was even poorer than Arakhala, a steep rise in the population was bound to have drastic results. What was the use of all her efforts to eradicate tuberculosis, leprosy and other diseases? It only aggravated the difficulties resulting from the already high population-growth rate. She knew that attention must be given to these problems, but what could she do? The villagers were all interested in family planning measures once they had three sons who had reached their teenage years, but until then, they had no use for it. Clearly, what the villagers were indicating was that family planning, as we know it, was a viable solution for them only if it could be demonstrated that their children would not die prematurely.

Gwen realized that the only way to meet this challenge was to teach the villagers modern health and hygiene habits. But there was one huge problem: modern health and hygiene presumes that there is a constant and adequate source of pure water, something that virtually every village in these hills was lacking. The only reason that she had chosen Tedhe Bojha as the site for the health post was that there were no other villages for miles and miles around that had adequate water. There was water in the mountains all right, but often it was a mile or more away from the village. It was very difficult for most of these poor villagers, even with government assistance, to afford to buy the necessary amount of pipe for a drinking-water system.

When Gwen came to Tedhe Bojha, she built a drinking-water system for the village. In the years that followed, Gwen observed that with a proper water supply, some diseases were virtually eliminated and other diseases that were common elsewhere were only incidental in Tedhe Bojha. Obviously, water-supply systems combined with health and childcare teaching would have a high payoff.

Gwen gave up her medical work and turned it over to the Nepalis which she had trained. Then she taught the Nepali staff to begin going to the surrounding villages with child care clinics. The results came quickly; the infant mortality rate dropped dramatically. Previously, in the Tedhe Bojha area, fifty-five percent had died before they reached age five. By 1978 this had been reduced to nine percent. As a result, the women no longer feared losing all their children and developed new attitudes toward family planning.

Gwen has now put her efforts full time into helping the villages build water-supply systems. Her goal of helping them to have good health and plan their families is finally becoming a reality.

For the villagers to put in a water system themselves was very difficult. In Arakhala, Daje had made a supreme effort and water was brought in from over a mile away. This project was possible to complete only because of a large number of retired and on-duty soldiers from Arakhala who gave generously. The new water supply had made a great difference in Arakhala for two years. Then they discovered that the shopkeeper in Bhairahawa had sold them the poorest quality of pipe; it broke hundreds of times. Although they put one man full-time on repairing the pipe, often there was no water in the village for days or weeks at a time. The supreme effort to which they had gone and the thousands of rupees in expenses all turned out for naught.

On a hot, misty day, Daje carries two 65-pound jugs of water back from the water hole.

With the road between Kathmandu and Pokhara now completed, it was possible for us to visit Major Thapa from time to time. Our house in the Kalimati section of Kathmandu was on the main road. When he came in to purchase medicine or for other reasons, he would drop in to see us. I had often told Pegleg about Major Thapa. Would this just happen to be his old army buddy? "What is his serial number? Is it 5469? I used to know a Nar Bahadur with that number," he would comment wonderingly.

In the spring of 1975, Pegleg happened to be with us in Kathmandu, helping in our work. I found out that Major Thapa had arrived in town so I searched him out. We invited him and his wife over for dinner the next day. Some forty years had passed since Pegleg and his friend were assigned to different units. Could Major Thapa, by some odd quirk, be Pegleg's friend? Would they even be able to recognize one another now? But I shouldn't have wondered. The minute Major Thapa came in the door Pegleg recognized his friend from long ago. Neither had reason to expect that the other was still alive, yet that day they met once again in our living room! It was a happy time for everyone.

When we returned to Arakhala again, we found that rats had gotten into our thatch roof. We killed seventeen, but the roof was already damaged so badly that it had to be changed. This time the children were thrilled more than ever with living in the village. Michael, like his sister, began talking the Magar language. There were goats, pigs, cows, chickens, buffaloes, dogs, cats and rats to chase or play with. It was a child's paradise.

They didn't mind dirt, and with crowds of kids to entertain them, it was like a perpetual party. The children loved to imitate the big people. They would get drums and sit down in our front yard or on the veranda with their little friends. The boys would beat the drums and sing while the girls danced in the traditional way of their older sisters.

One day we received a distinguished vistor in our simple village home. General Baral, the head of Nepal's police force, was touring the area. He had come to inspect the new police station built on an upper ridge and at the same time to visit his home village of Chuli Bojha. Chuli Bojha was another hour-and-a-half's hike up the ridge and was the poorest village in Arakhala *panchayat*. All the villagers were proud that one of their own had risen to such a position of responsibility, so they made a big celebration out of his visit. General Baral's father had been a Captain with the British Gurkhas. While living in India, Mr. Baral took the opportunity to receive a higher education and go on to earn a graduate degree. Despite the fact that his life was now worlds away from that of the villager, he never forgot his people. Every few years he would return to Chuli Bojha and do what he could to help them out.

At the time we did not know General Baral very well, so Barbara was a bit nervous. She had fixed various types of sandwich hors d'oeuvres and, after arranging them on a tray, had covered them with a tea towel. As we were talking, a neighbor man, the healer for the upper part of the village, had slipped in the side door. At a lull in the conversation, he addressed General Baral, saying, "My son is stationed in Kathmandu with the police force. Would you please have him transferred to the nearby station? We are having many difficulties with him so far away." I'm not sure what answer General Baral gave, and he probably isn't sure either. We were both sidetracked by the fact that the man in his nervousness had backed up and put his hand behind him to steady himself—right into the pile of Barbara's prize sandwiches!

While accompanying General Baral up the trail, we stopped once under a tree to rest. He was greatly disturbed as he gazed over the mountains at the tremendous amount of forest land that was being cut and burned for the villagers' temporary corn fields. "This must be stopped soon!" he said. "They have been given seven years of grace since the law was passed prohibiting such destruction."

He went on then to inquire what ideas I had for improving the villagers' economic situation. I had tried to introduce new varieties of seeds, chickens, pigs and rabbits, as well as a number of other things. Almost everything, though, had failed for one unexpected reason or another. I, too, was distressed at the sight of huge patches of the forest going up in smoke every spring. I wondered what solution there could be? A satisfactory one was not obvious; patterns of living that had been established since ancient times could not be changed overnight. But General Baral's searching questions got me to thinking and delving more into the economic patterns and problems in the Arakhala area.

After General Baral left, I made more inquiries and wrote up a small summary of my investigation for him. This was an area that I'd always been very interested in, but our main thrust here was supposed to be centered around literacy, not agriculture and economics. I didn't know it then, but this was a topic that was going to occupy a large part of my future time.

When the healer asked for his boy to be transferred, I doubted that it would ever happen. Many boys from

Inspector General of Police K.J.S. Baral poses with Pradhan Pancha K.B. Lungeli (Daje).

Arakhala were in the police force in Kathmandu. Furthermore, the man had mentioned neither his boy's name nor his serial number. General Baral was an extremely busy man. He had so many things to look after, and he'd made no notes of the man's request. If it had been me, I probably would have forgotten it immediately. But we never saw his boy in Kathmandu again. By the time we returned, he had already been transferred out. General Baral had not forgotten a poor villager's request!

May 1976 found us packing things away in Arakhala. Arrangements had been made for the plane to pick us up down at the Buling airstrip, but then we received the news that due to engine trouble, the plane would not be coming for us. Instead of going down the mountain, we'd be going up over the pass and down to the plains. By now, the East-West Highway running through that section of the plains had been completed. We hiked out and spent the night at Dhara Pani, a Magar settlement in the Terai. We were among friends there. Many of the people from Arakhala had taken free land there when it was made available seven or eight years before. From there, it was two days by bus to the capital. That three-day trip to Kathmandu was good for us, for in the future we were to use that route till it became second nature to us.

We had been back in Kathmandu only a week or so when we got unexpected news from the Rector of the University. The Central Government had not approved the agreement drawn up with Tribhuvan University to continue our program for an additional five years. Our work with the Magars was finished! We had known that it was possible that the extension might not be approved; nevertheless, it was a shock for us.

In Nepal, the main contribution we had been interested in making had never been realized. Our approach was similar to the one used in the Soviet Union in the 1930s. We had hoped to demonstrate the value of using primers and booklets in the minor languages. From experience gained in other countries, we knew that for the minority groups this would be the quickest and most productive way for them to attain a high rate of literacy in the national language, while retaining all that was best of their own language and culture.

This, however, was a ticklish job to undertake. The surrounding countries were noted for their friction and strife over minority languages. We knew that some officials were fearful of this approach, feeling that showing an interest in the multitude of minority languages might somehow encourage them to put their language into competition with the national language. SIL, however, realized that the situation in India or Burma, for example, was very different. The history that had produced their problems had not been the lot of Nepal. Under British rule, no effort had been made in those countries to bring about a common language. The solution they had tried had usually been to repress the minority language groups or else simply to ignore them.

Unwittingly, SIL made a bad mistake, perhaps the fatal one. In talking about their proposed literacy programs, they often used the term "bilingual education" in its Western context. By it was meant the use of the language of the home as a bridge to literacy and to the national language. This was commonly done in the Soviet Union and the Americas. In effect, the program was only a transitional phase in the whole education process. Only years later did we learn that "bilingual education" was used in some circles in Asia to mean quite the opposite.

The term as used in Asia referred to a government policy of using two official languages as media of instruction in the schools. The languages are always major languages, such as Mandarin and English in Singapore, or Tagalog and English in the Philippines. Thus in many countries in this area of the world "bilingual education" became a big political issue and a very emotional one at that.

The SIL approach was centered on taking each minority language as an individual case and developing whatever materials were needed to teach the children to read and write. After mastering the alphabet in their own language, the foundation was laid for them to continue their education in the national language. "Bilingual education," with virtually opposite meanings on different sides of the globe, was an unfortunate term. No doubt using a different term such as "transitional education" would have gone far to properly describe SIL's approach and alleviate the Nepali officials' rightful concern. It might have made all the difference; who knows?

It seems ironic that an organization that was founded to solve communication problems should have failed to communicate clearly. Perhaps their widespread success in other parts of the world lulled them into being unaware of the depth of the problem. The work had been slowed by an almost total lack of information on the Tibeto-Burman languages in the country. In many ways, they proved to be among the most complex and difficult in the world. In addition, travel in and out of the remote villages was hindered by the torturous terrain and unpredictable weather.

When the agreement came up for renewal, SIL had no shining examples of literacy wonders to show. Certainly there was a multitude of small things, such as the little Tamang boy. For a year his parents had to drive him off to school with a stick, but still he had been unable to make any sense out of reading Nepali. Then for a few months he had been taught using examples in his local language to bridge the gap. Suddenly he was not just another backward village boy; he could read! Confidence surged through him from that time forward as he strode off to school. In a matter of months, he was well along in reading Nepali. He was no longer just "another stupid Tamang" to be looked down upon. He was now a part of a nation and eager to take his place as a citizen of that nation. And now he had the tools to do it with: he could read Nepali, his national language.

But all that didn't matter now. The decision had been made and we accepted it. Within a matter of weeks, our colleagues began leaving; some went to reassignment in Japan, Korea, the Philippines and Indonesia. Others were headed for Africa, Australia, South America and other points around the world. In some countries, the local SIL branches had projects in need of immediate volunteers to start work in fifty or more different language groups. They hoped to fill some of these slots with experienced people from Nepal.

Finally, all of our household goods in Kathmandu, even including wedding gifts, were sold. The only items we kept were a few things we packed away in two drums. Somehow, I felt that we would be back; Nepal had gotten into our blood. The so-called "good life" back home had faded from our memories. Home seemed to us to be Nepal more than any other place. It was the land and origin of our children, our friends and our future goals. It was a country emerging from ancient times—a land of challenge, of mystique and of a people desiring to develop and change.

Finally, when everything was gone from our house, we left to spend our last night in Nepal with friends. Just before dark someone told me, "There's been someone standing at your gate for hours waiting for you to return." "Who could that be?" I wondered. "He is a muscular, heavy-set older man. The way he stands there with his *khukuri* knife in his belt, he looks like a soldier."

It must be Major Thapa! Weeks before I had written him that we were leaving Nepal, but I had never expected to see him again. He had always taken it upon himself to go that extra mile to show compassion, concern or to give help to others. Now, at the last possible moment he had arrived and nearly missed us. I went and got him. He came to say goodbye to Barbara, Tara and Hukum. He stayed just a few minutes and left. He was pale and thin, still recovering from a stroke that had nearly taken his life. Nevertheless, he'd made the hike and grueling five-hour bus trip into Kathmandu just to say goodbye.

The next morning we were on the jet as it lifted off for Bangkok. In a real sense, we were leaving home and going off to see our relatives. We were heading back to a busy, modern civilization, returning to a people who had progressed so much that they didn't have time for people and seldom found time to write us a letter.

Then I thought of the contrast in Major Thapa. I knew he would be aboard the bus winding its way slowly over the jarring, twisting road. It had cost him two days and a lot of expense and effort to complete his mission. As he toiled his way in the monsoon heat up the trail to his quiet little village that day, I don't imagine he ever once took thought of the sweat streaming from his face, his panting lungs or his aged, partially-crippled body. No, that meant nothing to him now; his mission had been successful. He had said "goodbye!"

CHAPTER 10:

HOME AGAIN

It was good to be back with our family again, but always we found our thoughts wandering back to Nepal. "How was the corn crop this year? Did they get a fair price for their ginger? How much livestock were the leopards killing?"

We had left Nepal with the anticipation down deep that we'd be back. After a few months we felt that we wanted to return and work for a limited time on some of our personal projects. This was contingent, however, upon getting a visa and providing our own travel expenses to Nepal and back. We had a one-month tourist visa in hand. "But what is the use of spending four thousand dollars to travel to Nepal for only a month?" some friends asked.

We bought our tickets anyway and left the U.S.A. exactly six months from the day we had left Nepal. The kids were really excited. Lee Maya, Bhumi Sara, Pot Bahadur, Bir Bahadur—soon they'd be playing with all of them once again!

When the plane landed in Honolulu, our son looked wonderingly out of the window and inquired, "Where is Nepal?" At Tokyo, Taipei and Hong Kong, the question was still the same. As we landed at Kathmandu, I happily announced, "Look, Michael, here's Nepal." In his three-and-a-half-year-old mind, this was not the Nepal he had

Michael (Hukum), Kalu and Pot Bahadur tease Lee Maya, Adina (Tara) and Bhumi Sara.

remembered, and nothing we could say would convince him otherwise. This was not Nepal!

In Kathmandu, we began looking for a place where we could fit in. Barbara had been a primary school teacher before we were married. She enjoyed it and had done some substitute teaching in the following years. Two weeks after arriving, a friend told us that an opportunity had unexpectedly opened up for him back home. He would be leaving his position at his school in about six weeks. This meant that they would be short a teacher, so we went to inquire. The principal was delighted to have someone with Barbara's background to teach, and so a week later we had our visa to stay.

We wanted to go back to Arakhala right away, but in the meanwhile I had broken my foot, though at the time I thought it was only a bad sprain. Two days later, at the house of some friends with whom we were staying, Michael fell backwards into a bucket of steaming water being heated by an electric immersion coil. When I hobbled into the bathroom where the housegirl had taken Michael, he was screaming hysterically. As I splashed cold water onto the burns, the hunks of skin were peeling off his thighs. After six days in the hospital, we took him home. A week later and we were on the bus bound for the Terai plains. The first-degree burns and most of the second-degree ones had healed; two spots of third degree burns would take longer. But he could endure that discomfort; he was going to see his friends.

We crossed the Narayani River and caught the bus heading west for Butwal. An hour later we got off and walked up to Dhara Pani, where we stayed with our retired army friend Captain Lal Bahadur, who had moved down from Arakhala.

Pegleg's younger brother Gopal had also moved down to the plains. He had settled illegally along with hundreds of others on cutover forest adjacent to the properly registered settlers. Though their little plot of land was second-rate for the area, they could still raise considerably more crops here than they could on their relatively large amount of land up in Arakhala. We arranged for his two sons, Pretty's older brothers, to carry our children over the pass.

My sprained foot had not healed. To keep up with the others, I found I needed a staff in each hand. I got a stick for one hand and used our umbrella in the other. It was March now and stifling hot down in the Terai. As we climbed to the 5,200-foot pass on the southern face of the Mahabharat, the glaring sun took the strength right out of us. Strangely enough, my foot didn't bother me while we climbed. If I was careful, it hurt only going downhill.

At the crest the cool breezes felt good. We pointed out Arakhala, barely perceptible in the hazy distance, but Michael didn't seem very interested. Sometimes he would run ahead to play hide-and-seek along the trail, but most of the time he was just content to ride on Tilu's back. He had come down with a fever the night before and in the morning had broken out with red spots. It was chickenpox, a minor disease common to the village. He endured the discomfort, though; after all, soon he would see his friends. Four hours later we came around the corner of the ridge just above Arakhala. Michael looked and his face began to glow. In his little mind the vague memories of the past suddenly broke

Barbara watches Michael getting a ride down the trail.

forth into recognition. "Look, Daddy! Look!" he shouted. "There's our home! There's Nepal!" and down the steep incline he raced, squealing with joy.

All day on the trail and tired; third degree burns; chickenpox and fever; all these were forgotten in a moment. Adina and Michael, now changed in name to "Tara" and "Hukum," ran off with their little friends. Even though it was dark, we didn't worry about them. We were home. They'd be back soon when the tiredness of the trip caught up with them and their excitement died down.

Going upstairs, I laid out the sleeping bags and slumped into bed. Coming over those fourteen miles with a broken foot had taken every ounce of strength. Barbara was left alone to take care of everything herself.

At daylight the next morning, the village children were twanging on the screened windows and rattling the door. "Uuuu Tara, come play," they called. In short order the kids bolted down breakfast and were out the door. It was

Michael's favorite pal is Pot Bahadur.

khimbu season now, and the mulberry trees in the village were covered with juicy black berries. For hours at a time they were gone, going from tree to tree with a flock of friends to pick the berries. One or two would climb the tree and throw the berries down for the others to share. At the house, everyone who came by had the same questions, "Where did you go? Are your mother and father well? When are you leaving again? Will you come back after that?"

The few weeks we had to stay flew by all too fast. We found that the leopards had again been tough on Pegleg. His original herd of twenty-five goats had been reduced to four over the last three years. He was so discouraged by this terrific economic loss that he didn't want to keep goats any longer. In a year of poor crops, a large goat could be sold for enough to buy corn to feed his family for two months.

Pegleg feeds his four remaining goats. Leopards have killed over twenty of his flock.

It is impossible for the villagers to spot the leopards on the steep, brushy terrain. Though the herdsman is nearby, most of the herd is still out of sight. Without a sound, the leopard catches and kills one goat after another. His jaws are so powerful that the victim is not able to make a sound when caught by the throat. Often, a leopard is able to kill five or six before one lets out a dying bleat. Alerted, the herdsman then shouts and chases the leopard away, but by then it is too late. In one year alone, the leopards killed fourteen of Pegleg's goats. This was his savings for a time of famine. We can't imagine how great the psychological shock must have been. Daje also was one who had suffered greatly from the leopards. In a single year, they killed six of his cattle, an equally great loss.

While we were still in the United States we had received a letter from Pegleg saying that someone had burned down Daje's house in January. He had been developing into an effective and respected leader of Arakhala, and so we wondered who would have done such a thing. Now we found out how it had happened.

In the village there was an extremely poor fellow who was of low mentality. Though he was not able to speak well, yet he was termed a "joker" because he would make others laugh with his antics. Daje, like many of the other villagers, kept bees in a hollow log suspended under the eaves of his thatched roof. Since the people are very short of meat and protein, many villagers keep bees, more for eating the larvae produced than for the honey.

In the middle of the night, this destitute fellow came to rob Daje's hive. Daje's corn harvest had been far better than usual that year. Just a few days before, he had finished hauling in the last of it from his fields. All of it was now safely stored away on the second floor of his house.

Outside, the man planning to smoke the bees lit the firebrand and began to open the end of the log hive. But while he was preoccuppied with the hive, a gust of wind blew the flames onto the veranda roof. The dry thatch ignited immediately. Frantically he tried to beat out the fire with his hands, but the swirling wind made it impossible. In a few moments the fire was racing across the roof. Fear overwhelmed him as he realized the consequences. Dropping everything, he fled.

All was peaceful inside. The family was nestled together sleeping soundly on their straw mats. It was cold outside with the wind blowing. It felt good to be near the dying embers of their fire. Daje was sleeping right next to the ladder which led upstairs. Suddenly he awoke out of a sound sleep. As he looked up past the ladder to the roof above, he first thought that the light he saw was the morning sun streaming in. Then it registered in his sleepy mind: fire!

Sacrifices had been offered and many other precautions had continually been taken to insure that neither nature, fate nor the gods would burn down their house. But there it was! The roof was a roaring inferno. First, he got the children out. Their tin trunk of valuables, a few water pots and cooking utensils were saved. Then the roof collapsed. A few minutes later and they would have been trapped in the flames!

Their year's supply of food was gone. Their clothes and possessions had vanished. Their house and adjoining cowshed was reduced to smoking ashes. The two buffalo cows, a couple of pigs, a few chickens and a dog were all that remained. Daje had five children to feed, and it was more than six months before the first of next year's corn would be ripe.

The villagers had all turned out to fight the fire with the few water jugs and buckets that they could muster. Fortunately, they had been able to keep it from spreading to the other houses which were crowded close by. A year before in the village of Chharchharya, where Tokolok Gurung had challenged Aganda to the eating contest, it had been a different story. That afternoon in 1975 a windstorm had blown sheets of flame in every direction. In a matter of minutes every house in the village was afire! Four people and most of their livestock were lost. And a 1971 fire in Arakhala itself destroyed seventeen houses on the north side of the village before the fire could be contained.

To prevent a similar tragedy, a sacrifice had been performed and a house-fire ritual reenacted for the gods. At the upper end of the village, they had built a replica of a house, along with a miniature rice beater. One man went up the hill with a small wooden bucket of water in hand and pretended to be cutting fodder for the animals. A second fellow, dressed as his wife, did the housework.

Pretending to cook rice in a broken clay pot, she laid a clay shard on top of a fire she had built in the wooden rice beater. In a few moments the whole house was ablaze and the wife began screaming, "Fire! Fire!" The man responded by stumbling and rolling down the hill with his water bucket in hand. His clowning evoked quite a laugh from the villagers. Perhaps it was intended to amuse the gods for whom it was being performed as well.

Arriving at the house, he said to his wife, "What have you been doing! Picking body lice?" This has cultural implications that caused everyone to laugh heartily again. After he had thrown his bucket of water on the house, everyone else joined in and helped to put out the fire. Beer and rice were then sprinkled on the ashes and a rooster was sacrificed over the remains of the house. This was to prevent the cycle of fate from repeating itself in the village. Unfortunately, it hadn't worked.

Daje was despondent over his loss. For the next few days he could hardly eat, but then the villagers' strong kinship feeling and appreciation for his leadership was demonstrated. Each family gave grain as it could spare. They carried rock, wood and slate for free. The housebuilders of the village worked at a reduced rate. Within a couple of months, Daje had the only slate-roofed house in Arakhala; he wouldn't have to worry about fire again.

Meanwhile, the man who had set the house afire had gone into hiding near Tedhe Bojha. A few days after the fire, he was apprehended when he tried to return home under cover of darkness. He could have been taken to trial and jailed for a number of years, which would have satisfied to some extent Daje's need for retribution after such a traumatic loss. Instead, he put the man to work, giving him only meals for his wages. After the man had worked for about four months building the house, Daje set him free.

Asking Daje about the fire one day I inquired, "Older Brother, why didn't you send him to court?" Reflecting the spirit the Magars have built up over the centuries, he answered, "Well, he's ignorant and without intelligence. He didn't burn my house down on purpose. Besides, he has very little land and not enough to eat. What would his wife and child do if he were in jail? It would be all the more difficult for them. So I just forgave him and sent him home."

Sitting around the warm fire inside his new house, I was much impressed by that statement. It was the same unfeigned magnanimity and greatness that I'd sensed in Major Thapa. Lesser men would have nursed a spirit of revenge, hate and hurt for years to come. But Daje had refused to live in the past—it would have sapped him of his imagination and energy for the future. Under his leadership, Arakhala had taken second place in 1974 for progress and development among the eighty-two *panchayats* of Palpa District. And in 1977, as part of the Nawal Parasi District, Arakhala placed third among fifty-one *panchayats*.

Daje had received no pay for this job; it was strictly honorary. If he hadn't had such a large extended family to lean upon and help support him, he couldn't possibly have done it. He had told me from time to time, "I'm going to quit next year. I spend all my time on *panchayat* business. I have no time for my own fields and I hardly ever get to go hunting." But the villagers wouldn't let him quit. In 1978 he was chosen to be the District Representative for the five *panchayats* of his area. As such, he would be on the District Council.

Daje's extended family was a good example of how combined families operate much more efficiently than a single, independent one. Daje was the oldest of three brothers. Some ten years before, land was being parceled out for free in the Terai about fourteen miles south of Arakhala. At that time, the youngest brother was sent down to look after the land they had received there. This was at the time the campaigns were in progress to eradicate malaria from the lowlands. The second brother, who just recently retired from the army, purchased a small plot near the first one. And down at Desot Stream, the old father herds about twenty-five goats and looks after their fields nearby. Thus with Daje looking after the large home in the village, the four men of the family normally live at four different locations.

In addition to this, there is a sixty-five-year-old uncle with his sons who are a part of the extended family. Years ago when the family was separating, he chose to continue to keep everything in common with Daje's father. The uncle lives up on the mountain in a doorless shed next to Pegleg's. There he grazes about thirty goats and twenty-five cattle. Two of his adult sons live with him on the mountain and help cultivate the fields they own up there. His other son is now retired from the army and lives down in the Terai next to his two cousins. Together, these eight men and their wives make up one extended family. The land,

Daje's uncle, Saha Bir, cooks corn meal mush for dinner.

dwellings and livestock are common property. Cooperating in the work, they have formed a miniature economy of their own.

When it is plowing-and-planting time in the Terai, a couple of the men bring one or two teams of oxen over the mountains to stay for three or four weeks until the heavy work is finished. In Arakhala, the villagers are always short of grain even in the best of years, so they make up for part of their deficiency from the excess grain grown in the Terai.

On the other hand, down in the Terai there is insufficient fodder to raise many animals. This becomes Uncle's and Father's main responsibility over on the mountain. When they need extra cash for something they can sell a goat or cow. When they need meat for a ceremony or at festival time it comes from their two goat herds. So at these times, many of those living in the Terai will come up to enjoy a portion of the meat available for the occasion. Some of the meat, however, will be cooked or dried and taken back down to the plains, to ensure that those who have stayed behind to look after the Terai houses will get their share too.

For all of them, home is Arakhala. They prefer to live in Arakhala and come back whenever possible. In the fall of 1978, Daje's youngest brother expressed his feeling of homesickness in an interesting way. The land he looks after is registered in his name, so he sold a corner of this highly valued land to a neighbor. Technically, he had every right to do this. But according to custom, he had no right to do it without the consent of the extended family. Upon hearing of this, Daje and his brother rushed down to Dhara Pani.

That was really what the younger brother wanted—to catch their attention. It was an indirect way of expressing his unhappiness in not getting to go home often enough. The brothers went to the man who had purchased the land and refunded the money, taking back the title to their piece of land. As soon as the rice harvest was in, the younger brother and his family were rotated up to Arakhala for a long stay. His primary assignment remains at the house and land at Dhara Pani, but from now on those up at Arakhala

On our way through the Himalayas we pass 24,184' Churen Himal

With the trail lost under new snow, our Tibetan porters wait under hovering clouds

Men carry loads across Major Thapa's bridge over the Marsyandi River

Even little girls can use a *khurpa* sickle-knife

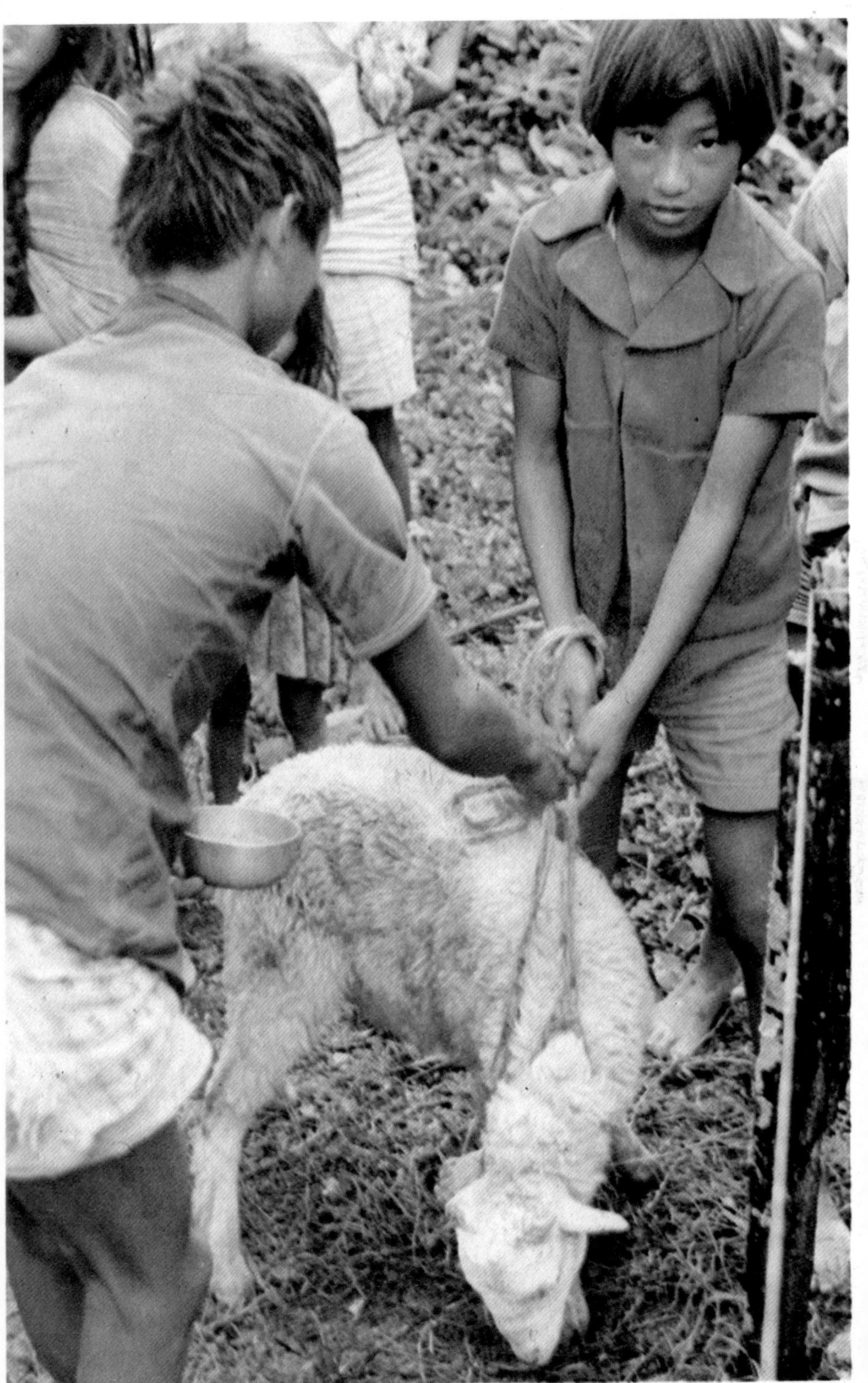

A young ram about to be sacrificed to the Great White Serpent

Adina thrills at a "merry-go-round" ride on the mustard oil press

"Mulberries are my favorite!"

Michael prepares to shoot his pellet-bow

Adina & her friends winnow rice

Michael carries the fish bag as Daje's brother prepares to toss his net

Michael's shirt "LITTLE THINGS MEAN ALOT!" tells a fisherman's story

will be careful to see that the ones working in the Terai get back home more often.

Home has been defined as "where your heart is." There is some inexpressible quality about these mountain villages that continues to draw its people back again and again. An example of this is General Baral, who himself had grown up in India. I heard him one day talking about home. Chuli Bojha was home for him, and he was saying that his grown sons should make a visit there. One son replied, saying something about "going to see YOUR home." General Baral retorted immediately, "It's YOUR home too!" That expressed his feeling on the matter. Chuli Bojha was his father's home, his home and his sons' home as well. Whether they had ever been there or not made no difference.

While travelling down the west coast of the United States visiting friends and relatives, Michael had plied me incessantly with the same questions: "Daddy, where's OUR house? Where's OUR home?"

No matter what answer I gave him, he wasn't satisfied. He knew Grandpa Ham had his home in San Diego, Grandpa Shep in Oak Harbor and others had their homes elsewhere. Only when we rounded the corner of the trail in the evening dusk some months later was his lingering question answered. "Daddy, there's our home! There's Nepal!"

It expressed very vividly not only his feelings and ours as well, but also those of countless others now working and living elsewhere. For them, the mountains of Nepal are, forever and always, home.

[illegible] seemed to [illegible] of the [illegible] in the Terai get [illegible] the major [illegible]

[illegible] been [illegible] [illegible] [illegible] some [illegible] about the [illegible] that [illegible] to [illegible] back [illegible] and [illegible]. An example of this is General Bahadur, who himself [illegible] up in India. I heard him [illegible] his [illegible] home [illegible] for him that he was [illegible] that his [illegible] sons should make [illegible] that [illegible] [illegible] to see OUR home. General [illegible] [illegible] home [illegible] [illegible] YOUR home [illegible]. This [illegible] on the matter. [illegible] his father's [illegible], his [illegible] sons [illegible] whether they had ever been there or not [illegible].

While traveling down the west coast of the United [illegible] visiting friends and relatives, my [illegible] and [illegible] me [illegible] the same questions: "Daddy, where is OUR home? Where's OUR home?"

No matter what answer I gave them, he wasn't satisfied [illegible] Grandpa [illegible] had his home in San Diego, [illegible] in Oak [illegible] and others had their homes elsewhere. Only when we rounded the corner of the trail in the [illegible] some months [illegible] his [illegible] [illegible] answered: "Daddy, there's our home! There's [illegible]!"

[illegible] only his feelings and [illegible] [illegible] those [illegible] others now working and [illegible] elsewhere. For them, the mountains of Nepal are [illegible] and [illegible] home.

CHAPTER 11:

HAZARDS

When school let out for summer vacation in the third week of June we were ready to return for another stay in Arakhala. The summer monsoon in Central Nepal is not nearly as heavy as it is in the east towards Darjeeling. There are a lot of clouds, but the rains usually come only at night or for a while during the day. In our house, the rain pattering softly on our grass roof made for a peaceful and snug feeling that summer.

Monsoon time, however, is also snake time. In Yangchok they would see a king cobra practically every year and two or three had been killed, but none while we were actually there. One snake I remember had made itself particularly unwelcome, as it had a habit of scaring the girls when they came to get water. After a few days of this a neighbor friend, who was back home on leave from the army, went looking for it. Sure enough, when he got to the spring, it raised up out of the brush in front of him and flared out its hood. He shot it through the neck, and after a great deal of thrashing about it died.

The snake, which measured nine cubits (about twelve feet), was so heavy, they said it took two people to tow it to the Marsyandi River to dump it. It is best, they say, to throw a snake into the river, because the poison stays in the snake's bones even after it has rotted away. Even months or years later, if a person steps on one of the bones with bare feet, they claim that the foot will get badly infected from the poison.

In Arakhala, as in Yangchok, someone gets bitten by a snake practically every year. Although it is greatly dreaded, I know of no one in recent times who has been bitten by a cobra, probably because its presence is comparatively rare in the area.

The worst of the snakes is a little green viper which doesn't grow much longer than two feet. Unlike most snakes, it does not flee when people approach. Being well-camouflaged in the heavy monsoon vegetation, it is easily stepped upon or touched when the villagers are weeding fields or cutting vegetation for their animals. Fortunately, the poison it injects is usually not sufficient to kill a healthy adult villager. What actually happens is that the victim often suffers for months and frequently is left with a semi-paralyzed limb due to secondary infection. But sometimes people are killed by that snake. One year a twelve-year-old boy and a young woman in Arakhala *panchayat* died from bites.

One day in early July, I chanced to overhear someone say that Daje's relative, Mohan Lal, had been bitten. It was our policy not to interfere with the villagers' ways and customs. So, as much as I wanted to, I did not go to him. Instead, following the village practice, I let it be known to those present that I had snake-bite medicine with me. After dinner that night there was a knock at the door, "Could you come? My father has been bitten!"

I took my only bottle of snake serum and a vial of penicillin. It was eight hours since he was bitten. He had tied a tourniquet above his ankle, and the foot was badly swollen. When I got there I gave him the serum and penicillin shots as well as some aspirin for the fever and pain.

Gwen had told us that she never bothered with serum shots because the fatal cases always died before they could reach her village. The main problem, she said, was the secondary infection aggravated by the tourniquet, which a villager will not take off for weeks. I encouraged the man to

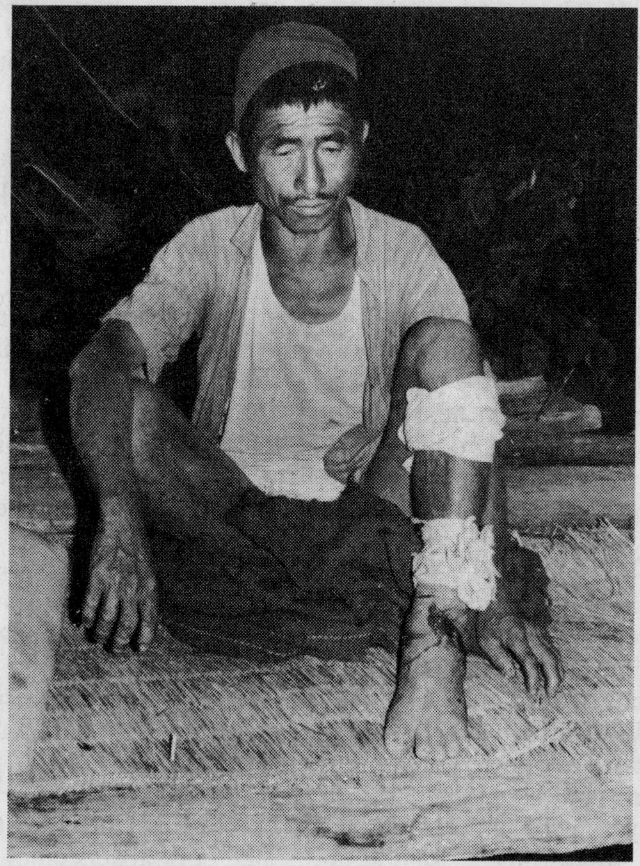

Mohan Lal, suffering from a snake bite.

loosen the tourniquet, so he moved it somewhat up his leg. The next day he was feeling fine except for the swelling and local pain. Nevertheless it was three days before he finally took the tourniquet off. After another week I was glad to see him able to return to work and with no aftereffects.

That was a difficult year, however, for Mohan Lal. That summer he lost sixteen out of his twenty-five goats to an unknown disease. Then in September his prize ox died suddenly. This was a terrific loss, particularly since he had less land than the average villager. Providing nothing else happened, it would take him four years or more to build back up to his previous level. Then, in addition to the livestock losses, he had been disabled by the snake bite at the peak work season. During the growing season, the villagers figure that for every workday lost there is a corresponding loss in yield equal to what one would eat in two weeks. Under this calculation, if Mr. Lungeli lost ten days of work, then he would also lose the grain that would feed him for twenty weeks. So the snake had cost him no small amount.

One of the strangest snake bite cases I heard of occurred in the village of Lower Arakhala. It was at night, so no one saw the snake bite the man in his bed. Just before he died the next morning, the villagers fed him some medicine of local concoction. Thinking that the medicine might still counteract the poison, the villagers delayed burying the corpse for three days. Apparently they believed that a person's spirit doesn't go far from the body until after three days have elapsed, so they waited to see if the spirit might reenter the victim's body and bring him back to life.

Pegleg, too, had many experiences to tell about snakes. One time while hunting, he and his friends killed a nine-foot king cobra. Another time he surprised a king cobra while climbing through the terraces. It came up after him, but he hit it with his crutch and it turned away.

In Arakhala, the life of the people is of necessity closely tied to nature and to the creatures of the forest. Of prime importance is the presence or absence of the carnivores. Though there were many jackals and a few wild dogs, I was told that the tiger and wolf were not commonly found in this area. Pegleg could only recall one case of a cow being killed by wolves during his entire lifetime. Every couple of years a tiger will frequent the area for a few months. They call him the *ghunggiya,* the "huge striped leopard." My guess is that nowadays they come up from the nearby sanctuary in Chituwan National Park when they are forced out by overpopulation. Tigers cause great suffering for the villagers because they kill so many buffaloes and cows. Leopards, however, are their main concern since they are more numerous and kill their livestock regularly.

Man-eaters were rare, but they did occur. In 1948, one came to a herding shed a little distance below that of Pegleg's. It was a warm night and a girl was sleeping in the open doorway. The leopard slipped up and, snatching her by the head, bounded off. She and her family screamed and shouted so loud that the leopard was frightened and dropped her not far away. She was tough, and miraculously her wounds were not fatal. If she had been caught by the neck she probably wouldn't have survived.

I was to find through the years that the Magars had developed an extremely high level of endurance to all types of pain. When hunting on the mountains we would often reach the 4,500-foot level after a two-hour hike and begin to hunt about 10 a.m. In the scorching sun, the men would chase the game up and down thousands of feet all day long. Sometimes they would not quit until it was completely dark.

As I was always one of the ambushers, I did not have to exert myself nearly as much as the drivers did. And though I was careful to sip slowly on the canteen of water I carried, on occasion I found that I was desperate for water before I reached home. On the other hand, they would go without a single drop of water all day long, with the result that I often heard them mention that their urine was so concentrated it burned when they relieved themselves. At work or play, they routinely set their wills to reach peaks of endurance that, outside a crisis situation, I never would have thought possible.

Exerting themselves and driving their bodies to the utmost just seems second nature to the Magars. I remember looking out the window of our house one day and seeing Daje's sixty-five-year-old mother coming up the trail with a load of wood that must have weighed at least fifty pounds. It was only two o'clock in the afternoon and I asked her where she had found such nice firewood. She replied that after the morning meal, she had gone over to the opposite mountain and gathered the wood. Then, carrying it a thousand feet down to the stream, she had made the fifteen-hundred-foot climb back to the village in the heat of the day, in order to get a good start at another job before dark. Her wizened face and thin legs would lead one to believe that her working days were over, but obviously that wasn't the case.

Carrying heavy loads is something that everyone does. The record long-distance carries I know of locally were made when five young men each carried a 101-kilogram bag of rice up from the plains. A single man, though, exceeded this with a 113-kilogram (248-pound) effort! The heavy exertion that the villagers regularly make burns up every single calorie of food value that they have eaten. Apparently, this is the reason that they can predict, depending upon what sort of food they have eaten, just how long they can work. They claim that a meal of rice will stick with them until about noon. If they eat corn, however, they can last until 2 p.m. And a meal of the heavy millet gives them energy to keep going until 4 p.m.

Due to this sort of exertion, there is no one in Arakhala that I would consider to be fat. This fact resulted in an event that gave me a chuckle one day.

Sometimes I would wear the Magar-type kilt in the village. One day I was sitting on the edge of a veranda with my kilt on, talking with some teenage boys. Since the kilt is short, part of my leg was uncovered. Seeing my white leg, the boy next to me began inspecting the skin on my thigh. Normally, at 145 pounds, I am considered by others to be skinny. But while living in Arakhala my weight usually drops to 135 pounds or less. Some friends consider me nearly emaciated at that weight, but compared to the villagers, obviously I was not. The boy next to me, having completed a thorough examination of my leg fat, turned to his friend and exclaimed, "Wow! That guy is obese!"

The time came for us to return to Kathmandu, and with it came the most unusual trip we'd ever had. Coming down off the mountain, we were still about an hour from the one and only stream crossing when a tropical storm thundered down upon us. The warm rain drove right through our umbrellas and soon was rushing ankle deep on the trail. No sooner had we forded a small branch of a stream than those behind us beckoned urgently for us to return. The main stream was already too deep to cross, they said, and the side stream could also rise and leave us stranded between

Wearing his kilt, Gary carries Michael on his shoulders.

the two. Showing us an alternate route, they led us to a point above the conjoining of the two streams.

The muddy water before us was white with foam and running chest deep. We knew that the Narayani River could flood and prevent the ferry canoes from crossing, so we had purchased airplane tickets from Bhairahawa for our return. Though it was much farther away, we didn't have to cross any large rivers to reach it. Our tickets were confirmed, so if we didn't get to the airport on the day of the flight we would lose our money. Standing there in the rain, I

Gary helps Moti Lal safely across the foam-covered stream.

wondered how this was going to work out. Then I glanced back up towards Peak of the Gods and saw a blue hole in the dark clouds. I knew then that the rain would soon cease, and about an hour later the flooding stream subsided sufficiently for us to make our way carefully across.

Early next morning, we were waiting down at the main highway when one of the oldest-looking buses I'd ever seen clattered up to the stop. The driver was a young, turbaned Sikh from northern India. Sikhs are noted in Nepal for their mechanical and driving skills. In fact, one time when I was taking the bus from Tansen to Pokhara, I marvelled at the Sikh driver as he guided the bus up the dark, narrow road. Changing gears as if it were a fluid drive, he had made maximum speed through the mountains with perfect safety. As I think back on it, though, the young Sikh driving this day must have been a trainee.

After riding for about an hour we topped a slight rise and the driver let out a shout. Gesturing to his partner who sold the tickets, he chattered on excitedly. Up ahead at the ford was a rushing river fifty yards wide. The churning brown water swirled into waves two feet high as it raced toward the nearby Narayani. Lined up beside the road were the 7 a.m. and 8 a.m. buses, a few jeeps and a road full of people waiting for the flood to subside. On the open roof of the old bus, which served as the luggage compartment, perched my metal trunk full of books, notes and important papers.

As the driver continued to talk with his friend, I assumed that we would stop and wait like the others. But instead of pulling over when we reached the ford, he blasted on the air horn for the people to move aside. Just as we got to the water's edge, he slammed on the brakes as if it had finally occurred to him that this was a foolish thing to do. As I was happily thinking that this was his decision, he suddenly gunned the engine and we plunged into the surging water.

As the water beat against the floorboards of the creaking bus, I was thinking how I would keep my two little kids above the water if we went over. I knew my notes representing years of work would be lost, but that didn't seem so important now. Meanwhile, the old diesel engine kept hammering for all it was worth. I watched the Sikh, his arms flying wildly one way and then the other. Actually, I thought, he wasn't doing too bad a job of keeping the old crate aimed toward the far bank.

Laboring up out of the riverbed, the Sikh stuck his head out the window and with a great shout of glee, waved back to those on the far shore. Now was his big chance. Groups of people who had been waiting all morning would get on HIS bus. As we pulled up to each stop, he shouted for everyone to hurry to get on. Then, to let them know they would be left if they didn't jump fast, he started to move off slowly. It was half an hour before another bus caught up with us. By then, we were packed in like sardines as we lumbered down the road towards Butwal.

At this point the road winds steeply up over a spur of mountains. When we were almost down the other side, an old thing that looked like a 1935 Ford milk wagon passed us when we stopped to pick up more passengers. It was a minibus carrying people on a local route. Up ahead of us, we saw him pick up a few more passengers and hurry on.

Our driver was upset; the other fellow was getting "our" passengers! When we came to a two-mile straight stretch, he gave full power to the engine. He had tried unsuccessfully to pass the minibus once before. This time, though, the road was straight and with our heavy load we had the advantage on the downhill slope. The whole bus creaked and shuddered; the poor engine whined with agony. Reaching at the very most 35 miles per hour, the Sikh was obviously pleased as we inched past the ancient minibus. Without a doubt, it had been a good day for him.

At the little crossroads at Sunaul, he shut off the engine and sat down at the roadside shop to celebrate with a cup of tea. But when he climbed aboard five minutes later, the engine refused to start. We all got out and pushed. Finally, the diesel fired and making an ear-shattering noise, began to run. The Sikh hastily turned the engine off and wondered what to do. To me, it sounded like a valve was stuck. After fiddling unsuccessfully with a number of different things, he decided that he was not going to let this stop him from completing his run. So, ignoring the terrible noise, he nursed the old bus on in to Butwal. It was a trip that we would not forget.

CHAPTER 12:

DEFORESTATION

In 1977, we were looking forward to the twelve-week winter vacation from school. We had planned to go back to Arakhala in early December, but wanted to see Major Thapa once again. It had been over a year since he came to say goodbye to us. We wondered how well he had recovered from the stroke.

We sent him a message that we were coming, so when we arrived with our car he was there waiting at the roadside. A couple of friends who had once visited us in Yangchok said that it was the nicest village they had ever seen anywhere in Nepal. When we climbed the hill, we found his village up on the ridge was as spic and span as ever. The pigs were fenced in and flowers were planted all along the trail. In Yangchok, we had a real problem: so many villagers wanted to have us for a meal that we had to eat until our stomachs nearly burst in order to please everyone.

In August I had been encouraged to submit an article to *Kailash* magazine on the religious customs of the Magars. In doing so, I was referred to Professor Dor Bahadur Bista. He gave me a number of suggestions and told me that I had so much information available that I should write something more than just an article.

With this in mind, when we got back to Arakhala I began probing more deeply into the areas Professor Bista had suggested. A few weeks later the Chairman of the district panchayat, Manohar Shrestha, came to Arakhala. He was making a tour of the mountainous *panchayats* on the northern border of Nawal Parasi. For a man like himself who had lived his life on the plains, it was difficult to climb the steep trails. The villagers snickered as they watched him come, limping along on aching feet. I was impressed, though, with his determination. He could have stayed in the plains and forgotten about the people up here, but he hadn't. He knew it would be hard, but he chose to come anyway.

When he wanted to talk with me I felt somewhat embarrassed; my ability to speak Nepali was limited. Magar was what everyone spoke around here, and it was the language I was fluent in. However, he was kind and patient and full of questions regarding the area. So with Daje often acting as an interpreter for me, we had some good conversations.

He, like General Baral two years before, was very concerned about the obvious deforestation of the area. I knew intuitively that to try to enforce the law against cutting and burning the forest would not work. But if that wouldn't work, what would? What answer could I give him? The reason that enforcement couldn't work was that on the average, the villagers only produced enough from their fields to feed themselves for six months of the year. From their slash-and-burn type of fields, called *khoriya,* they got another three months' supply of corn. For the other three months they got by with selling or trading bananas, oranges, sweet potatoes, ginger and the occasional goat. This still was not sufficient, so to survive they dug large quantities of the bitter-tasting *lakuwa* root.

Deforestation wasn't just a simple matter of cutting down some trees, it was literally "life and death" for the villagers. Without the corn from their slash-and-burn fields they simply could not survive!

This system of slash-and-burn agriculture, common in many parts of the world, is one that has probably been used by the Magars since ancient times. I asked Pegleg how they used to farm when he was younger. He told me that previously they used to get the majority of their crops from these *khoriya* fields. Their major crop used to be the *bhotiya* corn sown on these newly burned fields. Some of that land they reserved to sow their cotton and summer millet. Nowadays there is little or no summer millet grown. Instead, they grow a different variety, which is transplanted among the corn on their terraced fields and it matures in the fall.

In the winter, they used to plant lots of barley and some wheat. In the following spring they would plant a part of the old *khoriya* fields with a very small type of millet they called *samma* and *koni,* as well as with highland rice and the *pinalu* root. After this, these fields would be left to revert to forest growth for three or more years before they would be cut. The more the forest regrew, the greater would be the ash when it was cut and burned again. Consequently, that is where they would also get the richest yields.

Pegleg stated that they were very foolish with their land in the beginning. As the population increased and they needed more permanent fields, they would just take the less-sloping hills, put the manure on and plant their corn. The land had no rocks and a good cover of black topsoil. This gave a good yield for a few years until the monsoon rains washed all the topsoil away. "Only then," he said, "did we make the huge effort required to bank up the land and terrace those fields."

Likewise, with the constant recutting of the forests the trees grew back more and more slowly, and their *khoriya* fields also lost most of their topsoil. As the demand for food increased, they began to run out of suitable land for forest fields. With less topsoil and less forest to burn for ash their yields reduced dramatically. To make up for it they recut ever larger areas of the wasted land. It was a sad, yet classic case of working harder and getting less in return.

By the time Pegleg returned from the army they were already having a yearly food deficit. About 1942, friends and relatives in Rising, who grew large amounts of the winter millet, counselled the villagers to do likewise. Previously, they had been growing great quantities of mustard as their fall and winter crop. Now, in place of it they began to grow millet on their terraced fields. This helped relieve their food shortage for many years.

For as long as he could remember, Pegleg said that they had always supplemented their diet with the bitter-tasting *lakuwa*. This round, hairy-looking root grew right under the surface of the ground and could be found all over the forest. The much tastier *tarul* they seldom ate because it could be obtained only by digging very deeply into the rocky soil. Furthermore, in contrast to the *lakuwa,* it spoiled quickly and could not be stored.

Nowadays the situation has become alarming. There are no more of the mountainsides left that are profitable for terracing. In fact, some fields that were at one time terraced have now been abandoned as unprofitable. Also, some of the *khoriya* fields will no longer reforest. They have been reduced to rock and weeds by overcutting, overgrazing and the accompanying erosion. These areas hardly even produce *lakuwa* roots any more. Yet it is the *lakuwa* and *tarul* that virtually keep the villagers alive in years of poor harvest.

With the deforestation also comes the difficulty in supporting livestock. Because of the constant threat of leopards and jackals the villagers don't want to graze their animals where the forest is thick with foliage; the predators will get them too easily. It is the previous year's nearly bare *khoriya* fields that are the most popular spots for grazing. So, as the mountainside begins to reforest, those types of vegetation that are the best fodder crops are chewed up again and again and eventually destroyed. This ensures a continuously worsening situation for the future.

The prime reason that the villagers keep animals these days is for the manure produced. Of course the people must have the oxen to pull the plow, but since killing cattle is prohibited in Nepal, cows are not kept for meat. The goats are eaten when sacrificed but generally they are kept to sell when a person has a large expense such as a wedding, when building a house or during a famine. I have no information as to whether the total number of goats kept by the village has increased or decreased over the years. But it is a simple fact that stunted, underfed goats will not produce the amount of manure that large, well-fed ones will. The fact is, they are getting less manure from their herds whether the total number has declined or not.

The result is that a vicious cycle has developed from which the villager knows no way out. Their animals are producing less manure, which they desperately need to make their terraced fields yield well. And their forest fields are producing less *khoriya* corn as they are recut more frequently. And perhaps most ominously, the *lakuwa* and *tarul* get harder and harder to find. The only thing that the villager knows to do is to cut an even greater portion of the stunted forest for a *khoriya* field, and to give more sacrifices in the hope that the gods will bring favorable weather for their crops.

It was into this disturbing situation that we had come. The District Chairman was looking for answers. He wanted to know how the villagers in these mountains could be helped NOW! It is an easy thing to say that they need to upgrade their farming techniques with modern methods and leave it at that. But pat answers of that sort don't often get transferred into lasting solutions. I knew from experience that people who are walking on the brink of famine are not going to accept new methods overnight. They are always afraid that the new idea may backfire and put them into an even worse situation.

This means that to introduce any new method requires more than just teaching. It takes a demonstration in a real village situation. The villager cannot be blamed for being unwilling to gamble on something new; he is already living too close to the starvation line. The rich can gamble and if it works for a couple of years, then the others will follow along and eventually do likewise. But in Arakhala there is no one who can be labeled as rich. In 1974, after a much better than average crop, I found that only four families out of the ninety-seven were self-sufficient in grain that year. All the rest had to go down to the plains or elsewhere to buy rice or corn.

While living in Yangchok I had brought in ten white leghorn laying hens. The villagers were all excited about raising them when they saw how the hens laid large eggs almost daily. That was, until I ran out of the supply of commercial chicken feed I had brought along. Though I continued to feed the hens with the best mix of grains and feed available in Yangchok, nevertheless they produced considerably less than the local chickens which scavenged for their food.

Later, the two hybrid pigs I brought for Major Thapa fared even worse. Though he had more feed available than anyone else in the village, still there wasn't enough to satisfy their voracious appetites. We butchered one while it was small, but still there wasn't enough feed to satisfy the second pig. Soon he began to catch and eat the village chickens that came into his pen in search of insects. By the time we butchered the second pig, we owed the villagers so much for the chickens that our new venture was a total loss.

Raising rabbits also seemed like a good prospect. When I found out that the villagers valued rabbit meat above all other animals, I brought two does and a buck to Arakhala. They ate the dried grass and leaves in the hot spring when there was always a severe shortage of fodder, so this was very advantageous. It seemed like an excellent way for each family to improve their diet and perhaps even make a little cash if they liked. Within a year the two females had produced about eighty offspring, but due to the presence of the coccidiosis disease and the absence of the medicine to counteract it all but two of the young died. A great prospect had failed for lack of a simple medicine. Obviously the introduction of new methods and technology was far more difficult than met the eye.

One solution for the people in Arakhala was to move many of the people over the mountain to the land made available in the Terai for new settlers. The district chairman was in charge of this very thing and could help out. In fact, about ten years before, large numbers of people had moved when the land was first made available, and since that time many more had gone and settled alongside them in the prohibited areas. These illegal settlers would have to be taken care of first. To make more than just a momentary lull in the situation thousands of families would have to be shifted out of the surrounding mountains. In the meantime, the mushrooming population was daily making matters worse.

Nevertheless, if at this point the deforestation process could be significantly slowed down, much of the forest land would quickly cover over and erosion and landslides could still be kept to a minimum. Fortunately, the rainfall is sufficient and the weather warm enough that if left alone, the forest will grow back amazingly fast, even in poor, rocky soil. No doubt the best solution is to help them become self-sufficient in grain. This could be done through the use of fertilizers, insecticides and modern farming techniques. But under the present circumstances and with limited resources, I couldn't see how this would happen before a poor harvest of crops had first wrought suffering and tragedy across the mountains.

Another solution, or best of all, a solution that could go hand in hand with the first was that of producing cash crops. The chief cash crop of Arakhala has been ginger, dried over an open fire. When we first arrived, the dried ginger was carried on their backs the five to six days' journey to Tribeni on the Indian border.

The buyers, however, always held the upper hand. After such a strenuous journey, no one was going to refuse to sell his ginger to the rich shopkeeper. The shopkeeper made a huge profit by shipping tons of the ginger to the big markets farther south. But he was not forced to give the poor villager a price that was relative to his profit, for the ginger buyers worked together as a cartel and cooperated in setting the price rather than competing. Thus the price was the same no matter to whom it was sold, and instead of fixing the price according to the demand on the markets, they could even fix it according to the corn crops that year in the mountains.

So in 1972 when the corn crop was very poor, the ginger buyers were able to drive the price of dried ginger down to five rupees per kilo. Thus with the skyrocketing grain prices came plummeting ginger prices for the farmer. Those who had hopes that their ginger crop would help tide them over the crisis were deeply disappointed. Many of the villagers in the area survived the year only by restricting themselves for months to one meal per day.

After this, the villagers greatly cut back on their ginger production; it wasn't worth the trouble. So the ginger buyers began raising the price the next year in order to supply the huge market for it in India. The price rose from five to fifteen rupees per kilo in 1977. They had no opportunity to drive the price down because, on the whole, 1976 and 1977 were very good years for corn in this area. But 1978 was another poor year. So, aided by a glut on the Indian market, when the villagers went to sell in early 1979, the price of nine rupees the previous year had dropped to four.

Ginger is an ideal cash crop in this area because it is usually intercropped with their field corn. Yet the prevailing marketing system is such that it greatly discourages the villager from producing as he could. All over the world, this is the lot of the farmer living in preindustrialized societies. He is very vulnerable and usually at the mercy of the commercial elite.

With the present system the poor farmer is very much in the shopkeeper's power. When the year of very low prices comes, the ginger buyer will generously offer the farmer a loan to tide him over. The loan comes in the form of food and clothing sold at a price that gives the shopkeeper a very good profit. When the farmer comes the next year, he is then obligated to sell to that particular buyer. A good portion of his profit goes to pay back his loan and the high interest payment. The farmer is usually not fortunate enough to have sufficient money to meet all his needs in the following year, so he borrows again and again and again. Thus in some cases the rich ginger buyer is able to maintain great power over the villager.

How can the grip of the commercial elite over the poor be broken? How can a better marketing situation be secured? Such a condition would bring about a huge boost in the production of exportable products by the farmer. The resulting profit would give him freedom to improve his own lot and that of the nation. In 1978, Nepal made some major changes in its export and import regulations which were aimed in this direction. Only the future will tell whether the villagers are capable now of forming a cooperative to market their ginger. Or perhaps someone else, not belonging to the ginger buyers' clique, will enter the business and give the farmers a reasonable price for their product.

Another cash crop that is rapidly gaining ground nowadays is bananas. The bananas grown in the Mahabharat region are of a superior quality, and they have a ready market in the Terai. In the past, bananas and other produce from the mountains have been traded to the plains dwellers for some of their excess grain. But more and more, they are also beginning to sell for cash as well. Around Arakhala, banana production is catching on and in the last few years has increased many times over. One serious drawback, however, has been an insect larva which bores through the trunks of the plants and destroys them. The banana patch that I had was completely destroyed by this grub, as were those of many other villagers.

The cash crop with the greatest potential is probably silkworm-raising. The Korean government has been assisting Nepal to get the silkworm industry established and has sent a number of Nepalis to South Korea for training. I met the Korean expert, Dr. Lee, who was in Kathmandu at the time. He told me that a survey of Nepal showed that its climate was ideal for raising silkworms. Whereas in Korea only two batches may be raised each year, in Nepal three and even up to five batches are possible because of the favorable climate.

The advantages of raising silkworms are multiple, he claimed. First of all, it is a part-time job that each farmer can adjust so that it doesn't interfere with growing his normal crops, because the refrigerated silkworm eggs are hatched in an electric incubator in Kathmandu and distributed to the growers upon demand. Secondly, the life span of the worms is only about twenty-six days. For the first two weeks or so while the silkworms are small, they do not eat very much. So the period during which the farmer must care for them intensely is only ten days or less. This means he could raise a batch any time he knew he had a little slack time in his agricultural cycle. Thirdly, the mulberry leaf which the silkworm eats is from a hardy, fast-growing tree indigenous to Nepal. Already about eighty mulberry trees of a good variety are growing in Arakhala. It does well in poor soil and could be planted on waste land rather than on their productive fields. So this would be a natural plant with which to reforest some of the area around Arakhala.

Additional points that Dr. Lee made were that raw silk has a ready market at a good price in Kathmandu as there is an established silk-weaving factory. Also, raising the silkworm is labor intensive and a relatively simple matter. It requires little more than picking the mulberry leaves, feeding the worms at regular intervals and taking a few precautions to guard against disease.

Furthermore, spinning the silk can be done on a simple hand-powered machine. It is a job that the feeble, the lame, the deaf and dumb, as well as young and old alike can do. Those who are not able to stand the grueling hours on the mountains and in the fields could be profitably employed in the silk industry. Dr. Lee said that in the beginning it is normal for the farmer to produce a large proportion of second-grade silk which naturally gets a lower price. The Magar women, though, continue to practice the ancient art of growing, processing and weaving their local cotton. Dr. Lee felt that if they wove this slightly bumpy, second-grade silk on their handlooms, the product would sell on the foreign market at a higher price than the slick, first-grade silk.

When Manohar Shrestha, the district chairman, left Arakhala, I felt it my duty to provide him with the information he was seeking to improve his district. I took some time to inquire more fully into many areas and to make a survey of forty houses in Arakhala. Getting the proper information in the survey turned out to be much more difficult than I had expected. I knew the villagers, and

Weaving cloth requires the use of the feet as well as the hands.

they knew me from our years of presence in Arakhala. Yet some of them were still suspicious.

Why did I want to know how much corn they grew on the *khoriya* field? Was I going to report this all to the government and have them fined? And for the crops on the terraced fields, would they have to pay a new tax? If I hadn't had Daje and their ward representative along with me, it would have been impossible to get accurate data from some of the people.

Many told me straightforwardly, "I got so much *khoriya* corn, so much field corn, so much millet and I raised so much ginger." Some, however, wouldn't. The ward representative knew each family well and knew approximately how well each one's crops had fared that year. The fearful ones he reassured and helped me obtain a reasonable answer. Still, a few continued resisting. These would report a ridiculously low figure. So I would say,

"Well, I don't believe you. I'm going to write down such-and-such a figure for you," and I'd name a figure well above what I guessed they had produced.

Startled by this tactic, they invariably blurted out in complaint the exact figure, saying something like, "No! Don't write down twenty! I only grew thirteen *muri* of millet."

As I assembled the information and wrote up the background, my ten-to-fifteen-page paper grew to a fifty-three page report. I entitled it *Deforestation in the Mahabharat* and had it reproduced. In doing it, my understanding of the problems and my appreciation of the complexities involved greatly increased. From that time onwards, deforestation was a subject that wouldn't leave me at peace. Agriculture and the improvement of the economy had always been a side interest with me, and literacy had been my main interest. Education would open the doors to a new world, I had thought, but never had I taken seriously the fact that deforestation and the destruction of their environment and economy could make those treasured doors a mockery.

CHAPTER 13:

BLACK PEPPER AND WITCHES

Throughout the years that we lived with the Magars, we tried our best to understand life through their eyes. Although we have sometimes heard some surprising and strange things, we refrained from showing any attitude of disbelief or disapproval. If we did that, they would no longer confide in us. Besides, we felt that only after we first understood their viewpoint could we communicate anything to them in a helpful way. Anyway, strangeness depends upon one's culture, one's upbringing and one's point of reference. Many things that were previously strange to us seem completely logical and normal to us now that we understand their reasoning.

After we arrived in Arakhala, one of the first of many interesting incidents I observed concerned Pegleg and Daje's father. I always enjoyed talking with Daje's father, as he had so many interesting things to tell. The only problem was that he stayed in his herder's shed down at Desot Stream. When he did come up to Arakhala, it was only to stay for a few hours before returning to his goats.

One day I decided to go down and spend the night with him; that way we could have some lengthy talks. After an early dinner, I hurried down the trail to the stream. Darkness fell before I arrived, so I got lost in a maze of trails. After spending the night in an empty herder's shed I crossed the stream at dawn and went to see Daje's father.

When I arrived he was huddling around his smoky fire with two baby goats. We hadn't been talking long before Pegleg dropped in. He had temporarily shifted his cows down to the stream for grazing, so he was staying quite close by.

When someone drops in, the polite thing to do is to offer him something to drink. Until recently, tea was not available to the villagers. In place of it they offered beer, alcohol or hot salty water flavored with peppercorns. This latter custom they adapted to their tea making, so when they make tea now, they add some pepper to give it flavor.

When Pegleg arrived, Daje's father politely asked him if he'd care for some tea to drink. Pegleg answered that he would, so Daje's father set a little pot full of water on the three upright stones and stirred up the fire. Tossing a pinch of ground tea leaves in the pot, he inquired, "Would you like a little pepper too?"

Pegleg replied that he would. Pulling out a little smoke-stained pouch, Daje's father poured out ten or twelve black peppercorns. "Will this be enough?" he asked.

I had found out from experience that boiling the black pepper brings out its maximum strength. So when Pegleg registered his approval, I watched in silence, shocked as Daje's father ground the peppercorns on a flat rock and emptied them into the pot. After it was well boiled, he poured the bubbling brew into a high-lipped metal plate and set it down in front of Pegleg.

Pegleg gave it just thirty seconds to cool. Then, taking off his tattered cloth hat and using it as a holder to keep from burning his hand, he picked up the plate. Blowing the billowing steam away with a couple of puffs, he downed a mouthful with a big slurp!

But that was not all; I was totally unprepared for the next episode. Daje's father then politely queried him, "Second Son, is the tea peppery enough for you?"

After downing a couple more swigs with relish, Pegleg answered, "Just right, Uncle!"

To me, it would have been pure torture to drink that concoction of tea and pepper, but to them it was not strange at all. Doubtless it had the desired effect of warming him up on that chilly morning.

If there was one thing that didn't appear to make sense about the Magars, it was their fear of the witches. They could stand a very high degree of pain carrying monstrous loads up perpendicular mountains and they could chase a deer all day long under the blazing sun without a drop to drink. They had superb courage in facing the enemy in mortal combat; they would hold a position under utterly hopeless conditions just because it was expected of them. Those were the sorts of things they could do in the physical realm.

But the spiritual side was an entirely different matter—witches, ghosts and demons terrified them. These same men would not walk a hundred yards in the dark alone; or they might refuse to sleep in a room at night unless there was someone to keep them company. They might even refuse to do something just because it entailed going near a witch's house.

Many times I was surprised when a villager failed to do something simple which he had promised, such as bringing us a load of firewood. At first I took it to mean that the person was either ornery, stupid or just plain lazy. However, experience taught me to inquire behind the scenes. Almost always the real reason turned out to be that the person was paralyzed with fear; somehow a witch was involved.

Obviously if I was to understand the Magars, I had to understand their witches also. Pegleg was one of very few who would dare to tell me about this hidden side of Magar life.

First of all, a witch did not always have to be a female; men also would take up witchcraft if they had the chance. Male witches, however, were a definite minority. A woman could become a witch only after a demon had appeared to her. At that time the demon would promise to provide the prospective witch with material blessings. In return, the demon would require warm blood sucked from a living person or animal. This could be acquired only when the witch yielded her will and spirit to the demon. Apparently, only while in union with a human being's will and spirit was the demon able to drink the blood it desired from a living being.

When a pact between the demon and witch is made, the demon becomes her *mechhõda,* a familiar spirit. If the witch wants to put a curse on someone or something, she will send her *mechhõda* off to perform the misdeed. If the *mechhõda* is an "eye" type, the witch will stare at the object to be cursed. If it is the "foot" type, then she must touch the object with her foot. Details about witches were very difficult to come by. One fellow I asked replied curtly, "Don't ask me those questions! If I knew those sorts of things, I also would be a witch!" Whether he knew them or not, he was not going to reveal them to me. Who knows, perhaps he was thinking that I wanted to become a witch myself!

When talking about the witch, the villagers do not usually differentiate between the witch, the demon and the *mechhõda.* As I understand it, her *mechhõda* is the mysterious combination of the witch's spirit and the demon. It is as if the spirit of the witch, joining itself to the demon, becomes transformed into a third entity. As long as she stays in this transformed state she combines the best (or worst) of human prerogatives with supernatural spirit power. This combination endows the demon and the witch with abilities and powers greater than either one alone possesses.

In Arakhala I found that there seemed to be a general agreement on who the witches were. What peculiarities did the witches have, I wondered? What did they have in common?

In the village, we had found that there was very much giving of small gifts. But what we didn't realize at first was that the giving was always done on a reciprocal basis. If we gave an empty bottle or small tin to someone, we would commonly be surprised to find that person knocking at our door a half hour later. In their hands would be a handful of vegetable greens, an egg or a cup of flour. In their minds, all was even; now they would not be vulnerable. Socially speaking, we could not ask something from them that was difficult to part with; or if we did subsequently ask for some favor, they would at least have a turn coming to ask us for something valuable.

The rules of giving were such that we did not readily master them. We found that some people would try to take advantage of us and trap us into giving them something we wouldn't otherwise give. They might bring us bananas and when we asked the price, they would say, "Oh no, it's just a gift, it's free." But ten or fifteen minutes later, they would say something like, "I'm in a pinch. Could I have some sugar?" (Sugar was something of which we had only a limited amount, but which the villagers greatly desired.) This was like a game that we didn't know how to play very well, but it did not break their society's rules of giving.

In contrast, the witch would regularly break the rules—she was forever asking and taking things, but seldom giving something equivalent in return. She could do this because of the great fear she evoked.

Another thing that distinguished a witch was that she seldom if ever revealed her inner feelings. She far exceeded the prohibition against showing anger in public, making it a point to converse with a cheerful smile, regardless of how she felt toward others. I was surprised to find how perfectly this description fit Sailha's mother, the witch who had demanded the tin from Barbara.

Another dreaded witch with whom we became familiar in Arakhala was Kali's mother. She was so typical that we got tired of seeing her come, for we knew that she would ask us for something or other without fail.

When our little garden was producing well, we gave all the excess to our friends. One day we gave eight different families vegetables for their meal. But Kali's mother wasn't content with a handful of vegetables every so often, but began to ask for vegetables every day.

The villagers are so fearful of the witch's power that they will seldom refuse her request. If they do have to refuse her, they will find something to give her as a substitute, so that she will not leave empty-handed and angry.

Westerners' ways of doing things are forceful and direct. Magars have their own ways of being forceful, but they are never direct. That would be rude, because it provides the other person no escape. To them, consideration for the feelings of other persons is supremely important.

But we didn't understand the indirect ways of being forceful. As a result, we failed to respond immediately to the witch's ways of applying pressure. The witches, however, never realized that we didn't understand, so they became frustrated when we didn't buckle under to their high-pressure techniques.

In the end these witches would often resort to the crude, direct approach. We, in turn, weren't intimidated by the witch's power. When they asked for something, we didn't always give it. Though we disliked doing it, sometimes we would have to revert to our direct Western ways and just say, "No!"

By Magar standards, the witches were forward and pushy. When it came time to eat, they didn't always leave our house as most of the others did, so we learned to be pushy with them and insist that they leave so that we could eat in peace.

The easiest and surest way that the witch can be successful in placing a curse is to be able to see the food one is eating. When the food goes down into the stomach, so does the familiar spirit and the curse. As a result, some of the villagers are nearly paranoid when it comes to protecting their food from the witch. When the food is served up, it is covered with a leaf for protection. If they are out on the veranda while eating, they will usually face the wall of the house so that no one can see their faces or their food.

In any event, eating seems to be a race against time. A plate piled high will be gulped down in two to three minutes, and a second helping even more rapidly. This is imperative, because the witch is able to turn herself into a bird or animal and enter the place where they are eating. In this form she is able to put the curse on them without their even knowing it. So the faster they eat, the less vulnerable they are.

I had found out something about witches and the way they acted, but I wondered, too, if there was anything unusual about their background. When I asked about these two witches with whom we had continual contact, I was taken aback by what I heard. Sailha's mother had been known to be a thief from the time of her youth. On a feast day, she had stolen all the meat her grandmother had been saving to serve to friends and relatives. Grandmother wept bitterly over this, and it was three months before the granddaughter showed her face at that house again.

Later she married a young man in a village east of Arakhala. There she stole whenever she had a chance and when she was finally caught, her husband was brought to trial before the village elders. Even after that disgrace he was unable to control her, so eventually he beat her and sent her home. Next she married a fellow in a village west of Arakhala. She was there only a year before the same thing happened and she was sent home again. Finally she married a man in Arakhala and moved into his herder's shed right below Pegleg's. This man was poor and didn't seem to mind her antisocial activities, so she lives with him till this day.

Kali's mother had no better history. As is the custom, when she married she moved into the family home with her husband's mother and father. After she had a number of children, her husband and mother-in-law died. However, her father-in-law, a veteran soldier who had lost an eye in the First World War, was still living, and she did not get along with him. Even though he remained the leader of the extended family, perhaps she resented having to look after the old man.

One day after finishing half the plate of food that his daughter-in-law had served him, the old man's taste buds picked up a strange taste. Slowly it occurred to him: it was poison! The white sap of the *sajiwan* plant had been mixed in with the food.

Out the door he tottered to tell the villagers that his daughter-in-law had poisoned him. He soon found an antidote, goat's milk, and so the poison didn't kill him immediately. The sap, however, had burned holes in his stomach and within a month he died anyway.

Kali's mother was never brought to trial. Who could ever prove whether she had tried to poison him or not? Anyway, who would dare to bring a witch to trial?

One of the peculiarities about a witch is that she is reported to keep as her pets the little *ledhen*. The *ledhen* are elves that can fly and make themselves disappear at will. The witch keeps her elf in the attic and makes a little swing for him to play on. Whenever there is a shortage in the house of rice, corn, water, firewood or the like, the magical elf will steal it from a neighbor and bring it home.

As I pursued this elf of the Magars, I found myself led astray. I was trapped by the natural presumption that a Nepali word used by the Magars would have the corresponding Nepali meaning, but often this was not so. We had learned, for instance, that *mama* in Nepali is a male relative, but in Magar *mama* is a female relative.

This time, however, it was harder to catch on. Sometimes the villagers would talk about the *ledhen,* and in the next breath they spoke of the *jhãkari*. In Nepali, *jhãkari* is the word for a shaman, but in Magar a shaman was called a *lama*. The way that the Magars talked, the *jhãkari* couldn't be a shaman.

When I inquired about the difference between the *jhãkari* and *ledhen,* I came up with conflicting answers. Some said that they were the same being and that the only difference was that the *jhãkari* was the male and the *ledhen* the female. Others said that they were different types of elves, but couldn't tell me what the differences were. Still others said that *jhãkari* was the Nepali term and *ledhen* was simply the Magar term for the same thing. This latter answer didn't seem right, so I concluded that the *jhãkari* was a male elf.

We came to learn that these supernatural elves were much feared by the villagers. These elves were the owners of the forest and the herdsmen of the wild animals. If you met an elf in the forest, he was quite likely to put a curse on you, thus making you sick or even killing you. If a shaman met an elf, a terrible battle ensued as each used his magical powers to overwhelm and kill the other.

It was said that there are five brother-elves in the forest, keen hunters, called *pãcha bhaya*. These tiny hunters are particularly feared. If in the night one should perchance hear the tinkling of their hunting dogs' bells, one must be sure to wake up everyone in the house. Otherwise the elves would drive off someone's spirit while that person is sleeping and death would ensue.

Through the years, I heard some things from the villagers that I would readily classify as tall tales. At first it was difficult to refrain from displaying a look of incredibility, but I did my best to keep from smiling or in any way giving the impression that I in any way doubted what they were telling me, knowing that any hint of unbelief on my part could undermine their confidence in me. It could finish forever my friends as sources for understanding Magar thoughts and ways.

In the beginning, one problem was to determine who was telling stories for entertainment and who was reporting a real experience. In any event, I knew that what they said had its basis somewhere in reality. I always kept this in mind, and as a result it was quite by accident that I stumbled upon part of the reality behind the *ledhen*.

In addition to being a witch's servant-pet, the *ledhen* was blamed for a number of the villagers' troubles, including skimpy milk production by the cows and buffaloes. "The elf has come and milked my cow last night. See his tracks here on the trail," and the person would point out miniature footprints that resembled those of a human.

One day, the postman from Buling said that he had a skin of an otter that I could have if I liked. Being a Kumal from the valley floor and not a Magar, this man was apparently not familiar with the *ledhen*. When I saw the skin, I recognized it as that of the giant flying squirrel. Including the tail, it was slightly less than four feet long. He had killed it while it was crossing the stream and thus presumed it to be an otter. A few days later it occurred to me that this flying squirrel might be the source of some of their *ledhen* stories.

I showed the skin to Pegleg and asked him what it was. He confirmed my suspicions. Though he had only seen two or three in his entire lifetime, it certainly was a *ledhen.* He described for me how these animals ate their food with their hands like a person. And when they flew, they resembled a flying carpet.

When I was back in Kathmandu, I looked in *The Indian Book of Animals,* by Prater, and learned a couple of interesting things about giant flying squirrels. First of all, they are nocturnal and retire to their nests before dawn. This accounted for their tracks being common, while they themselves were seldom seen. Secondly, the book (p. 196) mentions that the squirrels are ventriloquial and difficult to locate. Presumably this is why the magical *ledhen* are said to be able to disappear. Their voice is heard in one place, then another, and finally the animal is spotted yet somewhere else. This gives substance to their stories and gives the reason why a witch could make use of such a creature.

Witches, elves and demons are things one might expect to have trouble with. But counting? That shouldn't cause much trouble, but it certainly did.

When it came to counting days, weeks or months, Magars count any fraction as one and begin with that. This means that women always have a ten-month pregnancy. If a woman gets pregnant on January 15th, for instance, she is expected to have the child about October 15th. Thus, beginning the count with January and including October, the total number of months counted is ten! For one's age, it is the same: the day he is born is his first birthday. As each year is completed, he becomes two, three, four, etc. So a person whom we would count as twenty years old would tell you he is twenty-one. If you press him to be exact, he might say, "Well, I have completed twenty years and now I have a hold on the twenty-first year."

Not having understood this inclusive method of counting, I told my porters one day, "Please be at the airstrip to carry up the supplies in ten days." But when we returned ten days later, there was no one in sight. Because of that, I had to carry both children up the mountain myself while Barbara carried the hand luggage. It was hot and we couldn't go very fast, so we had to spend the night along the way. When we reached Arakhala the next morning I was a bit perturbed, and asked why they hadn't come to carry for us. They replied, "We went to the airstrip when you told us to, but you are the one who didn't come!"

I had left on Wednesday, saying I'd be back in ten days. Wednesday, counting around to and including the next Wednesday, makes eight days. Thursday makes the ninth and Friday the tenth day. But I hadn't come until Saturday. That is eleven days!

Another thing that caused me much confusion was their reference to "tonight." It certainly gave me plenty of trouble when I was trying to unravel the present and past tense in the Magar verb system. I finally got a clue to the problem when someone told me about the dream he had "tonight." After endless questioning, it became clear that their "day" must begin at nightfall, not at midnight or daybreak. Thus, **last night** was literally "today's night," meaning the night that began today. **Tonight**, however, was literally "this evening" while **tomorrow night** was just that—"tomorrow night."

All in all, through the years there was probably nothing that took us longer to figure out than the Magars' conception of disease and its relation to diet. For years, we were constantly confronted with talk about "hot" and "cold" or "sweet" and "sour" foods. There were so many prohibitions against eating various foods that I sometimes wondered if some people ate at all. Finally I decided that I was going to have to make an all-out effort to solve this mystery if we were going to be able to come to a meeting of minds regarding the subjects of diet, health and disease.

First of all, I discovered that the terms themselves were a major source of confusion. The terms "hot" and "cold" for their foods were misleading, because that was only of secondary importance. We always heard people saying that they couldn't eat something or other because it would make them "cold." But what they were primarily concerned about was nature's balance of body fluids.

This balance was called *dihi*. If one had too much *di* (water) in the system, then his *dihi* (balance) was out of adjustment and he was considered to have a "cold" situation. A shortage of fluid created a "hot" situation. Hot conditions were generally cured by eating "cold" foods and vice versa.

We realized that their system had its roots in the ancient ayurvedic system of medicine, but it was nonetheless greatly altered by their own notions. I had thought that to solve the mystery I would simply make up a list of "hot" and "cold" foods. From that I would be able to draw some conclusions. But it turned out to be far more complicated than that.

My first list proved to have some glaring faults when I checked it with more people. I just couldn't get people to agree. In the end, I found that though there is some agreement on what is "hot" and what is "cold," for the most part each person has his own list. No wonder we couldn't make heads or tails out of it before—each individual had his own system! Some strong, robust people were able to eat almost anything and keep a balanced *dihi*. Their system would differ considerably from others who were affected one way or the other by almost anything they ate.

Why one food was considered hot and another cold was a mystery to me. One person assured me that oranges are cold, but a second person told me that they are definitely hot, and a third person said that they are supposedly neutral. Finally, another person explained that unripe oranges, being sour, are hot, while ripe ones are sweet, making them cold.

Basically, it appeared as though sweet, boiled and bland things were considered cold, while sour, roasted and spicy things were hot. However, there are many exceptions to the rule, and obviously each item is considered on its own merits. I found, for instance, that cow's milk is hot and buffalo's milk cold; honey is hot and sugar cane cold. (The degree of hotness or coldness depends on each individual.) Likewise, *malbok* bananas are hot and *ponggya* bananas cold; tea is hot while liquor is cold; peaches are hot and peach pit seeds cold; garlic is hot, while onions are cold. Likewise, fried chilies are hot and raw chilies cold; and whereas mushrooms that grow on logs are hot and mushrooms that grow on the ground are cold.

The way something is prepared also affects whether it is hot or cold. For instance, boiled corn or *tarul* root is cold, but roasting makes them hot. Boiled millet is cold, millet bread is neutral. Boiled wheat is neutral, but wheat made into bread becomes hot. As for meat, it seems to be important what sort of things the animal eats and what its habits are.

Generally speaking, it doesn't make a lot of difference if one gets on the hot side of the scale, as this can be easily corrected. But if one's body has gotten cold, it may be quite difficult to correct, which would be serious indeed. Therefore, the meats which can most rapidly restore the *dihi* of a cold person are often referred to as "big medicines."

Buffalo, sheep, pork and duck are cold meats, but goat, chicken and pigeon are hot ones. The animals and fowl which eat a variety of forest leaves and herbs have the greatest medicinal value. The meat of the barking deer and goral mountain goat is hot, but wild boar nevertheless is cold. Of the animals, rabbit meat is the hottest and most desired. Of the fowl, pheasant is reported to have seven times the medicinal value of chicken, and partridge meat is still better than pheasant.

Because of this system of "hot" and "cold," we found that although a person was in a serious condition and had come to us as a last hope, he still might reject our medicine. The medicine would be taken home and then tasted to determine whether it was bitter, sweet, sour, or whatever. On this basis, they would decide whether or not the medicine would be appropriate for their hot or cold conditions. Of course, half of the time, according to their taste test, we were giving a cold-tasting medicine for a cold condition and vice versa. Under their system, this medicine would only aggravate their problem.

They say that a person who has diarrhea or vomiting has a cold disease and his bone marrow is too watery. Therefore, contrary to Western thought, it is dangerous under their system to feed water or fluids to a person in such a condition. The disease the villager suffers from may only be minor, but the treatment he receives is all too often fatal. As a result, probably more people die due to simple dehydration than from any other cause.

When inquiring about these things, I sometimes discovered their reasoning for classifying foods as they do. The *lakuwa* root is hot because it is always mixed with ashes when it is cooked. Watercress is hot; it grows in slow-moving, tepid water. Porcupine meat is cold; he lives in a burrow in the damp ground. Goat and chicken meat is hot, as is cow's milk; these animals don't drink much water. The buffalo, however, drinks a lot of water and loves to lie in the stream or pond. The pig also likes to lie in the mud, so these animals are cold types. The potato grows underground and likes the dampness, so it too is cold.

When it comes to classifying drinking water, however, their conceptions are reversed. To the Magars, water from a cold-flowing spring is hot. That is, it is tasty, thick, and satisfying to drink. It tastes good and is considered healthy. In contrast, water from a warm source is cold. It often causes the cold conditions such as diarrhea and stomach ache. Interestingly, in an apparent contradiction to the system, as long as it isn't accompanied by diarrhea or fever, one is sometimes allowed to drink heated water or hot tea, even though one has a cold (watery) condition.

Obviously, their system of classification is very complex, and I am sure there are aspects of it which I still don't understand. Our first reaction after coming into contact with it was that their ideas were completely useless. I had that feeling when Major Thapa told me that he put a clove of garlic in his mouth to prevent cholera. Gradually, however, I came to see that there were certainly some benefits to be gained from adhering to aspects of their system. In 1978 something happened which soundly reinforced that belief.

Early in the year, I had a very bad allergic reaction from eating cape gooseberries. Never in my life had I experienced such a reaction and it took over a month for all the symptoms to disappear. Due to the open, weeping cracks in my skin, my body contracted an infection of boils, something else that I'd never had before. I took a course of streptomycin and the boils went away. But I had barely completed the course of medicine before the boils erupted anew. Next I tried a powerful dose of penicillin. The result was the same: the huge boils returned again soon after the course of medicine was finished. I endured them for a number of months until someone told me of a mutual friend who had gotten relief from boils by eating garlic. By then I was ready for anything.

Immediately I purchased a bottle of ayurvedic garlic pills, and that was the end of my boils! I concluded that if garlic could cure boils which streptomycin and penicillin couldn't, then there was no reason to believe it couldn't prevent cholera for Major Thapa. After that experience I concluded that there surely must be other remedies with their system. Perhaps they are better than the many wonder drugs that we've come to rely on all too heavily.

Another subject that I found of interest was the villagers' conception of the origin of the leopard and tiger. It all begins with the common house cat. They say that sometimes he will go wild and after a few years turn into a jungle cat. Later on the jungle cat will eventually change into a fisher cat (which looks like a half-sized leopard). After some years, the fisher cat will turn into a small variety of leopard. If given the chance, he will eventually become a full-sized leopard. Finally, in the fullness of time, the leopard will change into a tiger.

They are aware that at each separate stage the cat will reproduce young that will grow to the same stage as its parents. How a cat can change his spots and move up the scale to tiger size, they don't pretend to know. He just does.

(For many years I steadfastly refused to accept the evidence that tigers walked these mountains. But just as this book was in its final stage, one of the most experienced leopard hunters of the area happened to see a picture I had of a tiger. Beyond a shadow of a doubt he identified it as their *ghunggya* leopard. As a result, it just didn't seem reasonable for me to deny the tigers' existence any longer. If the Magars' descriptions and terms for the big cats are to be accepted, this area is also the range of a dark subspecies of the common leopard, the rarer clouded leopard and the sandy-colored golden cat.)

In the mountains around Arakhala live perhaps six types of leopard-like cats. They are the leopard cat, fisher cat, golden cat, clouded leopard, common leopard and tiger (striped leopard). We often heard of the livestock they had killed, and sometimes we saw their tracks on the trails, but only once did we actually see one. He appeared in broad daylight and right at our house at that. For a few minutes he really caused a stir. It all happened one quiet Sunday morning in January. Barbara and I were sitting on our upstairs veranda planning to have a peaceful day when down at the buffalo shed about thirty feet from our house there was an explosion.

Suddenly, with a big commotion chickens were flying this way and that and people were running everywhere. In all the ruckus I failed to hear them shouting to me, "Leopard! Leopard! Bring your gun!"

The animal was crouched on the other side of a stake fence beside our house, and peering down from the veranda, I couldn't quite see him. Then I saw the old, half-blind grandfather with his heavy sickle-knife in hand, crouching down and making a lunge towards the fence. Then someone else was yelling, "Here he comes! Head him off!" On the other side of the shed the old grandmother responded with a leap that would have qualified her for anybody's football team.

At this I raced down the stairs. Out in the yard I finally heard someone yelling, "Leopard! Leopard!" A moment later I was back with my shotgun, loaded with buckshot.

But I was too late. Just then I heard the thunk of a sickle-knife smashing the leopard's skull and the neighbor's satisfied response, "I killed him!"

The animal had been trapped in the corner of the fence, and I still couldn't see him, so I ran around to see the cause of all the excitement. They called it a young leopard, but at a glance I recognized it as a leopard cat, a large three-foot male. Our neighbor gave me the animal to skin. In doing so, I noticed that its left front leg was crippled and its right canine tooth was missing. He was also very thin. The leopard commonly hunts during the day, but the leopard cat is nocturnal and rarely seen. Presumably, with his handicaps this one had trouble getting his meals during the night and had resorted to daylight hunting.

A few days after our leopard incident we had a run-in with a thief of a different stripe. Happily for us, Kewal Singh, the policeman whose father had requested General Baral to transfer him to the nearby police station, was home on leave. Dressed in simple village clothing, he was over at our house talking with me when a stranger came to the door. Barbara went to ask what he wanted, but he talked so softly that she wasn't sure what he was saying. Since Kewal Singh was fluent in Nepali, I asked him to go talk with the well-dressed fellow. Kewal came back a moment later saying that the man wanted to sell us an idol.

Stealing ancient idols from temples and elsewhere was not an uncommon crime. There was a big market in the West for such relics, but the government had been trying to stop the smuggling. With a loud voice Barbara yelled in Nepali to the fellow on the porch, "No, we don't want any!"

I was about to do likewise when Kewal began making signs with his hands. "Come upstairs," he signaled. Once upstairs he whispered, "Look, this is a bad sort of guy. He wouldn't be afraid to beat up or kill someone if he had the chance! This is the sort of person we want to have locked up in prison." We went downstairs. Kewal did most of the talking, and I was surprised at how nicely he baited the thief. Talking in a low voice, he went on about how buying idols was a crime and so we must be very careful not to tell others about this. "Be careful so the white man doesn't get caught in this," he cautioned.

He then arranged for the thief to come back some days later. From the conversation, we understood that there were other men involved with him and that it would take some days before he could arrange to bring an idol. We were returning to Kathmandu soon and the thief said he would bring it to me before we left, but he never did. Perhaps he smelled a trap. I wonder, though, if some day I might find him standing on my doorstep with an idol in his bag. If it happens, I hope that it is when Kewal is home on holiday again!

CHAPTER 14:

CROW'S BLOOD AND LEOPARD'S MILK

When we first went out to live with the Magars, we had to make a choice as to what our role would be in their society. With our supposedly superior knowledge and training, should we take upon ourselves the role of a teacher? As the products of an industrialized society, there were many things that we could teach the people, but we refused this role. We felt that inevitably we would misunderstand their indigenous social systems, resulting in at least a certain amount of confusion, and potentially, outright failure of whatever program we sought to introduce. They would misapply some, if not most of our teaching; they might even end up worse off than before. We felt that we didn't want to be responsible for "throwing the monkey wrench" into their smooth-running society.

The other possibility was for us to assume the role of a scientific observer, which would reduce our interference in their society to a minimum. But should we hide our medicine and knowledge, while quietly recording all we saw and heard? Should we conceal what we were and pretend that, except for our white skin, we were exactly like them? Ultimately, that role would force us to be selfish and uncompassionate. We would be taking everything we wanted from their society, but giving nothing in return. In fact, this is what they assumed we had come for.

Innumerable times we heard, "What are you here for? You are going to learn our language and then go back and teach it to the people in America. You'll write books about us and make a lot of money, won't you?" We rejected this strictly scientific role. We would share with them what we could; as best we knew how we would give in return.

As I looked at their society, I thought of it in terms of a wheel intricately filled with many spokes. Each spoke represented one of the important systems of their life and thinking. There were the "spokes" of good and evil deities, their beliefs about diet and disease, their concern over forest elves, their method of forest management, their disclipine of kinship relations, their local authority patterns (religious and secular) and many, many more.

Each system consisted of a unique, complex way of thinking and acting. Each system had its multiple pieces which were specially tailored to form the spoke that held up their wheel of life. Just as an overtightened spoke on a bicycle would result in a crooked wheel, in the same way, any changes made in a spoke of their society would have ramifications all across their social system.

We knew when we came to Arakhala that we would produce a change in their society whether we liked it or not. Just the very fact that there were strange white people to stare at changed to a degree their habits of passing the time away. We accepted this role as an agent of change, and as such we realized that any change we introduced could have unexpected repercussions almost anywhere on any of the interlocking spokes in the wheel.

If a change we made resulted in a crack or break in a spoke, then it was our responsibility to somehow repair that crack, a next-to-impossible task in my opinion. They and only they knew their society well enough to adjust successfully the tension on their spokes. For this reason, as much as possible we refused the teacher role.

However, if the changes we introduced were made on the initiative of the villagers themselves, who better understood the spokes of their system of life, then they would at the same time make the other adjustments necessary. Thus changes made solely at the villagers' own initiative would give them the maximum amount of personal satisfaction. The quality of their life would be enhanced with a minimum amount of accompanying friction, trauma or fear.

But how could we leave it all to the villagers and still be of help? How could we share new information without becoming the "Big Teacher," with its accompanying problems? We felt there must be a middle ground between the roles of teacher and scientist. As I think back on it now, the role that we chose might best be termed the role of an "Example."

The founder of SIL, Cameron Townsend, had told us that when he first went to a poor village of central Mexico, he planted cabbages and fruit trees. In 1936, President Cardenas was on a tour of the countryside and chanced upon the village. He was amazed at the changes coming about as the villagers had begun to follow Townsend's pattern. Townsend chuckled as he told us how a few cabbage heads had made him the lifetime friend of a famous President. We had unconsciously decided to take Townsend's advice by trying to be an example.

If the things that we thought to be superior were indeed superior and useful at this point in the evolution of their culture, they should be able to demonstrate their excellence under conditions and restrictions similar to those under which the villagers themselves lived. I had thought that white leghorn chickens, hybrid pigs and rabbits would be useful for them. I took the chance and demonstrated to them that I was wrong, at least under the prevailing circumstances.

Some of the villagers had thought that the new hybrid wheat would do well around Arakhala, so they tried it. The wheat itself did well, but usually the birds came in such numbers that the crop was nearly destroyed. In other fields, though, the birds didn't get much of a chance; instead, the rats beat them to it! So, the villagers too had tried something new and lost out.

Rats were terrible pests, I discovered. They devoured huge quantities of grain both in the fields and in the houses. Poison was the only way I knew to control them, but rat poison wasn't available on the market in Nepal. Finally one summer I found some in Kathmandu. It was zinc phosphide, a very toxic poison for any bird or animal, as well as for human beings. Why, I wondered, did they have to import such a terrible poison for rats when much safer types could be obtained?

Since there was nothing else available I brought it out to Arakhala in the fall. The villagers had used this kind of rat poison before when they had gotten it occasionally from India, so I wasn't too worried. Nevertheless, I warned everyone who bought the poison. Still, the unexpected happened: a neighbor's wife mixed the poison with flour and left it laying on the floor while she went to do something else. Meanwhile, their dog slipped in and ate it up. The dog immediately became sick and vomited around the pig trough. Their breeding sow ate the vomit and died as well as the dog. Who could have ever guessed it? Yet, unpredictable things such as this invariably occur when new items are introduced into a society.

In Arakhala there is low productivity from their fields these days due to insufficient manure. Some fields get manure no more than once every three years. Obviously, commercial or compost fertilizer would be a big help to them. Our neighbor who had killed the leopard cat apparently thought so, too. One year he bought a couple of bags and put it on his corn fields. He said that he experienced an unexpected problem with it, though: he found that the weeds grew so fast that he could not pull them out quickly enough. The weeds ended up consuming much of his fertilizer. He harvested a profitable crop nevertheless, but not like the one he would have if he could have controlled the weeds. He had put the fertilizer on fields which were an hour's walk away from Arakhala. I told him that next time he should put the commercial fertilizer on nearby fields that could be frequently and conveniently weeded.

One day, though, he told me that he had learned that the commercial fertilizer ruins the land. This is true to a degree if no humus or manure is added to the soil. However, his line of thinking was faulty. A friend who had used it one year had gotten virtually no yield from his field on the second year, so he said. I counselled him that his friend had gotten two years' worth of corn with the fertilizer in the first year, and though he had nothing the second year, he wasn't behind. If, on the third year, he put some type of fertilizer on, he would get a crop.

His friend knew that with their natural fertilizer they get a small crop on the second and third year, even when no additional manure is added. He thought that the commercial fertilizer also should have a residual effect and give something on the second and third years. But since it didn't, he concluded the land must have been ruined. I told my neighbor that the land wasn't ruined; he just needed to put fertilizer on it.

But rumors start, and they pass from village to village and become a problem. If they aren't explained or countered, the introduction of helpful inputs and new farming techniques into the economy is greatly hindered.

One year I thought I'd experiment with the commercial fertilizer myself. I brought in a bag and gave a small amount to some of my friends to try on their bananas and orange trees. On any experiment of this sort, I have come to realize that if one in ten tries is successful, it is worthwhile pursuing further. Under village conditions, it is amazing how many things there are that can ruin an experiment.

One fellow's newly planted bananas were all eaten by the cows. I don't know what happened to the rest, apparently nothing of note. But the next year one friend gave me some nice bananas, exclaiming that he had my fertilizer to thank for it. When planting the banana tree, he had put only two cups of fertilizer around the tree. It had fruited wonderfully, and these, he said, were from that tree. In addition, alongside the first one, another tree had sprung up, flowered and was doing just as well.

This was the sort of example I had been hoping for. But in order to get it, I had to be willing to have numerous failures first. I found, however, that my friend would not likely be keen to spread the good news. The witches, ghosts and demons are particularly eager to find someone who is being successful. By making this public he would become vulnerable to the witches and ghosts looking for someone who had escaped incessant trouble and suffering. And since he might be doing well enough to be able to afford to give additional sacrifices, the good deities as well could be expected to come and extract more sacrifices from him.

At this point, I abandoned my role of an example and took up the role of a whisperer. I told some of my friends of his success. Likewise, when I learned that one of the villagers had found success in killing the insect that consumes about one quarter of their annual ginger crop, I told the secret to many of the others. It turned out that the commercial fertilizer they called *potas* kills the offending larvae if put on in sufficient quantity; this was good news.

But the next fall my friend Jõlya told me some bad news. Although he had put the potas on his ginger field, still he had lost everything. I was sad to hear of his total loss, but it occurred to me to question him further. When I did, he told me that he had put the potas on all three of his ginger patches. One field was completely destroyed by the worms and two were fine. This greatly puzzled me, so I went to look at his patch that had been ruined.

At the most, one-quarter of his crop was gone; the rest was doing fine. Some parts of the field were bare, while the rest was untouched by the worms. I recognized then that the exaggeration of his loss was just another means used to mislead the supernatural beings. If they thought he was doing poorly, they would not be so likely to cause him trouble.

I thought back to 1976 when the villagers had reaped the best crops in fifteen or twenty years. The weather was such that all their crops did well. Yet when I questioned them on how their crops had fared, the answers they gave did not reveal it. They would admit that their crops were better than the preceding year. But always they were careful to add a negative note that would lead a person and the supernatural beings to believe that they were suffering real difficulties.

This is the most common means that the villagers use in attempting to outmaneuver or manipulate the supernatural. In fact, exaggeration in the negative is so inbred into their thinking that I don't suppose they always do it primarily to deceive the deities; it is just the customary way to talk.

Village ways were so different from our way of thinking that sometimes I didn't know what to say. Their ideas about medicine were exotic, to say the least. When I trapped a jackal and brought the carcass back to the village, people crowded around asking for pieces of the animal. It was medicine, they said. The blood, large bones and brain are particularly prized as medicine, although the flesh was considered to have healing properties as well. It was reputed to cure arthritis and pain in the joints, and was either rubbed on the affected area like a salve or ground to a powder and eaten.

For sores and lesions of the tongue and lower throat, the leopard produces a wonderful medicine, so they claimed. The leopard does not feed its young as other animals do, for if the babies tried to drink its milk, they would eat the mother's flesh, because their teeth are so sharp. So the mother leopard drinks her own milk, then digs a hole and lines it with leaves or grasses. She regurgitates the milk into this bowl and the kittens come along and drink it.

Pegleg's father once found this yellow substance, and reckoned that he came upon it before the kittens had had a chance to eat it. He was overjoyed at the find and brought the valuable medicine home.

The tongue of the leopard will cure the same diseases as the milk, but it is not as powerful. The eye of the leopard, dried and ground, is also prized as a cure for those persons with certain eye conditions or for those who can't see clearly.

In buffaloes and other animals, there is a white angular thing that moves around under the flesh. This is called the *bit*. It is the thing that causes the skin on animals to twitch, and wherever the skin is twitching, there the *bit* is sure to be. Of all the things in a body, the *bit* is the last to die.

The *bit* in the leopard is what gives him his superior strength. After a leopard is shot, but still twitching and not completely dead, one can acquire its *bit*. The leopard's skin is slit open where it is twitching; there the *bit* may be seen moving. If one will take it out and make an incision in his own skin, the *bit* will enter his body of its own accord. From then on, he will have the strength of a leopard. There is only one drawback to this: anyone acquiring the leopard's *bit* will someday have to fight a leopard. In this fight that he is destined for, he may not be able to defeat the leopard. Thus, one's payment for receiving the leopard's *bit* might be to suffer a violent death.

A person who is always sickly can receive great benefit and healing by eating large quantities of bear flesh. Pegleg's relative was healed in this way. For very bad coughs or asthmalike conditions, the bear's gall bladder is a potent medicine. Mixed in equal parts with the navel of the musk deer, this medicine cannot be surpassed.

Another medicine of great benefit is crow's blood. This is helpful for a person who has great difficulty in controlling his body fluid balance. If he is "hot" today and "cold" tomorrow, he will find relief in eating crow's blood.

When it came to doing something or going somewhere, it always seemed that we picked the wrong day. We learned that the villagers believe that the deities have placed their land under certain restrictions. These restrictions seem to be innumerable and many are astrologically related. If they can just know what they are and follow these restrictions, they will be able to avert disaster and multiply their luck.

For instance, beginning a journey on a certain day will increase the success of the trip. Cutting forest products, with the exception of forage for the livestock, is out of the question on the third, twelfth and twenty-first of every month; that would surely bring bad luck to the offender. Many people have a day of the week on which they refuse to buy and sell, or to give and receive anything. "Today is my bad day. I'll give it to you tomorrow morning," I've often heard them say.

We found that a particular type of perennial bean was fraught with dangers for an uninitiated person like myself. One day the grandfather next door was picking the green beans. I was about to help him when his son stopped me. "Only old men are supposed to pick those beans," he said.

A few years previously I had been growing that type of bean in my garden. After it had been there two years, Pegleg's brother Gopal advised me to chop it down. "Otherwise, lightning will strike your house," he had warned.

When people told us things like this, sometimes we did what they instructed us to do and sometimes we didn't. On the one hand, we didn't want to cause trouble or a big commotion by being different. But on the other hand, we wanted to give them an example of another way of life from which to choose.

We found that just living in the village with our children gave us plenty of opportunities to give them an example to consider. The villagers would often ask, "Here, my child is one or two years older than yours, yet yours is much bigger and stronger. Why is that?" Thus we took the opportunity to tell them about our diet. I'd say, "Look, when you get rice, you eat the rice day after day until it's

Michael and Adina enjoy petting a new-born calf.

all gone. When your lentils are harvested, you quit eating corn or millet. Instead, you eat lentils morning and night until they, too, are gone.

"We, however, hardly ever eat the same thing twice in the same day. We dry our vegetables in Kathmandu and nearly always have two or more vegetables with each meal. Our bread is usually mixed with millet or buckwheat flour if we can get it. We preserve our meat and eat a little every other day. You kill a pig and instead of drying it, you eat until your stomach hurts and you get sick from eating so much fat. Think about how the pheasant eats (which is the very reason that they value its meat so highly). All day long he takes a bite of this and a bite of that. That's why he's so strong and healthy. Of course, you don't have the means to vary your diet to the extent that we do. But the more variety you put into your diet, the stronger you and your children will become." With this they heartily agreed, and I've noticed that some are beginning to mix their grains and make an effort to change their eating habits.

In the area of health and medicine, we knew that there were some things that needed changing in their ideas and habits if they were to have the best of health. However, we did not want to compete with their local healers. When their own ways failed to satisfy, they would seek other solutions.

Gwen had told us that the Nepali staff in Tedhe Bojha was holding maternity and childcare clinics in the surrounding villages. They were teaching at least one person in each village how to administer five simple medicines: gentian violet for cuts and sores, worm medicine, an eye salve, sulfa for diarrhea and an ear medicine. They were cheap and simple to administer. With these medicines ninety percent of their health needs were met, and best of all, they were met before the people became seriously ill. We really wanted to do likewise but we had no source of medicines and were not in the village for a continuous period to do follow-up work. We did notice, however, that occasionally a villager would make the effort to buy gentian violet for cuts and sores and bring it back to the village.

When I went hunting with the men up on the Peak of the Gods, we would traverse ten to twelve thousand feet in the day. Running up and down the thousands of feet in the heat exhausted me. Often my canteen of water would be finished before the day was over. Coming down to the stream in the dark, they would refresh themselves in the water and drink their fill. But I didn't dare drink the water; I'd tried it before with disastrous results!

All I wanted to do was make the climb up to Arakhala, have a drink, and if I wasn't too exhausted, eat something and go to bed. So sometimes I'd leave them and start up the mountain alone. They didn't like this, because of the danger from the ghosts and witches to anyone who is walking alone. Sometimes Daje or someone else would come along with me, but other times they wouldn't.

Through the years, they never ceased to ask me if I wasn't afraid to go it alone in the dark, and when on occasion I had come by myself to Arakhala, they wondered if I wasn't afraid to sleep without someone else in the house with me. They are very much afraid to be alone, so much so that one person will even wake another up if he has to go outside to relieve himself in the middle of the night. My answer to them about being afraid was that I trusted in a greater Power than their witches and ghosts.

Pegleg, my language helper, took this example for his own. On the Peak of the Gods, just a little way down the hill from Pegleg's herding shed, lives one person who is noted as the strongest and worst witch in the whole area. Everyone was afraid of her power, and her family was notorious for stealing things from their neighbors' open sheds. Pegleg had taken in two orphans, a brother and sister, to raise, and they had become teenagers now. The boy's best friend happened to be the son of the witch.

One day the witch's son, whom we will call Sailha, along with five other fellows, spent the night at Pegleg's shed, in order to have an early start the next morning to go cut the *ninggala* bamboo up on the more inaccessible parts of the mountain. Pegleg, whose habit is to sleep only about five hours a night, was lying awake in the crowded room when long before dawn Sailha got up and went out. He was absent long enough to have gone down to his own place and back. When he returned, he lay back down to sleep. A couple of hours later when everybody got up, Pegleg went to put on his new wrap-around kilt. He had hung it up on a peg when he went to bed at night, but now it was missing. When he inquired, none of the boys claimed to know anything about it. After eating, they left his shed and went on up the mountain to cut bamboo.

When they were gone, Pegleg told his wife that he knew that Sailha had taken his kilt. This was the perfect opportunity to accuse the young man. Through the years, they had often returned to their doorless shed only to find their salt bag empty, their oil bottle dry or a tool missing. They had figured out who the culprit was, but like everyone else, they would never dare to accuse the witch or anyone of her family. But now, unknown to me, Pegleg decided that he would no longer cower under the witch's power.

Pegleg's wife was petrified. She tried all day to make him change his mind, but he had decided and could not be moved. Finally, aggravated at her insistent nagging, he vowed, "I'll get a confession from Sailha if I have to beat it out of him. And if you don't shut up, I'll beat you too!" After that remark, she worried on in silence.

That night Pegleg waited until after everyone had eaten dinner. Then he accused Sailha and told him nicely just to bring the kilt back and all would be forgotten. However, Sailha steadfastly denied the theft. Pegleg then ordered one of the other boys to tie up Sailha's hands.

By now, Pegleg's wife must have been nearly sick with fear but she dared not interfere. As the boy continued to deny the theft, Pegleg's anger grew. Finally, Pegleg picked up a stick and struck him. At this, Sailha leaped up and ran for the doorway. But Pegleg was quicker: he caught the boy by the foot and he fell face down in the mud just outside the doorway. Immediately, Pegleg hit the boy again.

That was enough. Sailha's resistance crumbled under the old soldier's determination. Yes, he had stolen the kilt. Yes, he had stolen...and he went on to name a long list of other things as well.

Pegleg's part was over. He turned him loose as another boy came to Sailha's side to comfort and counsel him to bring the kilt back. In such circumstances, no one would

Pegleg's wife puts tea leaves in the pot.

require Sailha to return the kilt immediately. That would force an unnecessary split in their close-knit society by publicly recognizing him as a thief.

The next day, though, while no one was around, he had to return it by hanging it onto the same peg from which he had stolen it. This way there would be no public humiliation. Everyone would pretend that the kilt had been there all along. By all outward appearances the incident would be forgotten. Sailha would be forgiven and all relationships would continue as before, providing of course that he never stole again.

Pegleg waited. From time to time everyone left the shed to give Sailha an opportunity to slip in unnoticed and return the kilt. But a day and a half later, the kilt still had not appeared and Pegleg's spirit stirred again.

With his mind fixed only on the theft of his new kilt, no doubt he had forgotten about the bad omen four nights before: in the middle of the night his big rooster had crowed. Roosters don't crow at midnight except to warn of *dhokan*. An evil fate, bad luck was about to befall him. In an attempt to avert the evil, he had leaped out of bed and wrung the rooster's neck and left him thrashing there in the cage. But he had forgotten this as he thought about Sailha and his kilt. According to custom, Sailha should have returned the kilt within twenty-four hours. Perhaps he never intended to. There was only one way left now, the last resort.

Pegleg picked up his crutches and made for Arakhala. There he reported the matter to his ward representative. It was now a public case; according to custom, the matter would have to be taken care of immediately. A runner was sent off to call Sailha down from the mountain. A few hours later he arrived, his mother accompanying him.

With the return of the runner came word that the kilt had appeared back on the peg, but then it was too late. That evening justice had to be done. The old men all gathered together to voice their opinion and give judgment. In the center sat Sailha with head bowed. The light of an old kerosene lantern flickered just enough to reveal the anxious look on the faces of the men seated around him. The ward representative brought forth the accusation: "Sailha, did you take Pegleg's kilt or not?"

Sailha's mother looked on steadfastly and he made no comment. Obviously, his mother had ordered him to deny it. The question was put to him a second and third time, but still there was no answer. With a stern voice he was asked again. Everyone's eyes were upon him. They all knew. They'd all heard that he had already admitted to the crime. Finally he couldn't hold out any longer. "Yes, I took the kilt."

Immediately, the witch flew into a rage, screaming, "Kill him! Kill the thief!"

Chills raced up and down the spines of everyone present; their faces grew pale, their arms prickled with goose bumps. The old men were in deep trouble. They must punish the witch's son for the theft, and she in turn would bring great evil upon them. When she had burst forth in fury and screeched "Kill him," her words on the surface were directed against her son. But they knew her seething, malignant hate was really for them. Their flesh quivered at the thought; "Kill him" was really meant for them! Surely she would curse them and instruct her devilish familiar spirits to torment them in a dozen different ways. What could they do? Finally someone found the answer.

After fining Sailha twenty-five rupees, they immediately brought up another matter. "It is a grave thing," they said, "to hit someone with a stick without proper authority." It was no small matter that Pegleg had struck Sailha. They had to deal with the issue severely. Now they would humble Pegleg before the community. All the protests he made counted for nothing. Everyone heartily agreed that for this misdeed, he should also be fined twenty-five rupees. No doubt it was with a great feeling of relief that the old men returned home that night. Indeed, a very dangerous situation had been successfully avoided.

Pegleg was humiliated by that experience; his friends had abandoned him. He had challenged the witch alone, yet no one had shown appreciation. At his trial not a single word had been voiced in his favor. At daybreak the next morning he returned to his shed on the mountain, never mentioning to me a word about the trial of the previous night. The *dhokan* had been fulfilled. The affair was the talk of the village and everyone watched closely to see what evil might befall him or his family. When nothing else did, they concluded that the public chastening and fine of twenty-five rupees was the extent of the evil omen signaled by the rooster.

But what about the witch? Surely she would get revenge and disaster would strike. But it never did. Instead, the next year was a bumper year for Pegleg's crops. While others got hardly half as much corn as the previous year, Pegleg's corn wouldn't all fit inside his herding shed; he even had to build a special storage place out front to hold it all. Furthermore, for the first time that he could remember, the bears had not gotten into his corn. The bears came, all right, but not until the very day that he had picked the last of his corn. Instead, they had filled themselves on his neighbor's field.

For the witch, though, it was a different story. The villagers recognize a certain spiritual principle that we might call the "ricochet effect." This principle requires a demon to fulfill by any means necessary the curse he has been ordered to make. If the demon is unable to work the curse on the person he has been sent to, then he will return in anger and bring the curse upon his owner. This seemed to be the case with the witch. While Pegleg's house burst with corn, the witch's had none. In order to get enough to eat, she had to sell her son Sailha for a year's wage. The next year was no better and she had to sell him again for another year's work. In addition, while Pegleg's family continued to enjoy good health, she herself became desperately ill. She was sick for a prolonged period and even to this day it does not appear as though she has fully recovered.

All this must have encouraged Pegleg, because he took another daring step, this time against the *mayu* goddesses: he converted his herding shed into a house by installing a door. Since a tiger had snatched Jabar Singh off his veranda a hundred years or more before, no one had dared to put in a door. No one on the mountain had noticed anything missing since Sailha had been taken to trial, but just in case the witch's family got bold again, the new door would protect Pegleg's goods. Not only that, but it would also help to keep the cold winter winds out.

A change had started to take place in the power structure in Arakhala. Crow's blood and leopard's milk were still coveted medicines, but something more important had happened. The shaman's grandson had challenged the witch and won. At some time others might dare to do likewise and where it might end, who can say?

The spokes of Arakhala's society were tightening and loosening. They were changing and adjusting in ways I could never predict, much less hope to accomplish. It was not happening because of anything anyone had taught Pegleg to believe or ordered him to do; it was simply that he had seen an example he wanted to follow.

CHAPTER 15:

THE KING

While we were living in Arakhala, we watched another type of change taking place: that of the villagers' relationship with government officials. Previously an official held great power and could demand almost anything from them. If he wanted a goat or pig to eat, he took it. The result was that it was not unusual for a policeman of the lowest rank to live luxuriously in the area where he was assigned.

But this is all changing. In regard to the police, the scope of their authority is still being worked out. According to law, the police have authority to apprehend anyone suspected of committing a major crime. But concerning civil and minor offenses, the police are supposed to get permission first from the local *panchayat* leaders. According to Daje, this is one of the greatest blessings of their *panchayat* system.

One day we noticed that two policemen had come to Arakhala, obviously on business. We learned that a close neighbor's son had come home from the army and had gone to bring back his wife. She had been staying with her parents in another village. After two visits to the village, she still refused to return to his home in Arakhala. So one night we heard an old gun fire twice, announcing that a marriage had taken place. Even though it was against the law, the soldier had taken another wife, a girl from the headman's house. Now the police had come to arrest him.

When a marriage has not worked out, this soldier's action has been the usual practice. Pegleg's son had done exactly the same thing a few years before. It works like this: although the man legally has two wives, only the second will live with him. Without any divorce proceedings the first marriage is effectively, although not legally, annulled. Eventually the first wife will meet someone she likes and will run off with him. It is at that point that the divorce legally takes place. Thus in a single day she will marry her new husband and, legally speaking, divorce her estranged husband.

This custom worked satisfactorily because the men thus had only one wife in practice, so the prohibition against multiple wives was kept. However, a problem arose in that it was somewhat difficult for the estranged wife to get a new husband, because the man who courted her knew that he would have to pay the ex-husband a large compensation for wife-stealing. To avoid this, the girl had to get a proper divorce, in order that no such payment be required.

Divorce, however, is uncommon, perhaps because it would bring an unhappy situation to the community's attention. Someone would have to be judged as wrong and payment made. It would involve families and clans in a dispute that would inevitably force hard feelings into a community relationship that had been carefully nurtured for centuries. Nevertheless, in allowing this custom to continue, the villagers could not at the same time effectively prevent a man from taking an attractive second wife.

Jetha, a young, strong, handsome fellow from a very poor home in Arakhala, was just such a case. One day in 1978 when he had gone off to Narayan Ghat to buy some things, he went to watch one of the Indian movies. Fiction became reality to him as he watched the passionate love story and he began to feel he was missing out on an enjoyable life.

His wife had already given him a strong, healthy son and a daughter. That meant a lot in the village society. All the same, Jetha had his eye on a pretty young girl married to a soldier who was away at that time in the army. Just like the movie stars, she and Jetha ran off together. They stayed away for three weeks until Jetha's father had made the full payment to the ex-husband's family. The price was 1,350 rupees, an amount that put them deeply in debt. Of course his first wife was hurt, but she had no intention of leaving. Soon the second wife, too, was unhappy, if for no other reason than because they never had enough food to eat. When a girl runs away from her second husband, there is no charge of wife-stealing, so when she eventually left him for someone else, Jetha was out his money.

In the former case with the soldier on furlough, it was quite different. There were no children involved and the first wife wanted to be able to marry again without the liability of having the wife-stealing compensation hindering her. However, she knew that if she initiated a divorce before the village *panchayat,* she would have no defense for the charge that she had refused to live with her husband. She could get the divorce, but she would be the one judged at fault. The other way out was to avoid the local authorities and make a case against her polygamous husband to the local police, which is what her family had done. The problem arose because the officer in charge had gone down to Buling at the time. In his absence the sergeant in charge unwisely sent two men to bring the Arakhala soldier in for questioning.

By now Daje had become the district representative for five village *panchayats*. When the police came, he was gone to attend important meetings in these other *panchayats*. The accused soldier told the policemen that he would take the case before the village *panchayat* authorities. The police refused, however, replying that they had orders to bring him in. The new Pradhan Pancha and ward representatives came to the soldier's aid and an argument continued until dark.

Finally, the police prevailed and took the soldier and his new wife back to the police station. For three days they stayed up there, apparently waiting for the officer to return.

Late in the afternoon of the third day, the officer stopped by our house on his way back to his station. I chatted with him while our children begged a ride on his horse. Shortly after he left, Daje returned home. Hearing about the confrontation with the police, he ate dinner and left immediately for the police station to straighten things out.

The next morning the soldier and his wife returned to Arakhala. They said that the officer had handled the case, though, no doubt, with Daje's approval. The first wife agreed to a divorce, and so the soldier gave her three hundred rupees compensation. This has set a precedent now, and the old custom regarding divorce and remarriage is about to be superseded. I expect that after this it is unlikely that there will be many men who will dare to take a second wife without properly dissolving the first marriage. And fellows like Jetha, who have no excuse for taking a second wife, are going to be even more hesitant to do so; it could easily mean a stint in jail for them.

As for the relationships between the police, other officials and the local village *panchayat* representing the people, these too are changing. The villagers are careful to give due respect to officials and are eager to keep a friendly relationship. But on the other hand, changes have been set in motion such that the villagers are no longer willing to stand for officials who take advantage of the poor and ignorant.

The villagers feel they have the *panchayat* system to thank for this. This type of government is well adapted to meet the wide range of situations found at the village level in Nepal. In the north are the Tibetan cultures and on the south are those that have their origins in India. The problems of the Nepalis living on the Tibetan plateau in Dolpo District are worlds apart from those living on the hot Indian plains. How can a single set of laws and programs be made to work in such widely divergent situations?

This is where their *panchayat* system really shines. In many respects, the laws passed in the National Parliament often are no more in the beginning than standards and goals to be aimed at. It is up to the local *panchayats* to integrate the national laws into the local customs. In some cases immediate change is effected; in others there is little or no change over many years. This is not to say there will be no change; it is simply that the local leaders realize that their culture is so different from the national standard that to force an issue might bring about an unnecessary shattering of their society. Better to keep the peace and let the changes come slowly and naturally rather than with force and accompanying strife.

Recently a new system of taxation was introduced which gives maximum control to the villagers themselves. The land tax rates are originally set according to the productivity of the land. The tax money is divided up with 35% going to the central government, 10% to the district administration and 55% being allocated to the village *panchayat*. The 55% they receive is the village *panchayat's* own; they can use it for whatever community project they like. For large projects beyond their means, as before, the village still applies for additional financial assistance from the district and central government.

The villagers are very happy over this new way of allocating the taxes. It is a change that provides for a flexibility to meet local conditions in an admirable way. It is a change that exemplifies as well as any other the spirit in which the *panchayat* system was founded.

One may rightly wonder why nothing is mentioned in this section about the problems that can be found in the *panchayat* system. The answer is simple: we observed none worth noting in Arakhala village or *panchayat*. The problems we were aware of just didn't happen in Arakhala. They occurred either at the district level, or else in towns where the population was fractured among different ethnic groups or leaders.

When I first came to Nepal, I had many doubts as to how satisfactory this partyless government was to the villagers. Did it really meet their needs and expectations? That was the crucial point; whether it satisfied the ideas of a foreigner like myself didn't matter. When I asked Daje, I was taken aback at how definite his answer was, because I had expected a rather nebulous reply. But no, for the villagers the *panchayat* system was far better than the previous ones there had been.

Perhaps a major reason was that from time to time their *panchayat* system was adjusted as their needs changed. One important change made was the addition of a lower tier of representatives, making it possible for smaller units in the society to have their own leaders. In 1976 this adjustment went into effect in Nawal Parasi District. We were present in Arakhala that spring when those elections were held. What a difference it was compared to United States elections where there is so much hassle!

In Arakhala *panchayat,* all forty-seven positions were filled by unanimous vote. In fact, there were no ballots cast in Arakhala, a situation I discovered not uncommon across Nepal. When it came time to stand for election, the various candidates came and registered their names: for one position, five men registered; for another, two; and for some positions, none. Then the villagers began talking it over together. If it narrows down to two men who are about equal, they will make the accommodation that one will serve a term in office and then he will step down to let the other have a turn. In this case it took them three days to reach a consensus.

Jetha, my polygamous friend, complained to me that unknowingly he had been registered for a position no one had filed for. Though he didn't like it, he wouldn't refuse; he couldn't. The villagers had decided that they needed him, and so he would do it. In the end, everyone was in agreement with the names registered for the election. When the registration period for candidates was over, there was one name filed for each position, and the election was over! To the people of Arakhala, disrupting the group unity is unthinkable. The idea of a 51% ruling majority seems not merely strange; it is grossly unfair. They would wonder how anyone could successfully lead when 49% of the people were against him.

"Well," I thought, "this system certainly has some advantages, but it is the King who rules in the end. I wonder how they feel about that?" The answer to this

a day; it took years of living with
adequate answer. I learned that
st a leader in Nepal. There is
w people coming from countries
lly appreciate. He is the symbol
rs' ideal man with whom they
individual, it is not going too
e country and the country is
never seen him, he definitely
tector image.

Major Thapa's porch on
d into the evening news.
vith a quake in his voice
ed!"

seen more blood than I
news of the death of a
if the death of his own
uldn't empathize with
President Kennedy's
rowded around the
hile we wondered if
. But I had never

s in

had the sort of emotional attachm
Major Thapa had had to the Ki
were men and women to be elec
when the nation desired a chang

Some years later, friends
mandu and I took them out to
I had visited many times befo
been learning about Nepal,
Ever so slowly, Nepal was
beginning to understand its

As we came to the e
the section showing King
the last part of that secti
late King's fatal heart a
the photos, suddenly
welled up and swept
understand the peopl
Major Thapa's voic
Mahendra's death
comprehended, at
means to the peopl

With King M
plentiful as to hov
the Crown Princ
Durbar, the sea
absent from t
rumored that
known to tour
personally in
very early o
to Tribhuva
came drivin

"Why
the good
Why did
the bac
questio

In
called
was

Joshi, one of the King's secretaries. The secretary had studied in the United States and was now King Birendra's private secretary. We found Mr. Joshi to be a perfect gentleman with an unassuming manner; nevertheless, after we learned of his position, we tended to get nervous when we talked with him. However, our children often played with his and this helped to build a bridge for our conversation. It was through this man that we unexpectedly learned more about King Birendra.

One winter day I was chatting across the fence with Joshi's wife, telling her about some recent experiences we had had in Arakhala. As we talked, she mentioned that before King Mahendra's death, her husband was gone for three months every winter touring the country with the Crown Prince. "Sometimes my husband would not get his things put away from one trip before the call would come from the Palace to be ready to go again the next day!" she exclaimed.

One evening some time later, Mr. Joshi kindly invited us over. As we talked with them in their living room, I took this opportunity to inquire about King Birendra's trekking around the country before his ascent to the throne. Why this part of Birendra's life was not better known, I don't know; it intrigued me. I had heard tales from villagers of a laughable incident in which an illiterate old woman unknowingly ordered the Crown Prince to cut some wood for her. Now I had a chance to hear about it from one who was there himself.

First of all, Joshi expressed how unfortunate it had been that King Mahendra had not lived longer, in order that their plans to tour the whole nation could have been fulfilled. The usual group on trek included the Crown Prince, his two younger brothers, two bodyguards, Joshi and a doctor. Prince Birendra always insisted that a doctor come along to attend to the needs of the isolated villagers they met.

The men dressed themselves in soldiers' clothing to disguise their identity. Carrying their own backpacks, they travelled just like everyone else in Nepal. Reaching a village in the evening, they ate what was locally available and slept wherever they could find room. Up the rugged mountains and through the twisting valleys they went, no one realizing who they were or what they had come for. The Crown Prince saw all, heard all and felt all.

If one is to understand why the villager has a special spot in his heart for his King, he must understand the remoteness of the mountains of Nepal. He must realize the determination it took to endure the hardships found in trekking through the mountains the way the Crown Prince had done. This is a point easily passed over, but to the villager it really counts—their King made the effort and came to them.

In those years before there was scheduled air service to many of the areas, one could easily be two weeks of hard hiking from any road or airstrip. To give some idea of the ruggedness of the hilly region in Nepal (that which is below ten thousand feet), the road from Kathmandu to Hetauda at the edge of the plains is a good example. The paved road winds some seventy-six miles through the mountains just to reach a point only seventeen miles in a straight line from Kathmandu.

Once I made the trip in a light Toyota passenger car. There was little traffic that day and I kept the large engine going hard all the way. Including a short stop for tea, I made the journey in a little less than six hours. I had been able to average only fifteen miles per hour. But never again would I push that hard, for even at that speed, the tortuous curves were too hard on my car. Over terrain such as this, obviously it took a man of determination to endure the difficulties and to go on month after month, year after year, trekking through Nepal. Two instances in my own experience will have to suffice to give a feeling for what the Crown Prince must have endured many a time.

When trekking along some of the main trade routes in Nepal, little "hotels" can be found where the traveler may buy a meal and get shelter for the night. Once he leaves these few routes he is completely at the mercy of the local inhabitants, since there are absolutely no commercial accommodations anywhere. He simply has to move in with a family who will take care of him for the night. If he has food, they will cook it for him; if not, they will cook and give him theirs. Some will ask for money for the meal they provide. Others will refuse to take his money even when he offers it. If there is room in their tiny house, he may sleep around the fire with them. If not, he sleeps out on the veranda in the wind.

In the villages, they have no way to get rid of the vermin, so one never knows what to expect. In one house, I can remember catching and killing twenty-eight fleas before falling off to sleep. How many escaped and how many times I was bitten, I've forgotten. Then there was another time when I spent a sleepless night in a hotel. While I intermittently dozed, the bedbugs attacked relentlessly. In the morning, I counted over a hundred bites on my right arm alone! The rest of my body fared equally as badly. On the trail as well, one has to keep an eye out for leeches. The worst experience I've known is when my friend, Dave Watters, crossed a mountain pass. He later counted 114 leech bites below his knees!

These occasions are the exception, of course, and we always tried to avoid the worst. But the fact of the matter was that one never could completely avoid these unpleasant occurrences. It was in such places and over such trails that King Birendra walked, talked, ate and slept. He could have avoided it; in fact, most people I know would avoid it if they had any choice in the matter. The villagers remember that he refused to avoid hardship and discomfort in order to visit his people, and it meant much to them.

Lal Bahadur is the only fellow from our village who saw the King when he came to Parasi a few years ago. The crowd was so huge he could hardly make out who the King was when the people stepped down from the helicopter. Nevertheless, it was an experience of a lifetime. I've heard him repeat the story time and time again, and the villagers never tire of hearing it.

To the Magars, who must do very heavy work in order to survive, a good strong body is much desired. Even when looking for a wife, it is the girl with heavy shoulders, stout legs and a thick, strong waist who wins the contest. So when Lal Bahadur saw King Birendra, he was not disappointed. "Wow, our King's legs are THIS thick!" he would say. Going on at length, he would describe him as having features that were the envy of everyone present. Though the young man's description was no doubt exaggerated, his point was clear enough: King Birendra had endeared himself to the villagers of Arakhala.

Lal Bahadur is not the only one any longer who has seen King Birendra. Just recently nearly a hundred people from the immediate area made the two-day journey to Butwal to see him. Though the little town was a solid mass of humanity, still the villagers got to see their King. There were so many people there that they went twenty-two hours without a meal, but it was worth it; it was their chance of a lifetime.

Lal Bahadur, who once saw the King, weaves a basket.

Homan Singh & wife cut the forest sprouting among their millet on a slash-and-burn field

Gary weeds his vegetable garden in Arakhala

Waiting for trackers' report on leopard's hiding place, hunter in lower left weaves a fish net

Villager in home-spun clothing finds a leopard track on the hard dry ground

Michael hefts the leopard cat killed by our neighbor

Kali weaves a colorful design into her cloth

Adina helps Mommy with the wash

Adina watches a Nepali nurse administer medicine on our veranda

Adina operates a cotton gin while another lady fluffs cotton with a bow

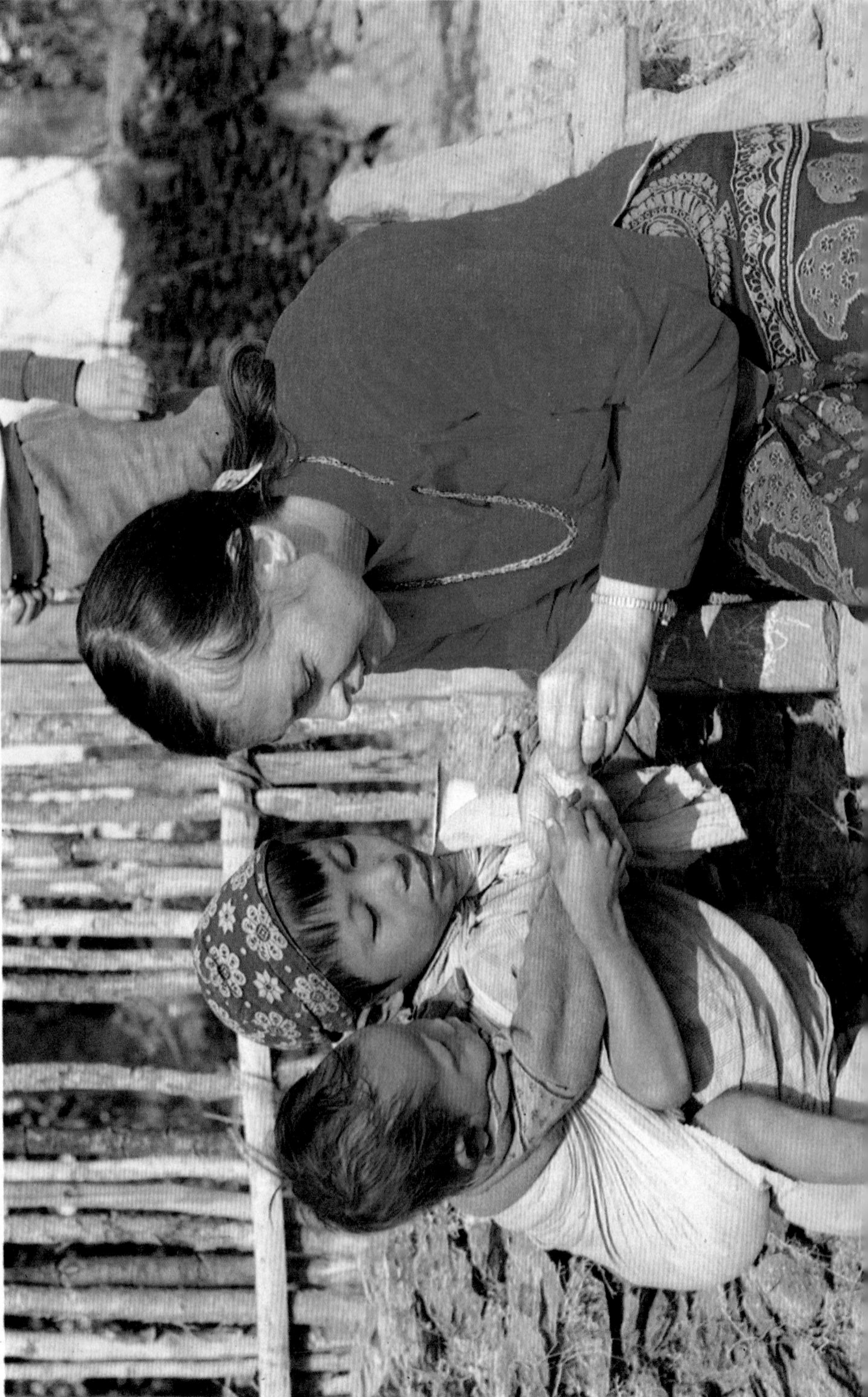

At sunrise fog fills the valleys between Arakhala Village & the Himalayas

Gary chats with Daje, the District Representative

Daje's daughter Sailhi dressed up for a festival

CHAPTER 16:

—

"NO MORE SACRIFICE"

As the years passed, changes of all types were occurring in Arakhala. One change came about when the villagers requested assistance for their defunct water system. Gwen arranged the finances to purchase top-grade HDP polyethylene pipe. Manufactured in Kathmandu from materials made in Germany, it was much cheaper and superior to that which could be purchased in India. The villagers replaced their worthless pipe and once again the water flowed.

Now the water taps were on twenty-four hours a day. On a full-moon night, I would wake up as early as 3 a.m. to the "phyat phyat" of a woman's wooden paddle beating her wash at the nearby water tap. In fact, there was hardly a morning when someone hadn't started out doing the wash before daybreak. Daily the number of children with shiny faces around our house increased, testifying to the fact that the water was being used for more than just washing clothes and cooking. Without a doubt, the general health of the village was going to be greatly improved.

When I studied the problem of deforestation, I came to realize the important part predators played in the villagers' agricultural cycle. I was amazed by what I discovered; there was so much loss caused by wildlife. But of all the numerous animals and birds that attacked their crops,

With plenty of water available, Darsuba washes clothes on a flat rock.

Women fill clay and brass pots at the water tap.

nothing compared to the devastation done by the rhesus monkey. When the corn was planted, troops of up to a hundred monkeys at a time would come along to dig up the kernels in the ground. I once watched a troop moving across a field of sprouting corn. They methodically made their way down the rows, digging up every sprout and eating the kernel at its base. Later on, the monkeys will begin to eat the corn from the time the ear starts to form in the stalk. They will pick even the miniature ears, devouring them one by one as they tramp across the fields.

I knew monkeys had a varied diet, but I was surprised to learn that it included lemons as well. My neighbor complained that the monkeys had gotten into his lemons, picking every last one off the tree. The ripe ones they ate, the green ones they picked and threw away! Earlier, they had done the same thing to his guava and papaya trees as well.

But it is the villagers' corn that takes the worst beating. In order to save their corn, the villagers must continuously guard the fields, losing an incalculable amount of labor in this unproductive way.

I knew monkeys held a place among the deities in Hinduism, Nepal's state religion, but I wondered what place they held in the minds of the Magars. They had accepted an overlay of Hinduism and claimed to be Hindus, but in practice attended much more to their forefathers' animistic form of religion. How did they regard the monkey? Was it a god or a demon, sacred or predator?

I knew that when monkeys came into their corn fields, they were killed if possible. Furthermore, I had heard that some people in nearby Bhartipur had taken to hunting them for meat. This practice had been reported with a note of surprise, but with no comment of disapproval. In fact, I heard it mentioned that if every village took to eating them, they would be wiped out in short order as other wild game had been.

I discussed all this with Daje, who as the leader was responsible for all that went on in his *panchayat*. I suggested that the *panchayat* put a bounty on the monkeys as is done in other countries to control predators. Daje thought this would be successful, but they didn't even have the money to fund their middle school, much less a new project like this. I volunteered to provide the initial money if they wanted to make it a *panchayat* project. They passed it in the *panchayat* meeting and set the bounty at ten rupees each, which would be paid when the tail was presented. When the word went out about the bounty, they also

Daje's father hefts the 40-pound porcupine that he snared. In one month it had destroyed a large part of his corn field.

reported, against my wishes, that I was the one who had funded the project.

Soon the rumors began flying around as to what kind of money-making scheme this must be that I was engaged in. Everybody had a different idea about what use monkey tails must have. Someone said that they were used on bicycles, another fellow thought that they would be used in the manufacture of automobiles. To add to the fun, I suggested the rumor that my friend had invented a method by which gold could be refined from the tail bones!

So the change started. The men began taking their old muzzle-loading guns to the fields with them. With high hopes of earning an easy ten rupees, they went after monkeys whenever a troop came by. I expected that if the hunting pressure became heavy enough, many of the three to four hundred monkeys in the *panchayat* would move out. My hope was that if the population were reduced sufficiently, a great amount of manpower could be reassigned from guarding their corn fields to producing more food. It actually would have a double effect: first, the large amount of grain and fruit destroyed by the monkeys would be saved; secondly, the additional manpower would make their fields more productive. After a few months, the project became so successful in saving their fields that the villagers decided to have the *panchayat* fund it.

I had told them that I would fund their predator project for only a limited time. Then if it was worthwhile, they would have to carry on with it themselves. But just when I was about to quit giving money to the *panchayat* for predators, heavy rains reduced their corn crop drastically. The *panchayat* had money for nothing. Furthermore, men began coming in greater numbers to tell me what a big difference the predator program had made on their crops that year. I decided to continue funding the program for another year. Besides, I was upset with the monkeys. I had planted peanuts on Daje's field for a demonstration of this nutritious crop, but the monkeys had wiped it clean!

At the same time as the predator project started, I began laying plans to start a silkworm-raising industry in Arakhala. Sericulture, as it's called, was worth a try, it seemed. I was able to get a lot of information when the Korean expert, Dr. Lee, took me out to Kopasi on the outskirts of Kathmandu Valley to visit the government silkworm station. The men in charge were eager to help the villagers establish silkworm-raising in Arakhala. They told me that although the profit potential was great, they were having difficulty persuading the farmers to make the necessary effort to get started. The problems were primarily in growing mulberry trees. Among the fodder trees, the mulberry is the first one in the early spring to sprout forth with leaves. Therefore, when other fodder is scarce, the mulberry leaves are in great demand.

When one farmer plants a field of mulberries, his neighbors are likely to steal the branches for their own hungry livestock. Furthermore, the only fencing material available in the villages are the wooden stakes cut from the forest. To fence a large area in this way is very time-consuming, and it will rot out within six months and have to be replaced. So the neighbors' livestock are always getting in to eat up the young mulberry plants that the silkworm farmer has planted.

I told the experts that in Arakhala many of those problems could be circumvented by making it a cooperative village project. Later, back in Arakhala, the people were stunned by the possibility that they could raise silkworms. A nearby large, steep hillside facing the village was selected. Anyone and everyone's animals entering the area would be in open view to all. The land was technically government forest land, but in fact it was owned as a *khoriya* field by some of the local people. I had thought that with the government prohibition against cutting the forest, the *khoriya* owners could simply be told that the village was going to reforest their *khoriya* with mulberry trees. But Daje warned, "No, that will never do. We must reimburse them."

All the terraced fields had been surveyed the previous year and registered by the government. The *khoriya* owners didn't have a legal leg to stand upon. But legal or not, Daje knew that to expropriate this land, which men had inherited from their ancestors, would needlessly force a crack in the structure of their society. Peace, cooperation and fairness must be maintained in Arakhala, no matter what the government regulations allowed or called for. Daje mustered the villagers for a meeting and simply stated that the land would be expropriated for the village silkworm-growing project and the owners reimbursed fairly. No objection was given; peace was preserved.

Now I began to wonder how much money the owners of the *khoriya* fields would want. It was common to rent a field for a season in exchange for a small pig valued at thirty or forty rupees. Daje thought one or two hundred rupees would satisfy the *khoriya* owners, depending upon the amount of land involved. That wasn't so much, but I knew that it would add up to a large amount over the years if reforestation and silkworm-raising projects grew in the proportions that I was hoping for.

Recalling how Major Thapa had appealed to his villagers to "do good for God" in donating their land at Ratna Chowk for Friendship School, I went to see Daje with the idea. I found him at the *panchayat* building along with a couple of ward representatives. Over the years I had learned a little about Magar logic and argument, enough to know that any reasonable appeal made on the basis of *dharma,* "doing good for God," was sure to have a strong effect. From what I had observed of the way that they had changed their custom when I had shot the deer, I surmised that it was important to have a special situation to set a precedent. Obviously, this was the opportunity to set a precedent in regards to their *khoriya* fields.

I presented my ideas to Daje and finished by saying "Look, Older Brother, we know that if the owners sell their *khoriya* to the village, they will just have a big feast and spend the proceeds from their ancestors' land. It will be irretrievably gone. But if they freely give their land to the village project, then in God's eyes that good deed will live forever. Everybody knows that. This is a big opportunity for them. Why should they trade it away for a single meal? Ask the ward representatives to take this approach with the *khoriya* owners."

The next morning when Daje saw me he said, "Your speech yesterday was very effective. One of the ward representatives who was with us yesterday happens to be one of the *khoriya* land owners. This morning he told me that by no means would he accept payment for his *khoriya* field. He would give it freely to the village for our silkworm project."

I was elated! I had guessed right. I thought everyone else would follow suit, and that acquisition of the *khoriya* fields for reforestation and mulberry planting would be easy, but once again I was proven wrong.

Before we could obtain the land we wanted, heavy rains ruined the villagers' corn crop. Following that disaster, the villagers' desires to "do good for God" were dampened. The man who had told Daje that he would donate his land did not go back on his promise, but it was impossible to get anyone else to follow his example. In the end, I donated two hundred rupees to the *panchayat* to purchase the *khoriya* land they wanted. We fenced the area with barbed wire and planted mulberry and other fruit trees. At the same time, the Canadian government gave me a grant of two thousand dollars to help get the sericulture project in Arakhala off the ground. A change that could and might have great effects on their economy had been started.

The villagers' religious system was another area where change was taking place. While we were still in Yangchok I heard a program on Radio Nepal which I asked Major Thapa about. He said the program was depicting the ways in which shamans deceive the people. The purpose of it was to break people away from their ancient religious practices by casting suspicion and doubt upon these religious practitioners who held great power over the villagers.

When we had first arrived in Arakhala I was in Pegleg's house asking for new words from his younger brother's wife. I got the word for the shaman's drum and then wondered where I could see what one looked like. She said, "There are none in Arakhala. We don't allow the shaman to beat his drum here."

"Why?" I inquired. She replied that when a shaman beats his drum, bad things happen. If a shaman did come and beat his drum, they would run him out of the village.

She never expanded on the subject, and I didn't inquire further.

Later, I found out that there were no practicing shamans left in Arakhala, though there were still some in other villages. Two men, one a grandson of Aganda and the other the man who owned the land upon which my house was built, had been shamans in their teenage years. But that had ended when they enlisted in the army. It just wasn't possible to keep the shamans' dietary restrictions in those circumstances, so when they enlisted, they both had to quit.

Now, back home on pension, they could resume their role as the intermediary for the gods if they so desired. But neither one had felt that it was advantageous. They would have to return to eating only one full meal a day and to periods of fasting, as their deities ordered them. In addition, there would be the exhaustion that followed being in a trance. My neighbor told me that if he would just light the incense and call upon the *mayu*s which were his teacher spirits, they would definitely come and possess him. Now it was different from what it had been in the beginning: then he hadn't been able to control them and they had possessed him at will. But now he could control them and make them come or go as he dictated. Nevertheless, he didn't want to call them forth; he didn't want to go back to the shaman's life.

In 1976 a shaman had been called to Arakhala to divine who had stolen the tailor's sewing machine. Rather than invite him to someone's home, they took him out to the school grounds at the edge of the village. While he was in his trance, the god addressed Daje and declared, "Brother-in-law, you've fallen into sin!"

After such an accusation, Daje got into an argument with the shaman and his god. Later he defended himself to the villagers with the retort, "Am I a relative of the gods?" His point was that since this part of the god's statement was obviously false, the other part saying that he had fallen into sin was false too. As one might expect, Daje, since that time the chosen leader of the area, has not been inclined to do the bidding of the shaman's gods.

So shamanism, the underpinning for Arakhala's religious activities, is slowly losing its hold over the village. The official government organ had at one time made fun of their religion. Local people are abandoning their allegiance and no one is replacing the shamans who are dying off.

For years I had been afraid that if fundamental changes were not effected in Arakhala's economy, a calamity would surely befall our friends there. Someday adverse weather was bound to strike and then they would face starvation. To my dismay, it came far quicker than I expected. First, they had a year of too much rain. Their corn didn't receive enough sunshine to mature the ear and so the harvest was about half of normal. This was followed by drought the next year. Thus the stage was set for the most unusual event ever known to occur in Arakhala *panchayat*.

"It's strange, it's wierd," Pegleg thought as he puzzled over the echoing of the drums in the valley far below. "It couldn't be a marriage or a procession for the Five-Blood sacrifice again, could it? What has gone wrong? I heard the drums only a few days ago. In fact, they were beating the drums last week too, and the week before that, and the week before that.... What in the world is happening down there?" he mused from his lonely mountainside home.

The next time Pegleg came down to Arakhala he learned the amazing news: Lower Arakhala was doing Five-Blood sacrifices—every single house! The Five-Blood sacrifice was one that was generally performed once every eight years by the villagers in Lower Arakhala. This they did as a cooperative sacrifice so that the cost was not too heavy for anyone to bear. In that small village two miles down the mountain they did not have the wherewithal to give as many sacrifices as they did up in Arakhala village itself. But why was every household now making a Five-Blood sacrifice? That was unheard-of; they must really be desperate.

The primary reason was that too much rain had spoiled the corn crops in the area the previous year. Now it was spring and everyone was beginning to suffer from lack of food. But there must have been other reasons as well. Perhaps some inauspicious signs had been discerned and they wanted to curry favor with the gods while there was still time.

Tulya, the young ward representative from Lower Arakhala, would tell me all. He was my close friend and for a short time had been my tutor. His sister had married Pegleg's son and his father was the village shaman. No doubt, his father was the primary one responsible for this unusual event. I started to ask Tulya another question, but then I saw the tears cropping up in his eyes; it was no small

From Pegleg's hut on Peak of the Gods, only a part of the massive gorge which separates him from Arakhala Village is visible.

amount of grief he'd been through. "No," I thought. "I know enough already. Why should I tear Tulya's heart out just to get some details?"

The answer their gods gave to the sacrifices and prayers they had offered was incomprehensible. Where had they gone wrong? They had done nothing perceptibly different from what their ancestors had done through past eons. They had been in trouble, out of food, so obviously the gods were not pleased. There was nothing that made the gods happier than a drink of warm blood from a sacrifice, so that's what they had done.

They had gotten together and discussed it, and a Five-Blood sacrifice from every house had been the suggestion. That was the ultimate that could be given and that would surely bring about a generous blessing from the gods. The bottom section of the village declined. How could they afford to do that when they were already on the verge of famine? But nine or so households from the upper section went along with the shaman. They wouldn't starve to death this year, but what about the next? They HAD to have a good crop this coming summer. A desperate situation called for a radical solution. They would pay the price and give the Five-Bloods.

And so that was how Pegleg came to hear the drums in the valley below. It was the Five-Blood sacrifice procession. Every few days, whenever it was auspicious, someone else would lead out the buffalo bull, a male goat, a rooster, a pigeon and a duck for sacrifice on the altar.

How fearful, how desperate they were can be gauged by the cost of these sacrifices. Tulya's bull alone was worth nine hundred rupees. The money they expended for the Five-Blood sacrifice would have fully fed their family for four months. Of course, some already possessed most of the animals they gave for sacrifice, but they were animals that could have been sold and the money used to buy grain. The animals they didn't have had to be purchased with money borrowed at high interest rates. And all this at a time when they didn't know from where their next meal was coming!

At great cost they had given these animals in sacrifice in order to gain a secure future, but it didn't turn out that way. Little did they know that they had just begun to give their sacrifices. The fear that had forced them to come this far was going to propel them even further down the road to debt and ruin in a strange and tragic pattern of events.

No sooner had the drums quit beating on the last Five-Blood sacrifice than a drought set in. The sun glared down unmercifully on their newly sprouted corn. It withered, curled up and died. The villagers went into action. Out came the drums and more sacrificial animals. Off they went to give the rain-calling sacrifices; the gods were still thirsty and had to be appeased. Time after time, the villagers called for rain, but the gods turned a deaf ear. The sun just seemed to burn all the hotter as they suffered through what was said to be the worst drought in a hundred years to hit that part of Nepal and Northern India.

But that was just the beginning. The drought had not passed before measles, that dread of every parent, made its appearance. From child to child it spread. More sacrifices. The worse a child was, the more valuable a sacrifice they gave. If he didn't recover with one sacrifice, then additional sacifices were offered until he either got well or died. Even the shaman's family was not exempted. Tulya's pride and joy, his only son, was among those who succumbed.

But the gods were still thirsty. Like an alcoholic's desire which grows with each drink of whiskey, it seemed that their gods would never be satisfied. Things went from bad to worse.

Before the last child had died of the measles, an epidemic of a pernicious typhoidlike diarrhea swept across the hills. Again more sacrifices, more sacrifices, more sacrifices. But for all the sacrifices they gave, the shaman was not to escape grief again. Tulya's daughter too was numbered among the many who were buried.

Up in Arakhala, twelve or thirteen children had died from measles before we returned to the village, but Barbara was able to save the rest. During the diarrhea plague not one died, but down the mountain in Lower Arakhala it was a different story. The fate that had befallen them was even stranger than the Five-Blood sacrifices a few months before.

It was as if their gods had viciously led them into giving the Five Bloods and then maliciously rewarded them for it by killing their children. In Lower Arakhala, among those houses that had given the Five-Blood sacrifice, ten children died. Among those ten were two of the shaman's three grandchildren. In the rest of the village, which numbered about twice as many houses, the death toll was zero.

Tulya had come up to get medicine for his dying children, but we found out later that he fed it to them only once; presumably his father had tasted it and decided it was the wrong type of medicine. Now, no doubt he regretted bitterly that decision. He knew we would not condemn him for giving the sacrifices, nor would we force our medicine on him. But he had come and gotten medicine, only to reject it before it could be of any help.

He was sorry now that he hadn't believed us; he didn't want us to hold it against him. That was what he probably wanted to say to me as we stood chatting on Daje's open veranda. But he couldn't say that; that was too direct. As the conversation dragged on, another way to express himself came to Tulya. Finally he blurted out, "My father said, 'No more sacrifices'; he's not going to appease the gods any more. I'll never give sacrifices again either!" he vowed with a quavering voice.

CHAPTER 17:

COMMUNITY DEVELOPMENT PROBLEMS

In our years with the Magars, we have attempted to help the villagers develop their community. Because of our understanding of village life, we have found insights which we now present with the hope that they may be useful to others who wish to assist developing communities.

Perhaps one of the greatest problems in community development is to get the facts and to find out what is really going on in the village. The root causes for the villagers' difficulty must first be uncovered. To determine these, surveys are sometimes made at great expense to "get the facts." But the thing that many people do not realize when they read these reports is that the "facts" themselves are often inaccurate. It may be possible to record with a high degree of accuracy the population of a village or how many trucks travel a certain highway, but much of the key data that are essential to ensure the success of a project are often very difficult to establish.

One important fact to secure is the population's attitude toward a proposed project; this is essential if there is to be local cooperation. But how can this be ascertained? The most important thing to a villager is to respond with the answer which will most please the inquirer. This is particularly true if the person is important or an outsider.

To reply with a factual answer may never even enter the villager's mind. Besides, if he is at all suspicious of the person making the survey, and it is highly likely that he will be, his answers will be calculated to lead anywhere but to the actual facts.

I was shocked when I surveyed forty houses in Arakhala to ascertain their agricultural production, and found it was no simple matter to gather that sort of data. I had supposed that because I had known them for years, because I spoke their language fluently and because the Pradhan Pancha and the ward representative accompanied me, I would get accurate figures, but this assumption was naive, to say the least. I don't suppose more than half of the people we interviewed gave us straight answers! For five days I carefully questioned the villagers. In the end I had data with an accuracy of probably no better than plus or minus twenty percent. With this in mind, I sincerely question how others can acquire valid statistics and produce sound recommendations from their surveys. Facts, some of the most important ones anyway, are in my opinion very, very difficult to pin down.

Obtaining information crucial to the success or failure of a project requires that one find out a great deal about the villagers and their way of life. In Buling, the *panchayat* adjoining Arakhala, the villagers petitioned the government many years ago to build a long canal to irrigate a huge, flat section of land above the river. The government sent a foreign firm to do a survey and write up a proposal detailing the feasibility of the project. When no action was taken on the report, the Buling Pradhan Pancha asked me to find out why.

The report was superbly done, full of the results of soil samples, rock samples and a host of other data. The canal layout appeared technically faultless, with detailed recommendations on how to ensure the stability of the canal along each difficult section. The project proposal, however, was given a poor rating because their data showed insufficient water running in the stream.

This took me by surprise because I knew how much water ran there. As I looked further, I found that the whole project rested on the assumption that the canal would be capable of irrigating the land for two crops of rice and one of wheat. This of course would be the maximum possible output of the land. But the surveyors found that during the dry season there was only enough water in the stream to irrigate twenty-five percent of the land for an early rice crop, and concluded that they could not justify the expense for building the canal. After the value of the corn presently being grown on the land was deducted from the value of one-and-one-quarter crops of rice plus one crop of wheat, the increased value in crop production fell slightly below the break-even point.

When I reported to the Buling Pradhan Pancha that his proposal had been rejected on the basis of insufficient water, he was stunned. "That is impossible!" he said. "Why, there is plenty of water for a crop of rice, then wheat and then corn in the spring. Three grain crops instead of one!"

I had expected this sort of reaction from him. As far as I could see, the people who produced the report had never considered this alternative. Apparently they had never asked the people in Buling what crops they would grow once they had water from the canal; or if they had, they discounted the answer. In Buling the villagers had never considered growing two rice crops. It was obvious to them from the beginning that there was insufficient water to grow an early rice crop. But what was too little for rice was more than enough for an early crop of corn. The villagers never considered subtracting the value of their corn crop from the value of the wheat and rice that would be grown; they had no intention of growing any less corn than before. (In fact, a little irrigation would enable them to increase their corn yields considerably.) They simply wanted to add a crop of rice and wheat to their present cycle. But the people who had made the report didn't consider this, and so the project was not taken up. The extra grain that could have been produced from that area in the last few years would have been sufficient to make up much of the deficit in the surrounding *panchayats*. Instead, the villagers have had to cope with constant food shortages and famine.

The case above was one which, in my opinion, resulted in a poor recommendation. The report was obviously the product of hard work and was crammed with technical details that I could not refute. It wasn't because the people who made the report didn't know how to build canals; it was just that somehow in all their efforts to produce a good report they failed to get a simple but crucial piece of information. They had failed to consider the villagers' alternative.

A poor understanding of the total life of the village is a major reason why people involved in development reach wrong conclusions. One case in point is this: I've heard the "fact" stated many times by foreigners that the villagers have plenty of free time. This is true to a point; there have been studies to show that the average villager is engaged in productive labor only thirty, forty or fifty percent of the year.

That fact, however, has been inappropriately applied. I have heard it said, for instance, that it is fine to install a drinking water system to improve the overall health of the village. But, because villagers have so much free time, there is no economic advantage to bringing the water into the village. They will just have even more time to fritter away, it is implied. I've heard this stated as hard, indisputable "fact." This could be true in certain cases, but please don't apply that notion to Arakhala or any of the other villages with which I'm familiar!

A crucial point has been missed that beautiful charts and paper statistics do not reveal. It is true that the villagers have a certain amount of free time in the fall and winter, but the important fact is that there is a period in their agricultural cycle when they are feverishly engaged in their work. In Arakhala, this is the spring planting and weeding time of April through June or July.

Furthermore, as far as drinking water is concerned, these also are the very months when their traditional water holes dry up. If the average time spent throughout the year collecting and carrying water for a home is two hours per day, during the dry spring months it can easily become eight or ten hours! In addition, most of the villagers' sicknesses caused by contaminated water are likely to occur at this season as well. A water system can save thousands of days' worth of labor by putting a stop to sickness and by bringing water right into the village at the very time in the agricultural cycle when there is a critical shortage of labor. Contrary to the statement I've heard, this can result in a significant increase in their agricultural productivity.

If there is a reason that one could pinpoint why invalid conclusions are reached, why deep causal problems are not seen, and why critical points are missed, I would think that "time," as much as anything else, is to blame. Village problems are not understood when the experts don't have time for the villagers. There are reports to make and goals to meet. Tremendous efforts are made to write up economic development proposals which will look good when submitted to the home country for funding. A five-year proposal, which as likely as not should be stretched out to ten years to be effective, is often trimmed to three years by those in the bureaucracy back in the home country. Then, with a flurry of great activity and at huge expense, the project is launched. But three years later, when the project is over and most of the goals remain unattained, the frustrated foreigners bemoan the fact that the villagers have not responded as they should!

The problem is that those of us from industrialized countries have no time to waste. We have no time to listen to a poorly clad peasant, no time to sit and watch what goes on at drawn-out village meetings. Many were the times I didn't want to go hunting with the men or listen to someone gabbing across the fence; it seemed that I had more important, more meaningful work to get done. But it was precisely at times like those that a comment overheard or a minor act observed was just what I needed to open my understanding to a confusing but important point in their way of life.

It's sad, but it would seem we have no compunction against wasting millions of dollars, as long as we don't waste any time. The result is that the local people are not allowed the time necessary to adjust to and assimilate the drastic changes we would force on them. We just don't have the time that is needed to come to a complete understanding of the root problems that villagers face.

In my opinion, the above points are all too neglected by those who would be agents of change in Nepal. Again and again, programs designed to control population, increase agricultural productivity and reforest mountains have had little or no impact. Proponents of such programs have gone back home frustrated, blaming everyone but themselves for the poor results. They assume that if a little teaching is good, then a lot is better. The idea seems to be to give a training course, some medicine, some miracle seeds or a truckload of seedlings and all will be well, but time has proven over and over again that it won't, unless there is a proper integration into the total structure of the village society. That, however, does not happen very often when the project is tied to a Western-style timetable. Such a project tends to become integrated in name only and its potential for success is minimized.

It is good to see that there is much more attention being paid nowadays to integrated approaches, but there is still another pitfall in the path of the development effort: the widespread assumption that knowledge is the panacea for every problem. Basically, it seems that the false assumption is made that true knowledge will be assimilated by a society. But fear can hold tremendous power over the villager. Head knowledge is seldom if ever sufficient to overcome fear, particularly fear of the type that has been experienced by the villagers. An adequate example may induce the courage to overcome fear and bring true change, but in the village, knowledge alone is not likely to produce much more than a superficial change.

We may expect almost any new thing introduced into their society to clash with a local social system. What this clash is with—witches, healers, jungle elves or something else—doesn't matter. If villagers don't have control of the change being brought in, anxiety and fear will result. So, rather than live under such a threat imposed by outsiders, they will generally try to neutralize its effect. Thus many a development project which could bring great benefit to the community comes to practically nothing. This crippling power of fear is, on the whole, a point grossly underestimated by foreign advisors. It's fine to talk about integrated projects, but if they are not truly integrated into the society (and only the villagers themselves will be capable of doing that) integration will remain a sterile theory.

Many years ago I heard the announcement that Nepal would begin initiating cooperative societies to help the villagers. I was quite pleased to hear this and was sure that cooperatives could do much to help village societies like Arakhala. However, the cooperative as it was introduced did not provide the sort of services that I had expected. When it was learned that a cooperative was to be established for Arakhala *panchayat,* there was a great expectancy among the villagers. Soon after the man who was to manage the cooperative arrived, I noticed everyone talking about the money they could get from him. At first I thought that the man was a manager for the Agricultural Development Bank rather than for the cooperative. In a sense, he actually was nothing more than an extension agent for the bank.

Since the villagers were generally short of food, they often were in maximum debt to whatever moneylenders were in the area. But with the new cooperative, they could suddenly increase their debt load many times over. (Fortunately, because the cooperative, which got its money from the bank, charged only 10-15%, the villagers' interest load probably didn't increase that much.) The villagers all grew ginger, and since the cooperative would give loans for that, they simply applied for and got the money. Many of the people had buffaloes and goats, and since they could get loans for that, they did so. The idea of the loans was to help the poor villager take on something new and build up his producing power, but what the villagers did was to get loans for things they already had. One friend got loans for growing ginger, a second for raising buffaloes, a third for raising goats and yet another to build an irrigation canal. The only thing that really changed was that my friend did have a canal built. Other than that, he just increased his debt load by a few thousand rupees.

After a while, it was found that the profit from the loans given by Arakhala Cooperative was not sufficient to cover the manager's salary and expenses, so the cooperatives from three *panchayats* were consolidated and the office was moved to Buling. Years later, the villagers in Arakhala wanted to start a cooperative of their own in order to build an oil and grist mill as well as to have a means to market their ginger, goats and other produce. Instead, the district headquarters for cooperatives instructed them to make use of the cooperative that was already functioning for the three *panchayats*. That was not feasable, though; the cooperative was run by outsiders from the Terai who had no interest in Arakhala except to make loans.

The problem was that cooperatives were formed from the top down. The very name "cooperative" presumes that the people involved are those who are used to working with one another. Three *panchayats* participating in a common cooperative will represent a cross-section of society that is not likely to have common goals and needs. If the main service the cooperative performs is to work as an extention of the bank, this is fine; but if it is meant to provide other services, then the villagers themselves need to have the opportunity to have some say in forming the cooperative. They would surely need assistance in setting up bookkeeping procedures and in other matters, but this should not be an excuse for control from the outside.

Cooperatives could perform a real service if they were allowed to be formed and run by the villagers themselves. Those villagers who already work together and trust one another could then form their own societies. These groups formed into formal cooperatives would be beneficial for their society. They would be able, with some initial help, to market village produce in such a way that the villagers could get a better price. And they could go into such money-producing projects as small water-turbine-powered mills and other cottage industry projects. Under the present situation, I don't think these societies would be allowed to give out loans except from their own savings. To give out loans in the way that is presently done would require someone sent or approved by the bank to manage their cooperative. But his salary would be such a heavy drain on the cooperative in its early years that this alone could cause it to fail.

Integration, it seems to me, really means nothing more than local control over local circumstances and local development. Lack of local control is the basic reason for the distressing change we've observed taking place in Arakhala—namely, that of the relationship between villagers and government officials. When we first came to Arakhala, the villagers eagerly welcomed any official, great or small. He was banqueted by the villagers and entertained by the local teenagers with singing and dancing. He was also provided a comfortable place to sleep. The official might have only been a lowly health worker or agricultural technical assistant, but it didn't matter; one and all were welcome. The villagers knew they needed outside help; they wanted assistance and were ready to make a substantial effort to please those whom their government had sent to

Arakhala leaders Capt. Lal Bahadur, Panchayat Secretary Gopal Singh and Pradhan Pancha Khadak Bahadur prepare to welcome a visiting official.

aid them. That has all changed now. The reasons are no doubt multiple, but none is as obvious as the attitude of the officials themselves. With the sole exception of the Agricultural Development Bank, which has somehow been able to gain a better reputation, all officials sent in from the outside seem to have failed equally.

The officials who have come to Arakhala are, for the most part, a new breed of men. In order to qualify for their job they have had to reach a certain level of schooling. This restricts the field largely to men under thirty, and to those who have grown up in a city, town or prosperous agricultural area where better schooling was available. As likely as not, they have come from a relatively well-to-do family. They have achieved in school, they have learned, they have surpassed their peers, they are the elite. As such, they have qualified for a government job and a steady salary. They are hired and sent out to the mountains to help the backward villagers make progress. Unfortunately, it doesn't happen.

When the young man arrives at his post, he is shocked by the low standard of living he finds there. Good food and water, good homes and friends of a similar background with whom to pass the time away are nowhere to be found. All this is an affront to his person and he is unable to maintain a good attitude toward the people and the place to which he has been assigned. His resultant demanding attitude is quickly felt by the villagers and they soon lose all incentive to cooperate in whichever program he may be involved. To him it doesn't make much difference. The requirements of his job are easily met by correctly filling in an occasional report and by going through the motions of performing his job. Achievement and progress in the village or *panchayat* have no bearing whatsoever on his monthly salary. Besides, if anyone should point out that the progress of his program in the village ranges close to zero, he always has the uncooperative villagers to point to as an excuse.

The change in the villagers' attitude toward officials sent in from the outside is most easily seen in Arakhala's primary and middle school. This, more than anything else, demonstrates their deep dislike for interference from the outside. The situation was entirely different before the big change in the national education system took place. At that time, the children paid their moderate fees, the local school board hired and supervised the teachers and the government paid the school staff salaries.

In those days no one in the *panchayat* really qualified as a teacher, with the possible exception of Daje; he had completed fifth grade, which was more than anyone else. From a village two days' walk away they hired the headmaster, a bright, smiling young Brahman lad who had completed the eighth grade. He would never have come for the meager salary he was given, but the village enticed him with extras. Everyone took a turn, and in and out of season he was provided with vegetables, lentils, rice, firewood and water at no cost. On festival and sacrifice days he was either invited to someone's house or given a portion of the meat. As a result, he had no living expenses, and every bit of his salary could be saved to take back home.

To supply the rest of the staff at the school, Daje and some retired soldiers were hired. This worked well for them because they could earn a small salary and still work their land before and after school as well as on holidays. Though the soldiers had never passed first grade, they did have schooling in the army. They had no problem teaching the lower grades and demanded a high standard from the children. The children came from villages two hours' walk away to attend school in Arakhala. It was hard for the Magar children to conquer the strangeness of the Nepali language, but they came, and those who bridged the gap often went on to complete all five grades.

Then came changes in the education system. They reflected the commendable goal of raising to a common level the teaching standard in schools nationwide, and were expected to be of particular help to schools in remote areas like Arakhala. The change implemented by introducing an array of teacher-training courses and by raising the qualifications for teachers. No doubt the new policy achieved certain goals, but for Arakhala it was disastrous. The first thing that happened was that the power to hire and fire teachers was effectively taken from the hands of the local school board. This was done by raising the education requirements for teachers. Daje and the soldiers no longer qualified; in fact, no one in the *panchayat* could qualify. Of course they could have, if they had been willing to go out to the district center and attend school for another year or more, but that was impossible. They would have been happy to go out to take a teacher-training course for two weeks or a month, but such long-term courses as were required for them was just too demanding. They had no choice but to resign.

To replace them, the district hired young high-school graduates as teachers and sent them out to Arakhala. They had book knowledge and were proud of it. The men they replaced, however, had parachuted from planes, ridden huge ships across the ocean and been around the world. The soldiers' experiences seemed to the new teachers more like fairy tales in the books they had studied than reality. These young fellows were from the towns down on the plains and had their own type of food, their own language and their own culture. They didn't like it in Arakhala and wouldn't stay. It was not difficult to find some excuse to run back to the plains where they would stay for weeks at a time. Absenteeism was so bad that it was unusual to find even half of the teachers present on any particular day. Of course, their monthly reports never showed their absences and they continued to draw their full salary.

When the local school board lost its authority to hire and fire, it also lost control over the school. In turn, it refused to be responsible to supply the staff with vegetables, firewood and other amenities that would have made their stay more pleasant. The Brahman headmaster who had been hired no longer qualified and he had gone back home. He had been a welcome and valued member of the village society, but this was not the case with the new teachers. Before, if the villagers had any complaint the school board corrected it immediately. Now it was helpless. Furniture and blackboards were left outside to be broken or ruined by the weather. No longer were the grounds swept daily and the rooms whitewashed regularly. The results were predictable: many of the children quit attending school and the families refused to pay the school fees.

The villagers made due complaint to the district headquarters, but even with new teachers to replace the old, no improvement was seen. Outsiders had come to Arakhala in the hope of helping, but now it had come to this. The villagers had built their school with sweat and toil and the investment of thousands of rupees. They took pride in their school, and now this had happened. Ironically enough, it had all come in the name of progress! It happened because village leaders had lost control over those government employees who were sent to serve them.

Whether the people who were sent out by the government were involved in education, agriculture or health, the situation was basically the same and the results no different. Typically, the young government worker thought of himself as superior to the simple villager. In the early years, his attitude and attempts to force the village elders and *panchayat* leaders to meet his demands were excused; after all, they wanted help. But over the years when they failed to find much usefulness in him, they began to ignore him. In fact, if they had had their choice in the matter, they probably would have just gotten rid of him.

It seems so strange, when I think about it. From the top levels of government, sincere and long-thought-over policies were adopted to raise the living standard of the peasants. Considerable effort was expended and much money spent, but somehow after it had arrived on the villagers' doorstep, it had come out so poorly. It seemed more like a villager's curse of black magic than reality. Who should be blamed for it? It doesn't seem fair to lay the blame on the central government, nor even on the young men that are sent out to the village and do nothing. I think the culprit lies primarily in the philosophy of development.

Perhaps a fatal mistake has been made in assuming that outsiders (even if they are their own countrymen from the other side of the mountain) can do very much to pull the peasant up to a new level of life. Perhaps the climatic, social and linguistic barriers are too much. The central government has had the responsibility of building the nation up from the roots. It has tried hard and sent some of their best-educated people to the villages. But in Arakhala, the villagers don't want anything to do with those young men who represent their nation's best. Couldn't there be a different approach?

What would happen if the government and the village reversed positions? What if the responsibility for Arakhala's school were truly back in the hands of the local school board? What if the responsibility for local health and agricultural extension services were in the hands of the village or *panchayat* leaders? What if they had the option of choosing between a man sent out by the District or someone else, regardless of school qualifications? What would happen if these local officials had to perform to the satisfaction of the people they served or else risk losing their jobs?

To do such a thing would be a radical step. The whole philosophy of government services would have to change. Instead of the idea of "We will help the villagers," it would become "We will help the villagers help themselves." The government's position would shift to one of supporting the village workers in the form of short-term and on-the-spot training. In addition, material support in the form of salaries and technical assistance would be required. Perhaps such a shift would look more radical on paper than it would in practice. The real change would be that the administration of the village-level workers would no longer be from far-away district headquarters, but would shift to the hands of the village *panchayat* who would have the opportunity to pick the best of their people to fill these jobs. The district's responsibility would be to give them periodic training.

One advantage of this approach is that every bit of effort put into training a local person is an expense that will reap profits for as long as the man lives. Since that man will likely stay in his village, whatever skill or bit of technology he has learned will also stay to benefit the village. Even if he should quit the post after a few years, he will not quit his village. The man from the outside, though, is prone to quit his post as soon as any new opportunity shows itself.

And when he quits, the village loses the benefit of the expense and effort that was put into training him.

In addition, when a government employee fails to serve the people, the villagers put the blame for it right on the shoulders of the central government. If the employee were a local man this would not happen. And best of all, if the employee didn't perform, the villagers would always have the option of finding someone else. Such a policy shift would certainly have its own problems, but it would go a long way toward alleviating some of the blame the government presently receives and would do much to solve the problem of the villagers' degenerating attitude toward public-service employees.

Closely associated with the problem of village integration is the problem of village decision-making. Generally speaking, the villagers cannot do all the things we would like to see them do—at least not all at once—so they need to have at least some idea of the alternatives available to them. But as soon as an outside expert, whether foreign or Nepali, attends such a meeting to give counsel and advice, the whole decision-making process is likely to be derailed. The reason is that the outsider is usually not sensitive to the dynamics of village decision-making.

It may be different in other parts of Nepal, but in Arakhala, village decisions are made something like this: Daje, the leader, brings up the topic and itemizes briefly the alternatives and their relative difficulties and advantages. In doing so, Daje will be careful to be completely impartial and by no means will he publicly reveal his own ideas, even if they are well known.

Then, if some honored person is present, Daje will feel obligated to ask him to express his opinion. This is only a courtesy. At this point in the meeting no leader or honored person should ever express his opinion, but decline the invitation to speak at such a time; or if forced to speak, just go over the alternatives as Daje did. The most he should ever do is just to clarify some fact that is unclear to them. Then the floor is thrown open for discussion. Everyone is invited to speak his mind and express his opinion, but in fact, no one who is in a position of leadership will express an opinion. To do so would shut the discussion down immediately, because no one with less authority would feel like saying anything to the contrary in public.

If an honored person makes an opinion statement early in the meeting, he can be fairly certain that the village decision will concur with his opinion. In this case everyone knows that the decision is not the consensus of the village; it is only a face-saving device to appease him. He might be pleased that the villagers adopted his pet solution, but later on nothing will ever come of it. The resolution will never be put into action! This is something that many outsiders don't realize. When there is no action taken on a decision, outsiders commonly are puzzled and they put the blame on poor leadership or something else. It seldom occurs to them that a resolution duly passed in a meeting could actually mean "decision aborted" to the local people present.

The social dynamics of decision-making require that all nonleaders have the first opportunity to voice their opinions freely. Daje sees to that by continually urging other persons to speak whenever the discussion starts to lag. This has two purposes, it seems: first, the feelings of the public are fully aired and the popular support for and viability of the various alternatives are thoroughly tested. Secondly, leaders can sit back and nurture their own ideas, altering their own positions without public humiliation, which vacillation would involve. After the nonleaders have had their say, those with a certain amount of authority will begin tactfully to express their support for one alternative or another.

When the leaders have finished, Daje will make one last call for anyone to express his opinion. Only when no one else has anything left to say will Daje begin to speak. To speak his mind beforehand would be to risk the high probability that a pseudosolution would be arrived at, which would be unworkable and of no benefit to anyone. (However, I've known of people purposely breaking the rules of decision making when they want a no-action decision. They break the rules and attempt in some way to lead the discussion around to a pseudosolution.) When Daje begins his speech, he starts by recalling each of the important points that have been made and giving praise to their logic and value. When this is finished, he will weigh the comparative values and bring forth his suggested solution. Only if Daje has missed a point will anyone say anything to the contrary. Daje's solution will be accepted and passed by all. It will be a solution that brings forth action and support from the villagers.

If Daje has failed to convince everyone in his speech, the consensus will be a false one. Most likely no one will disagree at the meeting, but when it comes time for action, the dissenters will refuse to join in. Then it becomes necessary to call another meeting in order to air grievances or complaints and to reach a decision that is truly unanimous and that accommodates everyone.

A problem in village decision making arises if an outsider presumes that Daje's request to speak at the beginning of a meeting is a true appeal for his opinion. He must realize that this is only a formality and resist the temptation to speak out. If he doesn't, the usefulness of the meeting will almost surely be ruined. Even though they might have several good reasons for not wanting to adopt his suggested solution, no one will dare mention them once he's given his opinion and revealed his bias. For this reason, if they want to see an integrated approach really integrated into the village, they who are honored as experts or authorities must be very careful how they express themselves. Otherwise they will very likely not hear the other side of the story, and what they fail to hear will be the very thing that will cause serious problems later on.

As I've thought of it over the years, my ideas toward village development have become more and more basic. If there were anything I personally could do about it, there are two areas that I would surely major in—rat control and local food storage. If the rats destroy ten, fifteen or twenty percent of a crop in the field, it seems to me that it would be cheaper and easier to increase food production by destroying the rats than it would be by adding expensive fertilizers, insecticides and other inputs.

What is the value of growing a surplus? In these remote areas if there is a bumper crop one year, about the only thing that the villager can do is make it into alcohol for drinking. If he doesn't do that, the insects and rats will surely consume it for him. In the mountains, during the hot springtime corn is quickly devastated by weevils, and the problem is the same for legume crops and winter wheat.

Simple, relatively cheap storage containers can be built out of ferrous cement or other materials. Until each family has a means to store its grain safely, a bumper crop one year will be of practically no use in helping tide the family over a slump the next year. And as long as the population of grain-fed rats continues to boom, all efforts to increase the villagers' standard of living through an increase in agricultural production will face an uphill struggle. *Warfarin,* the relatively safe poison we used at home, or something like it, is the only satisfactory answer I know; perhaps there are other solutions too. All I know is that we can not expect to see much progress made in the agricultural sector so long as twenty, thirty, forty or fifty percent of their crops are destroyed before and after harvest by rats and insects.

Our story comes to a close now. We must stop with Tulya standing on Daje's veranda looking back, grief-stricken over the loss of his children. For us, life with the Magars continues and where it will lead us who can know? More importantly, where will it lead our Magar friends? The future looks bleak—very bleak. Two successive years of crop failure have destroyed their economy and put tremendous stress on their community-minded society. For two years they haven't paid a penny of their land tax. Their landslide-pocked mountains are becoming less and less fertile as more soil is washed away each year. Their livestock do not have enough to eat, so the animals are not supplying sufficient manure for their fields. In addition, a week doesn't go by that a cow, goat or pig isn't devoured by the pair of leopards living near Pulmadi Stream or the pair up on Peak of the Gods. Lastly, the price of their major export, dried ginger, is at an all-time low.

But there is hope. When Gwen saw the results of the terrible drought, she interested the United Mission to Nepal in running a Food-for-Work project for Arakhala and Buling *panchayats*. How much this will relieve their food shortage remains to be seen. There is also the proposed introduction of silkworm raising and the proposal to install a mini-hydroelectric plant.

Then there is the packet of corn seed that I gave to Daje. It was a variety developed in Nepal for use in the hills. Not only did it survive the drought, resist local diseases and ripen three weeks early, but in addition it produced just about double that of the local variety planted next to it. But will the corn, the silkworms or anything else prove out in the years to come? I hope so, but that is another story that only time will tell.

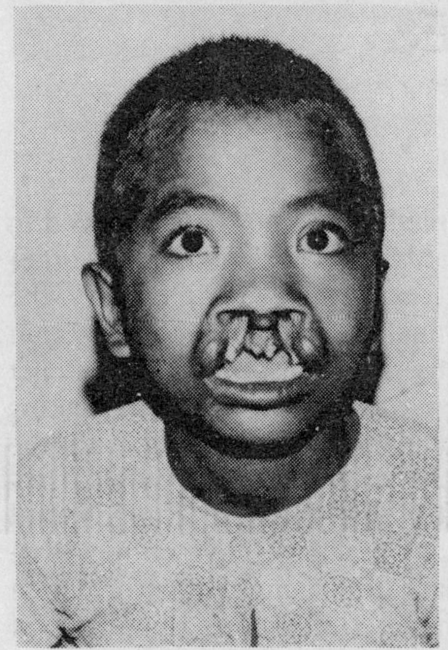

A village boy, born with a double hare-lip, whom we brought to Kathmandu for corrective surgery.

After surgery, the same boy with his grandfather. The latter is one of the few soldiers who survived the Irrawaddy River battle.

APPENDIX I:

HUNTING DEITIES of ARAKHALA

The following list was copied from one that belonged to Lal Bahadur Lungeli of Arakhala. He stated that other people had lists too, but that each list wasn't exactly the same. I have added an explanation about the deities that was not actually written on his list. The purpose of his list was to insure that no deity was omitted when making sacrifices. Some hunters would try to remember all the deities' names and pray to them continuously while they hunted. This list contains fifty-eight names. Lungeli had another list of deities for which the village gave cooperative sacrifice. That list had only forty-four names, most of which were the same as the hunting dieties. More than half of those deities are *bayu*s, ancestor spirits which have yet to reach their heavenly home.

1. *Tin Kannya Mayu*: The three goddesses of Peak of the Gods, the highest peak in the area.
2. *Siddha*: The sentry to the above's home.
3. *Baday Chuli Mayu*: A goddess of a nearby peak.
4. *Sunay Jhãkari*: A high-caste jungle elf.
5. *Dhokya Budha*: The doorkeeper of the *mayu*'s cave.
6. *Palu Budha*: The owner of the deer and mountain goats.

7. *Mahãraja*: An old king whose spirit now lives in the Terai.
8. *Lakadha Budha*: An ancient ancestor.
9. *Lata Jhãkari*: An elf who herds deer and mountain goats and who is dumb.
10. *Namurung Budha*: A shaman of long ago.
11. *Gosaĩ Budha*: A shaman of long ago.
12. *Bhũyar*: King of the earth; the earth-god.
13. *Jhãkari*: The most powerful jungle elf. This non-specific name is perhaps used to include all elves.
14. *Arma*: A jungle elf whose "dogs" are the bears and leopards.
15. *Aytesing Lama*: A shaman who was a famous hunter.
16. *Deota Budha*: A shaman who was a famous hunter of long ago.
17. *Bhaguwan Barajyu*: The Creator and older brother of the *mayu* goddesses.
18. *Jala Bhũyar*: King of all the water; the water-god.
19. *Bijay Budha*: A famous ancient hunter—not a shaman.
20. *Jabar Bhũyar*: A Gurung who was killed by a tiger while grinding grain on his porch.
21. *Somay Siddha Jhãkari*: A jungle elf.
22. *Ram Chandra*: A king of ancient times.
23. *Lachiman Deota*: The younger brother of *Ram Chandra*, a famous Hindu god.
24. *Pãcha Bhaya Jhãkari*: Five brother-elves who are great hunters.
25. *Bala Siddha Jhãkari*: An elf who, in order to gain power, did penance by never marrying.
26. *Jala Siddha*: An elf who lives in the water.
27. *Dadagon Debi*: A powerful goddess who lives near Dadagon Village.
28. *Dudhe Jhãkari*: An elf who drinks milk instead of sacrificial blood.
29. *Dhãdako Siddha*: Two elves who are father and son.
30. *Tolandi Debi*: The goddess of a nearby stream.
31. *Mandali Barajyu*: A terrible male witch who killed his grandson.

32. *Man Singh Barajyu*: The son of *Mandali*.
33. *Disaykoti Barajyu*: The brother-in-law of *Mandali*.
34. *Mandali Buje*: The wife of *Mandali*.
35. *Budha Barajyu*: All the dead ancestors.
36. *Pureni Buje*: A witch who drowned in the stream.
37. *Bankata Bajyu*: The original settler in Ban-Kata. He was killed by a leopard while herding goats.
38. *Chepi Budhiya*: A powerful witch. She was swept away by the stream.
39. *Bhariya*: The deity which carries *Chepi Budhiya*'s belongings.
40. *Susuling Budha*: A powerful shaman.
41. *Godami Budha*: A powerful shaman.
42. *Jaisi Budha*: A proficient astrologer.
43. *Bõlha Budha*: The famous shaman, Aganda.
44. *Lama Budha*: A shaman and Aganda's father, Jokhya.
45. *Chãdi*: The Mother Spirit.
46. *Deorali Mata*: A female Hindu ascetic.
47. *Dahar Gaidu*: A spirit that leads everything along the paths.
48. *Chyu*: A hunting dog-spirit that was killed by a barking deer.
49. *Dhãdako Siddha*: An elf that lived in a huge cave.
50. *Ranani Budhiya*: A witch who got lost in the jungle and was never found.
51. *Phodore*: A shaman.
52. *Mani Ram*: A shaman.
53. *Phal Budha*: A shaman from the village of Chharchharya.
54. *Dhole Budha*: A shaman and famous hunter.
55. *Wantaki Lama*: A shaman of Chuli Bojha Village.
56. *Kala Bhairum*: A god who guards the north side of the village.
57. *Chature Saru*: A man who was killed by a leopard while digging yams.
58. *Ayari Budha*: A healer and famous hunter.

APPENDIX II:

SACRIFICES PERFORMED by HUNTERS

The following is a brief explanation of the sacrifices and ceremonies required of the hunters in Arakhala. In recent years they have not been keeping them regularly.

A. *Ban Phoroni Dhar*

Before hunting for the year is begun, the hunters go down to Desot Stream and make an elaborate offering which includes cow dung, rice, string, milk and fire. This offering is for all the various deities.

B. *Ban Phoroni Puja*

A while later, a sacrifice of one female goat is made at the stream to the *mayu* goddesses to insure success and safety while hunting during the year.

C. *Sikhari Puja*

On an altar at the stream a huge sacrifice of pigs, goats, chickens and pigeons is made to each of the fifty-eight deities. To properly fulfill the requirements of this ceremony, at least one sacrifice should be given to each of the fifty-eight deities.

D. *Kana Khur Jatke*

Whenever an animal is shot, the animal is ceremonially cut by the lucky hunter. He cuts the animal between the hooves, across the nose and tongue, and across the ears, making sure to draw the knife toward himself, in order to please *Arma,* the herder of jungle animals, with the hopes that he will bring along another animal for the hunter to kill. It is also said that *Arma* is able to bring back to life dead animals, but after this ceremony is completed *Arma*'s magical power is foiled.

E. *Dhar Yakhe*

This is a complicated ceremony. Various parts of every animal killed are chopped up fine and offered to each of the deities. Beer, ginger, salt and spices are offered as well as the meat. The backstrap of the animal is cut up into small pieces and offered to *Bhũyar, Arma* and *Jhãkari.* If the meat is cooked instead of offering it raw, the hunters divide up and eat the cooked meat after it has been offered to those three deities. Raw meat which has been offered to the deities is left for the ants to eat.

F. *Kuri Puja*

When the hunters have bagged a total of eleven wild animals, a sacrifice of pigeons, chickens, goats and pigs is given to all the deities. It is similar to the *sikhari puja* above, except that it is held under a shade tree near the village. All fifty-eight deities are given a sacrifice by the hunters.

G. *Thang Lokhe*

Whenever Magars are having bad luck in hunting, they perform this ceremony to obtain success. An altar consisting of a long strip of cow dung is laid down with nine sets of hoof-prints imprinted in it. Rice, string and milk are put on the dung and some incense is lit. A young chicken is sacrificed and more incense lit. Then another person comes along leading a straw deer, followed by a hunter ringing a bell attached to the hunting dog's neck. The straw deer is thrown down and immediately shot with a gun. The hunter with the dog quickly brings it up to worry the carcass of the straw deer. Then the village guns are lined up beside the altar. Following a prayer for a successful hunt, a rooster is sacrificed and the blood is sprinkled on the guns. This reenactment of a successful hunt with the accompanying sacrifice "throws away" the curse of bad luck upon them.

H. *Lama Batke*

When the hunters fail to get game, they presume that it is due to supernatural intervention, so they have a *lama* go into a trance to divine the matter. The deities speak and tell who has sinned or how some deity has been offended. When the proper sacrifice has been offered, the hunt is resumed.

APPENDIX III:

SONGS and DANCES and THEIR RELIGIOUS SIGNIFICANCE

In Magar, each type of song has its corresponding dance and tune. The song, dance and tune are all called by the same name. Some types of songs are limitless in verse; the words are made up as they go along. There used to be strict rules as to what times of the year a particular song could be danced. However, some of the religious significances are being lost and these days the younger people do not always follow the old customs. All of the songs are sung in the Nepali language, though there is a man in a village an hour away who knows verses of two types of songs in the Magar language.

A. *GHÃTU*

This is a very important dance performed by the teenage girls in the month of *Baisak* (April). In some ways this is similar to a puberty rite or coming-of-age ceremony. After the girls have completed this dance they may be married. Many of the girls do not dance the *ghãtu,* however; their families are too poor to feed the relatives they would be obligated to invite. Though it is not required, the girls may continue to dance the *ghãtu* every year until they are married. During the dance and for a period afterwards, they are not supposed to eat garlic or pig meat nor drink liquor. The old women lead the singing while the

APPENDIX IV:

ENGLISH-NEPALI-MAGAR WORD LIST

The following is a comparative (Swadesh) word list in English, Nepali and Magar as spoken in Arakhala. Retroflexed stops are represented by capital "T" and "D". Nasalized vowels are indicated by a tilde over the vowel. Velar nasal is represented by "ng". Single "a" is mid-central vowel, "aa" is low-central vowel. The "h" in Magar words indicates aspiration, breathy syllable or both.

	English	Nepali	Magar
1.	I	ma	ngaa
2.	you	timi	nang
3.	we	haami	kaan
4.	this	yo	ise
5.	that	tyo	hose
6.	who	ko	su
7.	what	ke	hi
8.	not	-na	maa-
9.	all	jammai	patta
10.	many	dherai	dherai
11.	one	ek	kaat
12.	two	dui	nis
13.	big	Thulo	karhaang-cha
14.	long	laamo	lhot-cha

	English	Nepali	Magar
15.	small	saano	maar-chha
16.	woman	swaasni-maanchhe	maasto
17.	man	logne-maanchhe	lenjaa
18.	person	maanis	bharmi
19.	fish	maachhaa	disyaa
20.	bird	charo	gwaa
21.	dog	kukur	chyu
22.	louse	jumraa	sik
23.	tree	rukh	sing
24.	seed	byu	chhoyo
25.	leaf	paat	lhaa
26.	root	jaro	mi-arkak
27.	bark	bokraa	me-khok
28.	skin	chhaalaa	mi-chhaalaa
29.	flesh	maasu	mi-syaa
30.	blood	ragat	mi-hyu
31.	bone	haaD	mi-rhus
32.	grease	boso	me-sos
33.	egg	phul	mi-rhu
34.	horn	sing	mi-ryam
35.	tail	puchchhar	mẽ-mẽ
36.	feather	pwããkh	mi-khar
37.	hair	kes	mi-chham
38.	head	Taauko	mi-taalu
39.	ear	kaan	me-nekep
40.	eye	ããkhaa	mi-mik
41.	nose	naak	mi-naahaa
42.	mouth	mukh	me-nger
43.	tooth	dããt	mi-syaak
44.	tongue	jibhro	me-let
45.	fingernail	nang	mi-aarkin
46.	foot	khuTTaa	mi-hil
47.	knee	ghũDo	ghũdaa
48.	hand	haat	mi-hut
49.	belly	peT	mi-tuk
50.	neck	ghããTi	mi-dunggaa
51.	breasts	dudh	dut
52.	heart	muTu	mi-gin

	English	Nepali	Magar
53.	liver	kalejo	mi-sin
54.	drink	pyu-nu	gaa-ke
55.	eat	khaa-nu	jya-ke
56.	bite	Tok-nu	jik-ke
57.	see	her-nu	daang-khe
58.	hear	sun-nu	se-ke
59.	know	jaan-nu	waar-khe
60.	sleep	sut-nu	mis-ke
61.	die	mar-nu	si-ke
62.	kill	maar-nu	saat-ke
63.	swim	paũD-nu	pããdis-ke
64.	fly	uD-nu	bhur-ke
65.	walk	hiD-nu	hwaa-ke
66.	come	aau-nu	raa-khe
67.	lie	sut-nu	polo-khe
68.	sit	bas-nu	ngu-ke
69.	stand	ubhi-nu	tong-khe
70.	give	di-nu	yaa-khe
71.	say	bhan-nu	de-ke
72.	sun	surje	naangkhaan
73.	moon	chandramaa	gyohõt
74.	star	taaraa	tugaa
75.	water	paani	di
76.	rain	paani	naamaas
77.	stone	Dhunggaa	lhum
78.	sand	baaluwaa	baluwaa
79.	soil	maaTo	jhaa
80.	cloud	baadal	dĩbu
81.	smoke	dhuwãã	dhwãã
82.	fire	aago	mhe
83.	ash	kharaani	baadaap
84.	burn	bal-nu	dhaa-ke
85.	path	baaTo	laam
86.	mountain	paahaaD	dããda
87.	red	raato	gyaa-cha
88.	green	hariyo	phi-cha
89.	yellow	pahelo	or-chha
90.	white	seto	bo-cha

	English	Nepali	Magar
91.	black	kaalo	chik-cha
92.	night	raat	naambik
93.	hot	taato	khaan-chha
94.	cold	chiso	chyok-cha
95.	full	bhari	ping-chha
96.	new	nayaa	minaam
97.	good	raamro	se-chha
98.	round	golo	tokolok
99.	dry	sukeko	chhok-cha
100.	name	naam	aarmin

APPENDIX V:

A NOTE ON ONOMATOPOEIA IN MAGAR

Compared with English, the Magar language is liberally equipped with onomatopoetic types of words. These are colorful and descriptive expressions whose sound is meant to convey something of the meaning of the word. This sort of phenomenon in language has also been described as an ideophone. In the grammar, these words appear almost exclusively as adverbs modifying a small set of verbs. Phonologically, they are generally longer than other word types. Commonly they occur as a reduplication of one or more syllables. Some examples of onomatopoeia are:

phowak phowak yakhe	to pat softly
padiyak dungke	to slap
dadhak dudhuk dungke	to hit many times
bhuk dungke	to hit once (hard)

Many of these words do not appear to have a direct relation between their sound and the meaning they convey, such as:

jhamarak jhumuruk bikke	to have paralyzing pain in the legs
thyanglang thingling bikke	to have strong pain in the knees
not notta bikke	to have heart-burn

Other words are clearly a close representation of the meaning they express, such as:

ghururuttai kherke	to run fast
dhyamma pachariske	to smash into the ground
ghagarak ghuguruk chyakke	to have a noisy stomach

Speakers of Nepali also use similar expressions in their speech. Some of these are shared with Magar, such as:

jhowat	instantly
sowat	cut cleanly in two

As in the example above, it is not uncommon for words to differ only in their initial consonant. Another example is:

suwing rakhe	to dive as a bird
chuwing rakhe	to zip by, as a bullet

An interesting feature is that there are pairs of words with similar meanings which have the same consonant pattern, but differ in the vowels. The variant in meaning between these is sometimes one of scale. Two such pairs are:

chitik chitik bikke	to have **slight** pain
chotok chotok bikke	to have **strong** pain
hululuttai padhike	to enter a narrow place, of a **small** animal
hololottai padhike	to enter a narrow place, of a **large** animal

These modifying words are bound so closely and in such a way to the verb that they have the effect of creating new verbs. That is, whereas English will have descriptive verbs about **walking** such as **to slip, to limp,** Magar is inclined to take a single verb **to walk** (hwake) and modify it, such as:

kentek kentek hwake	to limp
phalet hwake	to slip

Listening to a dynamic speaker, one easily receives the impression that these words are made up on the spot from the fertile imagination of the orator. But investigation proves that these words are standard vocabulary and are known and understood by all. For instance, if you were to ask someone, without giving the context, what **sutuk sutuk** meant, he would likely reply that something was sneaking along stealthily like a leopard. Whereas if you asked what **sulululttai** meant, he would likely answer that something is crawling like a snake. These expressions have the function of making the language very precise with, compared to English, an amazing economy of words. This is possible because each expression, of which there are a huge number in the language, paints in the hearer's mind a complete picture of an exact situation, action or series of actions. Among the Magars, an expressive, exciting speaker, the one who gets the most attention and the most laughs, is the one who punctuates his speech with a steady stream of these descriptive words.